Some Must Die

A Marine Correspondent On Okinawa

James S. Nutter
PFC, USMCR

Hoosick Falls, New York
2017

First published in 2017 by the Merriam Press

First Edition

Copyright © 2017 by Jerry S. Nutter
Book design by Ray Merriam
Additional material copyright of named contributors.

All rights reserved.
No part of this book may be used or reproduced in any manner whatsoever without written permission, except in the case of brief quotations embodied in critical articles or reviews.

WARNING
The unauthorized reproduction or distribution of this copyrighted work is illegal. Criminal copyright infringement, including infringement without monetary gain, is investigated by the FBI and is punishable by up to five years in federal prison and a fine of $250,000.

The views expressed are solely those of the author.

ISBN 9781576385739
Library of Congress Control Number: 2016962644

This work was designed, produced, and published in
the United States of America by the

Merriam Press
489 South Street
Hoosick Falls NY 12090

E-mail: ray@merriam-press.com
Web site: merriam-press.com

The Merriam Press publishes new manuscripts on historical subjects, especially military history and with an emphasis on World War II, as well as reprinting previously published works, including reports, documents, manuals, articles and other materials on historical topics.

Contents

Foreword 5
Chapter 1: Okinawa Invasion Force 7
Chapter 2: Into the Setting Sun 17
Chapter 3: Skyscrapers of the Deep 25
Chapter 4: Mid-Pacific Holiday 45
Chapter 5: Through Perilous Waters 53
Chapter 6: Mighty Armada 63
Chapter 7: Target Run 75
Chapter 8: Invasion 87
Chapter 9: Baptism of Blood 99
Chapter 10: Victory at Motobu 117
Chapter 11: Eagles and Vultures 131
Chapter 12: Purple Heart and White Crosses 145
Chapter 13: Dauntless Defenders 161
Chapter 14: Air Victory Over Okinawa 173
Chapter 15: Bartering Blood for Victory 189
Chapter 16: The Fall of Sugar Loaf and Half-Moon Hills 201
Chapter 17: Japan's Empire Crumbles 211
Chapter 18: The Atomic Bomb and Victory 225
Addendum 233

Foreword

Some Must Die stresses the reality faced by the men gathered from every region of the United States and every walk of life, to become the fighting men in the final months of World War II. James (Jim) Nutter, my father, was 34 years old when he joined the Marines in October of 1944. When the announcement came that men of his age were about to be "called up"—drafted—he chose to enlist in the Marine Corps rather than be conscripted into the Army. He and a few others were at first turned away, being told that their age group was no longer needed. But the fever of patriotism was strong, and these men insisted as a group to be taken (see photo). And so he left for the war, leaving behind his wife, two children, and his job as Publicity Manager for United Airlines in Seattle. For many years Jim had been a Speed Graphics camera-carrying news man, and a writer for the Associated Press. Now he was immersed in the greatest story of all.

After boot camp at the Marine Corps Air Station, El Centro, California, PFC Jim Nutter was assigned to the intelligence section of Headquarters Squadron of the Second Marine Air Wing, Marine Aircraft Group 43 (MAG 43), now tasked to join the invasion force of Okinawa. He was issued a typewriter, and a field desk, and assigned various report writing duties. Before long his experience, his age (many ranking superiors were younger), and his lighthearted, infectious personality, won him increased freedom and access to the stories unfolding around him.

His account of the battles fought to secure the Island of Okinawa is often grim, but always with an eye for the determination and spirit that animated these citizen warriors, lifting them to the acts of sacrifice and heroism that fill these pages—the raw stuff of our victory over Japan.

Jim Nutter completed *Some Must Die* in 1945 but could not find a publisher. He died in 1950, and for some 70 years the manuscript sat on various shelves, shuffled through many moves, a time capsule preserving the stories of the men he got to know. It is a testament to the valor, the sensibilities, and quite a lot of the innocence—even prejudice—of that era. Nothing has been changed.

Jerry Nutter
Ashland, Oregon
1 July 2016

Chapter 1

Okinawa Invasion Force

The restless Hawaiian breeze whispered softly over the dark green cane brakes, and Donald J. "Shamrock" Coyne was singing: "Over the sea, let's go men; we're shoving right off, we're shoving right off again."

But only a few of us marines joined in the rollicking song as our long, open troop truck swung through the guard gate of the Marine Corps Air Station at Ewa, Oahu, Territory of Hawaii, and rolled briskly toward Pearl Harbor.

Nothing on the stoical faces of the leathernecks revealed their thoughts. But you could feel a certain tenseness—something as live and unmistakable as a portending thunderstorm.

Perhaps it was because the Leathernecks were quiet, weren't even bitching (graphic marine term for griping), that you knew they were thinking, and wondering about their forthcoming invasion.

For our Marine Aviation Headquarters Squadron was leaving the Hawaiian Islands to become part of the biggest invasion fleet ever to strike in the Pacific. We were embarking on the invasion of Okinawa.

The strategic island of Okinawa, some 62 miles long and dotted with airfields, lies 350 miles south of Japan proper, about 350 miles north of the Jap-held fortress of Formosa and 350 miles east of the Jap-held China coast.

"Yes, Fellows, it's no longer scuttlebutt that we're going overseas," chirped PFC Dick Koch-Church, the former New York kid who was "Dizzy" on the Henry Aldrich radio show.

We laughed, but I suspected that Dick and some of the others had prayers on their hearts, and home on their minds. The ex-juvenile radio and stage actor now looked mature and warlike in his slate-green dungarees, his pack and bedroll, camouflaged steel helmet, bayonet, cartridge belt, rifle and two canteens.

"I feel like a Nash-Kelvinator ad," he said.

A few of us knew what the mission would be—which beachheads would be invaded. Others had heard scuttlebutt (rumors), and ventured guesses—some of which were wild. But all of us knew it would be rough.

Yes, we were more quiet than usual. That is, all except Technical Sergeant Shamrock Coyne, that blithe, effervescent descendent of old Erin.

A San Francisco fireman, he spoke with a New York accent acquired from his father, who was born in Ireland and lived for a time in New York. Shamrock was a solid, ape-like hulk of a man, with just a touch of extra flesh. Twenty-four years of age, he was exactly six feet tall and weighed 200 pounds.

He played football at San Francisco University, but a broken knee ended his grid career. Later he played baseball at San Francisco State Teachers' college. Fast despite his large hulk, he played center fielder.

His back muscles were strong as steel bands. He had been a crewman two years at Balboa high school in San Francisco.

"Hey! Bill Carver," shouted Shamrock. You dropped your watch chain."

Coyne's freckled face showed sympathetic dismay as he pointed dramatically at a mountain of huge, rusting anchor chains in one of the many stockpiles we passed as we neared Pearl Harbor.

"Thanks," grinned Bill, a former bush league baseball player and button salesman from The Bronx, N.Y.

Nothing could dim Shamrock's Irish wit. It was as much a part of him as his tousled, black hair, his baseball cap which he wore a dozen different ways for as many moods, and his blue eyes which twinkled mischievously ever. Why, I believe he'd do a tap dance in front of a firing squad, or sing one of his favorite Irish songs even if seated in an electric chair.

He knew our invasion would be rugged...knew what war is about. He had been out 18 ½ months before, and 17 of it was in the thick of the Guadalcanal and Munda campaigns.

Smart as well as witty, he knew a good sense of humor is the best companion you can have in the combat zone. So he was helping cheer us all—sometimes by saying:

"Hello, toilet-face."

As our truck caravan rolled to a dusty halt at the edge of the bay, a Marine band was playing. It was an unexpected surprise to all of us, who had left San Diego only a month earlier without any fanfare.

"Yep, there's the band," ejaculated Shamrock. "This is a real war, just like in pictures. I guess it was an imitation when I was over before."

We dismounted from our trucks, and made ourselves as comfortable as possible while we waited. Waiting—that's the thing you do most in the service. Wait in chow line... wait in show line... wait to be sent overseas... then wait to be sent back home.

Some of the men squirmed out of their heavy packs and crapped out (reclined) against them. Others backed up against trucks and leaned there, resting their loads.

Then the band was playing again, and of all things: "Don't Fence Me In!"

Dick Koch-Church and I traded lumpy looks of dismay and I said:

"I can't think of any song more inappropriate, right when we're really going to be fenced in for a long time..."

Dick shook his head and said nothing, but we both smiled as Shamrock began singing the words snappily and doing a shuffling tap dance despite his heavy pack. For a finale, Shamrock inserted his own words: "Don't HASHMARK me. "

Now humor is no respecter of persons, ordinarily, but upon occasion it does run according to rank.

All the buck privates and PFC's and corporals laughed, because most of them still had two or three more years to go before donning the four-year hash marks. But the staff sergeants, technical sergeants and master technical sergeants didn't see much humor in it. Many of them were not so many months away from their hash marks, and approximately one-fourth of our men had been out in the combat zone before.

Dick and I edged away right after the muster for roll call. We saw Sergeant Major Bob Wray and MT Sergeant Carl Hamilton, the bull gang boss, approaching for a work party to carry our deck load boxes, sea bags and bed rolls aboard the LCT landing boats for transfer to our ship lying farther out in the harbor. We were both PFC's—fair game for any crap detail.

"You know I don't mind heavy work, Jim but I'm temperamentally unsuited for it," laughed Dick.

The sergeant major, a darned good Joe, considering the tough job he had, wore a concerned look. His was the responsibility to see that all of our men and all our supplies get loaded, quickly and efficiently.

"I want a dozen men to help with this loading," said Sergeant Major Wray.

Only a couple of the crapped out Leathernecks stirred.   Now mind you, none was averse to work, and yet none was averse to having someone else do the work.

"Damn it, get moving," yelled Wray, the first time I ever hear him swear.

"We're not going to mail you invitations."

Some of the most accomplished dope-offs (goldbrickers) of our outfit sprang forward and formed a working party. But once the party was formed, all members worked like demons, and our supplies were loaded in a trice.

There were soldiers at the point of embarkations, and we learned they would be on our ships. They were loading their supplies aboard other LCT's, and another outfit of Marines, also a Headquarters Squadron, was going aboard with us in our flat-bottomed LCT.

There were plenty of army and Marine Corps high ranking officers. Industrious Seabees were directing the loading operations of heavier equipment.

Suddenly a moan ran through the crowd of more than 500 Marines and soldiers waiting to embark. The band had started playing: "Give my Regards to Broadway."

"I thought I'd die when they started playing that," Dick said later. And Bill Carver chimed in:

"Man, I could just see myself marching right down Broadway and turning into Jack Dempsey's saloon for a shot of bourbon."

It's surprising how many people have been to New York City, and there's a nostalgic camaraderie among them. As Dick expressed it:

"Why there are only two kinds of people in the nation—those who've been to New York and those who haven't. And those who haven't ought to get on the ball and see it.

Just before we went aboard, Major W. L. Turner addressed our squadron:

"All right, here's the word. When you get on board ship, go to hold A102L."

"You'll remember that," quipped Shamrock. "You'll feel like you're 102 years old, after swarming up the side on those embarkation nets."

Then the word sounded:

"Marine Headquarters Squadrons, go aboard."

Our LCT had nosed up to the dirt bank, and dropped its front end, draw-bridge fashion. It was just one long step from the bank to the bobbing, metal platform. Then in we moved through the craft's gaping mouth. Under our weight, the craft's bow settled into the sand. Now the band was playing "Anchor's Aweigh."

A winch started, and heavy chains pulled the front wall of the LCT up with a loud clatter. There was a lurch as the craft pulled free of the bank. Now we were in the bay, and the band was playing the

Marine's Hymn—"From the Halls of Montezuma." We stood at attention.

Then, as we turned and began bumping along the bay, we heard the strains of "Auld Lang Sync."

I turned to MT Sergeant Norris Fry, my NCO (non-commissioned officer) in charge, and asked what his emotions were at going out a second time. Before, he had been on the Bougainville invasion, going in on D-Day, and had spent considerable time in the southwest Pacific.

"I don't have any emotions about it yet," replied this tall, genial and well-educated Texan.

But for us Malahenes (Hawaiian for newcomers) there was subdued excitement in the air, a feeling that this was the start of an experience never to be forgotten.

The uninitiated always marvel at the number of ships of all kinds in Pearl Harbor, and now we had a close-up view. There were destroyers, net minders, mine sweepers, troops ships, freighters, tankers, tugs, landing barges, small boats and a long, sleek warship which I first thought was a battle wagon, but which a sailor identified as a heavy battle cruiser.

Our landing craft pulled up alongside one of the troop ships, near the bow on the port side. It was an Amphibious Personnel Assault craft which was literally infested with small landing craft of the Higgins, boat type. Our "home" for many weeks to come was the USS Allendale.

As soon as our lines were secure, the ship's crew dropped two embarkation nets over the side, and we began climbing aboard, emerging by the number one cargo hatch, right back of the forecastle.

The first trip up that chain and wooden ladder with full pack is a real experience. The two nets, lowered side by side, were the equivalent of eight narrow ladders. It was a climb of about 20 feet from our bobbing bark to the ship's topside. With full pack, it was a bit tricky on that swaying ladder. But all made it without difficulty, the Shamrock negotiated this trapeze-like stairway with all the spryness of a monkey in a zoo.

Only one slight mishap occurred. Chief Pharmacist's Mate Lee Rutberg of Los Angeles lost his helmet and blanket roll. They slipped from his pack and landed on the edge of our barge-like boat, outside the railing. Major Williams F. Feasley, our squadron commanding officer, retrieved them and sent them up on a rope.

But as a sailor was pulling the load upward, hand over hand, the helmet slipped loose, fell and sank into the bay.

"Doggone," said Chief Rutberg. "This is my third combat tour, and that's the first piece of G.I. equipment I've lost in five years of service."

No sooner had we complete our new acrobatic trick then Dick, Bill Carver and I were sent back down the ladder on a working party to be stevedores loading rope nets with cargo.

As the first load of empty cargo nets came down on a pulley lowered on cables from a huge crane, it was just like seeing a friend from home. For there on the enormous pulley with its big hook, was written in raised letters: "Young Iron Company, Seattle, Washington." Seattle is my home city.

Four corner loops of the first cargo net lowered were tied together with stout cord. I was right there to take hold and get the job started.

"Which one of you commandos has a knife," I shouted. At that instant a Marine captain, supervising the unloading, whipped out a knife and slashed the cord. I grinned and winked at Bill Carver, then slid discreetly into the background. My verbal barb had almost boomeranged.

That cargo virtually flew up the side of the Allendale, and the ship's captain was pleased with the Leatherneck longshoremen.

I don't remember what we had for chow, but it was very good. The Navy put on a swell introductory spread which we knew was too good to continue. It didn't, either, although our salty veterans said it was the best food, day in and day out, that they ever had aboard a troop ship.

After chow we returned to our quarters in the top front hold, right below the forecastle. All of the more desirable bunks had been taken, and all left for me was a lower, and I do mean lower! Our bunks were four high, with the top man running the risk of butting his brains out against the steel ceiling if he sat up too quickly, and with the bottom man some four inches from deck.

I unrolled my bedroll and crawled into my new sack (bed). The strains of music came back to me: "Don't fence me in." Say, I never had been so fenced in before in my life. But more about that later.

Bill, Dick and I slept on the open deck that night. Someone had left an extra bed roll atop the number two cargo hatch. I used the small mattress pad and the water-repellent shelter half, while they took the wool blanket. It rained on us for awhile, but we stuck it out, rather then sleep in that tiny hold with some 150 sweating men, all breathing the same air despite the elaborate ventilation blowers.

Our ship was new, and clean. We could see why. After dark we saw sailors—marines usually call them swabbies—painting one of the Higgins boats while another held a flashlight for them. Those swabbies always were painting something.

We rode anchor in the harbor that first night. We had boarded ahead of schedule so there would be no last-minute delay. The next afternoon we got underway—weighed anchor. Quipped Shamrock Coyne: "Hey, fellow, they just weighed anchor. It hasn't lost much!"

Now we were turning, at first with the help of two tugs, for Pearl Harbor was crowded. Then we steamed away on our own power, circling Ford Island air field, and then heading out the narrow channel to the sea.

I looked down at oily water in Pearl Harbor. It seemed dyspeptic... a bilious green. But now we were passing the dirty harbor water. To our left were white coral sands, over which raced frothy waves like the flowing manes of white horses.

Where the water was a little deeper, it was of vivid pastel green tint, changing abruptly to a pastel blue where it was still deeper... and then, finally, the Pacific Ocean itself—darkest of indigo blues.

Where it was changing from the pastel blue, it reminded me of Crater Lake, the spectacularly beautiful volcanic lake in southern Oregon about 100 miles from the little town of Ashland, Oregon, where I lived from 1920-1930, and where my mother still resides.

Ships were coming and going in that busy Pearl Harbor channel, but one especially fascinated us.

It was a submarine. We gathered on port side of our ship and stared as this rapier-like demon of the deep slithered past. The very sight of it seemed to make us shudder inwardly, even though we knew it was on Uncle Sam's great Pacific Fleet team. It looked murderous as we gazed in awesome curiosity.

Now we were on the Pacific and a bobbing little boat pulled alongside and picked up the harbor pilot who had guided the ship out the narrow channel. He went down a Jacob's ladder and swung expertly into the bouncing craft. It is a common practice to have harbor pilots in ports where the channel is narrow or tricky. They are specialists who know every ripple.

I looked back at distant Waikiki beach, the swank Moana Hotel and the beautiful Royal Hawaiian Hotel which once was a tourist mecca of world renown, but which now was home for hundreds of battle-weary submarine sailors and a gawkers' paradise for thousands of restless, bored servicemen on their infrequent liberty days in Honolulu.

We had been on the island of Oahu a little more than three weeks. Personnel based there permanently didn't like it. It was neither stateside, nor considered "overseas," for it was now well out of the combat zones. There was no social life for enlisted men. Many of the Hawaiian girls were beautiful, but for the most part they remained proudly and discretely aloof from their pale-faced visitors.

You heard it on every hand. Honolulu is fouled up worse then even San Diego, because there are too many men and not enough woman. The ratio was reported as something like 100 to 1.

Just before we arrived, the first contingent of Woman Marines reached Ewa, and more arrived before we left. Some of the Marines liked the idea, and some didn't. I guess the biggest trouble with the Woman Marines is that there aren't enough to do much good, as far as social life is concerned. It's swell for a few of the men, but just a tantalizing reminder for the great bulk of fellows.

But I had enjoyed my brief sojourn at Hawaii. One day I lunched with Grant McDonald of Seattle, one of the top Associated Press cameramen. We talked of pleasant times at the Seattle Press Club- the days when he was an Acme photographer and I was handling publicity for United Air Lines.

And the night we arrived at Ewa I was overjoyed to find one of my closest Marine Corps buddies-Chuck Jones of Seattle. Chuck and I met at Marine recruiting headquarters in Seattle the morning we were sworn in. We lived in the same tent at boot camp, furloughed together at Seattle afterward, and then were stationed together at Miramar, Calif., for some time.

Chuck and I sipped rum and coco cola together at Honolulu and cast appraising glances at native women, fancying ourselves professors of pulchritude... epidermis epicures.

We swam together at Nimits Beach near our camp, and sat under the bright Hawaiian moon after taps many a night and talked—largely about our post-war plans.

Together we visited the Royal Hawaiian Hotel. From its windows, whence vacationing school teachers, office girls and starry-eyed debutantes formerly directed their romance-seeking glances, now fluttered the white underwear which sailors had washed and hung to dry.

And on the vast veranda, where once sat wealthy tourists from many lands to gaze at Waikiki beach in dazzling sunlight or shimmering moonlight, brusquely stood a boxing ring.

A couple of servicemen were banging boogie-woogie on a pair of grand pianos nearby, arousing a flicker of interest from the mid-afternoon crowd of sightseeing servicemen. There were about 300 of us; and three Red Cross ladies.

Other servicemen swam in the surf, or lolled in the sand. But once-romantic Waikiki beach was minus the comely, sylph-like bathing beauties in tight-fitting suits.

We left quickly. We saw what it had been—what it would be again—and had no desire to remain longer with the herds trampling the glamour of the place under military heel.

Chuck arrived at Ewa two months ahead of me, and now was remaining after. He wanted so much to join our outfit and go along. Several from his squadron were transferred into ours, but not he.

At Ewa we were given only one day of Liberty in six—9 a.m. to 7 p.m. (it was 6 p.m. for buck privates and PFCs). But I enjoyed the midwinter sunshine, the warm evenings, tennis and swimming—when I had time. We were pretty busy getting ready for the big invasion.

And in Honolulu I bought a string of beads made of delicate pink, white and purple shells for Barbara, my 10 year old daughter in Seattle, and a carved teakwood turtle from China for my pride and boy, Jerry, who is six.

But I hadn't seen any native entertainment...no supple-hipped hula dancers with poetically gesturing hands!

As our ship rocked and dipped on choppy seas, I looked back over our trough toward the high rugged hills of Oahu; back at picturesque Waikiki Beach with its frothing breakers, its backdrop of palms and coconut trees and emerald gardens; back at Diamond Head which juts majestically southward, forming a natural breakwater for Waikiki beach; and back at the huge, cumulous clouds which rode swiftly across the assure skies like great white sails.

I looked back on all this... and said Aloha.

Someday I plan to return—by air—and bring my family to enjoy Hawaii when peace-time tourist attractions abound, and the place is not fouled up by war.

Until then, fair island, Aloha.

Chapter 2

Into the Setting Sun

Our tiny convoy steamed south-southwestward from Pearl Harbor, and soon our speculation as to its probable size ended. There were three troop ships—two other amphibious personnel assault ships similar to our 12,000-ton craft—and a small destroyer-escort, the USS Vernon.

Except for the guns aboard our ships, this pocket-sized destroyer, with only on smoke stack, was our sole protection against submarines. Our guns would be effective all right, if any enemy sub surfaced. But a submerged sub could be flushed out only by depth charges, which light, speedy destroyers can lay with the agility of spawning fish.

However, we still had little concern for submarines. At least I didn't, and none of the crew nor troops seemed to give a second thought to enemy pig boats. But of course there were the regular dawn and dusk alerts, and the complete black outs of our ships during hours of darkness.

As we steamed from Oahu toward the central Pacific, the other two APAs followed in single file. I had seen newsreels of such processions, but never before had been a part of one.

Our three ships were rolling and pitching slowly, and to me were reminiscent of a string of circus elephants. Over the white-capped waves and medium-sized swells we paraded like undulating pachyderms, swaying noticeably from side to side, but pushing always onward at ponderous pace.

And leading this plodding procession, with the grace of a prancing, short-skirted drum majorette, was our destroyer escort, describing a wide zigzag course a half mile to a mile in front of us.

This tireless DE immediately won our admiration, respect and affection. It gave us a sense of security—like a mastiff watch-dog in your home, or a .45 caliber six-shooter swinging at your side.

On and on ran our tiny escorting warship, back and forth over the waves like a swivel-hipped, All-American halfback.

Our speed was 14 to 16 knots an hour, but the DE was going faster to cover a wider area. Occasionally it would vary from the zigzagging course, and, as if reversing the field, steam in a circle completely around us.

The waves and swells had only moderate affect on us. But not so our gallant escort. When it presented a side view we could see the bow and the stern, alternately, almost disappearing beneath the water line as the ship rose on the crest of one swell, then dipped into the trough of the next one. Spray flew high, washing the decks constantly.

And when this toy bulldog of the seas was headed straight away from us, we saw its single mast rocking back and forth like a pendulum of a huge clock. The mast with its cross-bar reminded me at once of a crucifix—a crucifix tossing and writhing as if tormented with thoughts of evil and a guilt-stricken conscience.

One thing we knew. No enemy submarines would care to surface and tangle with us. And we also knew that our Pacific Fleet ran down and exterminated Jap subs with dispatch, once they showed their heads.

Chow was good again that evening, particularly the dessert of pie.

Afterward we lolled on the main deck, the well decks, the forecastle, the fantail or any place we could find standing room or a place to crap out. Some were writing letters—letters which we thought might not reach their destination for weeks, possibly months.

Before we left Pearl Harbor we had been permitted by our censors to write something like this:

"Don't be alarmed if at some time in the future you don't hear from me for many weeks at a time. We may not be near a mail box, but just keep on writing, and I'll do the same."

That was as close as we could come to hinting that we were going to be part of a massive invasion force.

However, now that we were aboard ship heading westward, we were able to say in our missives that we were "going into combat." No further details could be mentioned. But to ease the mind of my wife, June, and my children, Barbara and Jerry, whom I knew worried much more than they should, I added:

"In Marine Aviation we have it pretty safe and easy, going in and setting up airfields and operating them after the Marine infantrymen have stormed the beachheads and faced the enemy's guns. They are the men who have the tough job, and they are the real heroes—not we typewriter commandos who come in later."

But I knew the chances were that some of us would follow very close on the heels of the Marine infantrymen, and that we would be within easy bombing range of the Japs for many days... and nights:

After chow our little coterie was having a bull session on the main deck, near the number two hatch. Now Leathernecks speak lightly of death; banter each other about it. From the second day in boot camp we learn that our military justification for existence is to kill Japs. It was Shamrock who brought up the subject.

"Bill," he said, addressing Tech Sergeant Carver, "you're a rough and tumble character from The Bronx; how would you like to kill a Jap with a knife?"

"Swell," replies Bill. "I'd like to jab the yellow sons of bitches, and watch them curse and die!"

"What if hot blood gushed all over you?" asked Shamrock, who had a knack for ghastly realism.

"So what?" barked Bill. "I'd just like to kill some of them."

"And how about you, Dick,?" Shamrock asked Koch-Church.

"I'd like to stab a Jap," replied the tall, slender New Yorker, "but not get his blood on me." Then, to convince us—0and possibly himself—that he had no qualms about such a grisly ordeal, he added: "I'd like to stab my knife in and give it a twist."

Dick had been whetting his bowie knife, and also a pearl-handled pocket knife with a four-inch blade, since the day we arrived at Miramar from El Centro, Calif. In his pocket he carried a small emery stone. He took the invasion seriously.

Bill hadn't turned knife-carrying commando yet—we knew knives would be issued to us later—but he left me no doubt that he would use one avidly if the occasion presented itself. He added:

"I'd like to stab one of those Jap bastards and then kick him in the face."

I expressed my sentiments:

"I used to help dad butcher hogs and cattle down on the farm at Ashland. It wasn't exactly pleasant, but a necessary job. And I'd certainly rather kill a Jap than an innocent porker."

Turning to Shamrock, I asked:

"How about you? You've been in the combat zone before. How would you like to slash a Jap's gullet?"

I'd do it gladly, but it would be an unforgettable ordeal," he said seriously... with clouded countenance.

"I saw a Jap hit in the stomach with a burst of .45 slugs from a Thompson submachine gun. Guts flew in all directions. It made me a bit sick."

Technical Sergeant Grover Mounger, a chunky Marine from Houston, Texas, broke in:

"I'm not going to get close enough to a live Jap to use any steel, "I've got my .45 six-shooter, and I'm wearing it all the time after we hit the beach.

We wished that we also had side arms in addition to our M-1 rifle or carbines.

All agreed we would like some souvenirs from any Japs we killed. A fancy knife, his rifle, or if an officer, his jewel-handled saber. They say the Army fights for victory, the Navy for glory, but the Marines fight for souvenirs.

At this juncture MT Sergeant Don Poorman, a short, fat, argumentative Marine who wears the Legion of Merit for setting up communications under Jap fire during the Guadalcanal campaign, added some grisly humor to the macabre discussion, saying:

"Jim, your kids will razz the other kids at school and say: "Yah, your daddy was only killed by a German. My daddy was killed by a Jap."

Roars of laughter greeted this remark. Then Koch-Church said:

"Say, I just heard that we're likely to be on board ship 55 days. That will give You a month longer to live, Doyle."

"Well, " replied Donald Doyle, buck sergeant from Milwaukee, Wis., a lad of 18 who acted much older, "I'm going to die of old age."

"Yes, but you age rapidly when Japs are shooting at you," quipped the volatile Shamrock.

Just then 210 pounds of Marine rolled up to the group in the person of PFC Marion Stevens of Wichita, Kas. Rolled is the only way to describe the self-propelled locomotion of his portly frame. But for all the roll, it was an easy, graceful swaying motion he described when walking, and his belt bit stubbornly a full two inches into his prodigious paunch.

"I insist on holding the line there," he would explain, smiling like a sunflower from his native Kansas.

Coyne cast a quizzical eye at the corpulent Stevens, and then surveyed the comparatively scrawny frame of Koch-Church.

"You know," said Shamrock, "crafty Koch-Church thinks we might go where there are cannibals. He's gone on a hunger strike so they'd pass him up and eat Stevens first. Now just look at Stevens—wouldn't he be a dish for a cannibal?"

"I don't know," said MT Sergeant Ralph Plumb of Indianapolis, Ind., who had just joined the group. "They might eat Koch-Church right away and save Stevens for a Sunday dinner."

We knew cannibals still existed on parts of Formosa, and it would be possible for shipwrecked members of our invasion force to drift ashore there.

Then arose the usual conjuncture as to whether or not the Aviation Marines would go in on "D" day, right behind the invading Marine infantrymen, or D-plus three, or D-plus six.

"When I go in, it will be D-minus 10...minus 10 dead Japs," said Bill Carver. "You know, we Marines don't die for our country—we're going out to make those damn Japs die for their country."

Every Marine going into combat where the going will be rough, knows that some must die. But each one insists he won't be among them, But in their hearts, they sometimes wonder.

We saw our first "casualty" much sooner than expected. He was Staff Sergeant Roman N. Paulson of Thief River Falls, Minnesota, the benedict of our outfits. He married Miss Joyce Lucille Mickkelson of Seattle, Wash., at El Centro and three days later kissed her goodbye to leave on our "cruise."

Paulson, a tall man with angular features, was standing near our group listening to the sanguinary conversation. A wrench slipped from the hands of a sailor working on a landing boat far above Paulson's head, and hit him on the crown of the skull ripping a deep, bleeding gash.

The big ex-football star stood there dazed a moment, with a silly grin on his face.

I don't know why, but we all laughed!

Next the conversation turned to Iwo Jima, that tiny island 750 miles southeast of Tokyo. It had been reported by Jap radio that Iwo Jima was invaded, but the American forces were "repulsed."

"What the Japs will find out is that the American Marines are not repulsed, but repulsive," said Shamrock.

Every day thereafter the question on every tongue was: "How goes the battle of Iwo Jima?"

It was one of the chief topics of discussion where soldiers, sailors or Marines gathered in tiny knots to shoot the breeze and while away a few idle moments. It was almost as if the battle for Iwo Jima were our battle. For ours, we knew, would come next. What the Marines encountered there, we soon would encounter, in like proportion at Okinawa.

The strategic importance of Iwo Jima was obvious. Its capture would bring us within fighter and dive bomber reach of Japan, and hasten the day when the American Eagle would soar unchallenged over Oriental skies.

We knew, instinctively, that Iwo Jima would be another of those rugged campaigns, that the Japs would sell it dearly. We knew that many of our invading forces must pay the price—the toll of human lives which war ghouls extort as the price for victory.

From day to day the picture unfolded more clearly. It was as we foresaw. Leathernecks storming the beaches through cross-machine gun fire amid tremendous outpourings of mortar and artillery fire. Then Leathernecks fighting face to sweating face, and blade to dripping blade with the stubborn, fanatical defenders of that rock.

And Leathernecks in dearly-won machine gun positions, or lying prone with their M-1 rifles, unleashing terrific blasts of hot steel bullets to keep the Japs low while other Devil Dogs with hand grenades, flame throwers and demolition charges crept forward under the shadows of enemy guns to burn or blast the Japs from their caves, crevices, fire trenches and sturdy pill boxes.

The Japs at Iwo Jima not only fought with the zealous fervor of ancestors-worshipers protecting their homeland, but they had new defensive surprises—pill boxes with walls four feet thick, ..and 1000-pound rockets.

The Marine hurled tanks, artillery, mortars and anti-tank guns into this largest and bloodiest battle in the 169-year-old history of the Corps. And the Marines hurled themselves—with their machine guns, their rifles, their bayonets and their bowie knives—to uproot the tenacious defenders and advance over their seared and crumbled defense. . . Their dead and dying bodies. . . To press onward and capture the island.

Grim glances were exchanged aboard or troop ship as we heard the daily news reports and particularly when casualties were announced. It was significant that few Jap prisoners were taken. It was a fight to the finish.

And when the Marines' ghastly job was done and the island secured, there was a surge of pride, mingled with an unuttered feeling of grief and awe for our fallen comrades.

The Marines had done it again... just as they had stormed and conquered so many other Jap-held Pacific Islands, themselves, or spearheaded attacks for the Army. Now blood-drenched Iwo Jima headed the long list of Leatherneck conquests—a list etched in crimson.

The list included Guadalcanal, Bougainville, Tulagi Tanambogo, Govutu, the Green Islands, Eniwetok, Roi, Namur, Florida, Rendova,

New Georgia The Russell Islands, Majuro, Vangunu, Vella Lavella, Emiran, Tarawa, Guam, Saipan, Tinian and other islands, in the perennial battle back across the Pacific.

The final score in the Iwo Jima campaign was 4,189 dead Marines, and more than 20,000 dead Japs. Also, 15,000 Marines were wounded in that roaring inferno, but half of them returned to combat after receiving medical care, and helped blast the foe from that rock in the 26-day campaign.

But that score soon swung even more lopsidedly in our favor as our planes from those blood-ransomed airfields struck again and again at the Jap home island and surrounding islands.

Yes, Iwo Jima was to us another point of Marine assault...battle...victory...sacrifice.

Some must die that our shores and our homes be protected from attackers... that our freedom-loving nation endure...that international justice prevail.

While our daily news reports told of the battle for Iwo Jima, they also carried news of the Allied breakthroughs of the Siegfried Line and the Yanks' speedy drives into Cologne and across the Rhine; of the great Russian offensives, and carrier plane strikes against the Jap homeland.

Later these carrier plane strikes against Japan, and then the Ryukyu Islands chain, were to become the focal point of our news interest. We knew these were softening up strikes to pave the way for the Okinawa invasion. But the grim preview on Iwo Jima of what we would meet face to face on our beachheads was the all compelling story of the moment.

The story of Iwo Jima was just starting as we left the Hawaiian islands and began that long, oceanic caravan toward our objective.

As we stood there that first evening on the main deck of our mildly tossing and rolling ship, the sun slid swiftly downward on our fore starboard side.

Hawaii is a land of beautiful sunsets, and now we witnessed another majestic one in the making.

The fast-moving clouds, as usual, covered only small patches of the sky overhead. But above the horizon they seemed to stack up, and finally to trail off into the distance like a light gray blanket, covering all.

The blood-red sun dropped behind one of the closer clouds—a white fluffy, cumulous cloud. Now the sun's fading rays were painting the scattered scud above us with all-encompassing strokes of scarlet.

Rays of light streamed forth on all sides of the cloud behind which the sun was descending. Some of the long square fingers of light reached down and touched the calming sea. Others stabbed the evening sky like brilliant beams from giant searchlights.

Thus outlined with gilt, and limed against the darker horizon, the cloud now took a fantastic form upon which several of us remarked. It looked exactly like an amoeba, one of the lowest forms of animal life.

Yes, in the skies above us, as though it had germinated and come into existence in this battle stagnant fen, appeared for a few moments in the shape of this primitive organism.

Then, as if by a miracle, it began to change shape and become transformed before our eyes.

The outstretched rays of light still outlined the cloud in bold relief, but now its form had changed and its ashen gray color was infuse with flaming red. Our cloud was taking the unmistakable form of an eagle in full flight.

Its neck stretched out ahead, and the tail protruding squarely. It flew on broad, powerful wings.

Our tiny convoy had shifted to a more westerly direction, more toward the land of the "Rising Sun," and shifted to echelon formation.

And now, ahead of us, in the dazzling pyrotechnics of a Pacific sunset, symbolically and prophetically flew this fiery monarch of the firmament. It flew challengingly into the setting sun, and our ships followed, relentless fingers of vengeance, scorn and justice.

With a final burst of flaming anger, the sun illuminated our winged harbinger of might with a crimson glow. Then Sol sank suddenly below the horizon amid a profusion of afterglow... first magenta... then pinkish purple... and finally battleship gray.

We remained there—silently, meditatively—and twilight descended apace.

A shrill whistle, piped by the bos'n's mate, sounded from the ship's speakers. The Skipper's stentorian voice sounded staccato commands for the twilight alerts:

"General quarters. All hands man your battle stations. Darken ship. The smoking lamp is out on all weather decks."

We steamed westward—toward the setting sun.

Chapter 3

Skyscrapers of the Deep

Ships are small cities all unto themselves, with their own utilities—generators, water manufacturing machines, ship's stores (there's really a waiting line there) laundry units and provisions enough to last several months.

The USS Allendale was a medium sized ship, 455 feet long. Gross weight was almost 12000 tons. To get a picture of 455 feet, just remember that the playing surface of a football field is 300 feet long.

There were some 900 troops aboard, plus a crew of about 500-a total of 1400—more populous than thousands of small towns in the United States.

Our APA was seven stories high, from the bottom cargo hold to the hurricane deck atop the superstructure. Above this rose the masts. Looking at a cross section of a ship's plans, you see it as a skyscraper of the deep.

"She's well-constructed—a good ship in every way," the engineering officer Lieutenant (j.g.) A.H. Jones of Chula Vista, Calif., told me. And he knows his ships, being an old salt who came up through the ranks.

When general quarters is sounded, a troopship seemingly becomes a bedlam—like New York's Grand Central station between 4 and 6 p.m.

There is feverish activity, but little confusion. Troops stand clear of passageways for a few minutes while ship's crew members, wearing their bulky life jackets and steel helmets, dash to their battle stations.

Some man the guns, the life boats and life rafts, while others deploy as fire crews to extinguish any blaze which might occur. Medical corpsmen stand by at various locations to administer first aid and to man stretchers. After giving the crew a couple of minutes to reach battle stations, the troops on deck quickly lay low to their compartments.

Then is when it really gets hot, stuffy, sticky, steamy and smelly! Humanity was so thick in the troop-carrying holds that two-thirds of us had to roll into our bunks to avoid complete traffic jams. There were about 150 in our small hold, with our bunks stacked four high.

It doesn't seem so hot steaming through tropical waters—not nearly as hot as El Centro in southern California's Imperial Valley where our outfit formed and trained. But we sweat like a fat man in a Turkish bath—particularly when crammed in there for general quarters. We could smell the steam arising from our own and other perspiring bodies. Most of us developed mild attacks of pimples and heat rash at first.

Luckily there was water enough that everyone could shower daily. Otherwise the body odor would have caused a putrid stench.

Perhaps to forget the discomforts, our bull sessions during general quarters often assumed a sadistic flavor, with Technical Sergeant John Martin of Washington, D.C., frequently serving as the sacrificial target for our vitriolic banter.

Although only 22 years old, he was prematurely bald. His sandy-complexioned face would flush crimson as we ribbed him about his shinny skull, which was adorned only by a few forlorn strands of silk. Well-muscled, but only five feet, four inches high, he was what we call a "feather merchant" in the Marine Corps.

"Say, I thought I hit that one into the south pocket in the billiard game back at Ewa," said Shamrock Coyne, grinning apishly and pointing to Martin's naked scalp.

"I'd like to put my fingers in his ears and go bowling," said Dick Koch-Church. And Bill Carver chimed in:

"Say, a flea wouldn't have a chance on that simonized job."

The hold was in an uproar of laughter.

"I presume you fellows are enjoying yourselves with that crude attempt at humor at my expense," replied Martin primly. Although a good sport, he never quite cast aside the cloak of formality which he acquired as a cleric in a governmental department at Washington, D.C.

"Aw lay off the kid," I said. "He can't help being bald—his mother was frightened by a billiard ball."

We howled with delight, while the Martin blush extended over the top of his skull and disappeared into the fuzzy hairline, far back on his head.

"Hey, flat top; the planes are peeling off for landings," continued Carver, who perfected the art of razzing years ago when coaching third base and ribbing opposing pitchers in bush league games in The Bronx.

Incidentally, Bill was a better than average ball player, having hurled 11 straight victories in the two years he played for Tottenville High School at Staten Island. Later he played in the Yankee Stadium league with the Goodyear Reserves.

"Let's look for ostrich eggs," suggested Shamrock, with a look of satanic cunning. Then he lumbered around like an anthropoid, and suddenly placed his hand on Martin's head.

"Quauk, quauk," he bellowed. "Dis one is about to hatch. See de tail feathers comin' out de back."

"Johnny won't be a feather merchant much longer," interjected Koch-Church. He's losing his feathers."

"Now Johnny, just a bit of friendly advice," cooed Coyne. "Get on some camouflage before you get caught in a hair raid."

And so it went. Tech Sergeant Martin cringed at the quips, yet reveled at being in the spotlight. The only trouble was that it sometimes scorched. We really liked Johnny very much, and frequently vowed we would take pity and lay off. But he was too appealing a target, and there is so little else to do for amusement aboard a troop transport.

Another endless source of merriment at his expense was to roust him about allegedly amorous forays south of the border into nearby Mexicalli, Mexico when we were based at El Centro.

The report was that the usually bashful Martin grew bold and bought a few drinks for one of the charming senoritas in a Mexicalli night club—if you could dignify those somewhat squalid combination café-saloon-dance halls with that term.

But by the time we got through building it up, it sounded like an affair of greater proportions than the romance of Mark Anthony and Cleopatra; more soul stirring than the passionate devotion of Romeo and Juliet; more dashingly delicious than the lascivious love of a De Maupassant libertine.

Martin's nickname became "Cisco—the Don Juan de Mexicalli." Big John Runciman a Tech sergeant from Detroit, always took a prominent part in accusing Martin of indiscreet amours. Runciman's bunk was right below Martin's, and he would nudge the hapless victim with a knee in the back for emphasis.

An expert and rapid typist, Martin was a conscientious an efficient worker, and a youth of high morals.

One evening he said to me:

"Jim, I admire your wit, but you can't seem to conduct sane verbal intercourse with anyone. You always twist everything around and make a joke of it."

I replied: "Well, John, I understand you thoroughly. You are an educated gentleman who held an estimable position as a cleric of no mean repute in a high governmental department at our national capital.

"You are a man of parts and learning, to whom the finer things of life hold great appeal. You are erudite and learned, well read, have a taste for fine literature and culture, are an interesting conversationalist, have impeccable manners, and you are a veritable lexicographical genius.

"It must have been considerable of a shock for you to suddenly be thrust into the Marine Corps and be subjected to the ribald humor of some of these Leatherneck louts."

I kept a straight face while delivering this gushing mock eulogy, which I fancied would leave him shaking his head. Instead, he sat there for a moment with an ecstatic glow on his countenance. Then he said:

"Nutter, that is the finest thing I ever heard you say."

I didn't have the heart to laugh.

Martin inadvertently heaped more hot coals on his sensitive skull by arousing the ire of Tech Sergeant Bill Carver one day. Buying some candy bars, Martin accused Bill of having taken some candy previously from beneath Martin's mattress.

Now Carver is the last man in the world who would stoop to thievery, particularly petty thievery. So he said nothing, but kept watching Martin. Bill climbed into his sack, and peeked over the end just as Martin was placing the candy bars under the head of the bed.

"Oh, get away, Bill," shouted Johnny, "I'm not going to put these away with you looking."

By this time the other Marines watching the by-play were nearly in hysterics.

Bill huffily stalked out, but stopped at the fountain near the hatch and looked back just as Johnny was again hiding his sweets. Their eyes met. Martin seized his treasures and fled until later.

That noon at chow Carver gained further revenge by giving graphic, four letter descriptions of the food Martin was eating. Now the mess hall is just as stuffy and steamy as the troop sleeping compartments, and you have to have a strong stomach to eat some of the concoctions served.

Martin's stomach was of the sensitive variety, and PFC Koch-Church and Tech Sergeant Runciman, who incidentally holds the purple heart medal for being wounded by shrapnel at Roi island, joined in the sport.

Poor Martin finished only about a third of his meal. Then he fled.

Sleeping in our compartment—that fen of steaming humanity—took as much out of us as a 10-mile hike. I remember the first night at sea after we left Pearl Harbor.

There I was, onto the bottom bunk, with three Marines stacked above me. There was about a foot and half of clearance between each tier. My feet were pointed toward the bow of the ship, but each rise and dip nudged me backward.

Seasickness seemed the fad that first night. I kept sliding back so my head protruded into the main passageway, where it was kicked or bumped by every floundering fellow who got up during the night in the blacked-out ship and sought the head, as we call our toilets. (Soldiers say latrines.)

I slept in my underwear, with no covers over me. Yet I was a mass of perspiration in 15 minutes, and remained that way until morning—fenced in and roasting. As we dipped farther southward, it became hotter, and stuffier.

After that I re-joined the quick-forming host of troops who slept outside on the deck. We would take our bedrolls out at night, and return them to our hold in the morning. It was pleasant out there, under the moon and stars. We soon forgot about not having springs under us.

There always is a breeze whipping across the dock, and by morning we were reaching for blankets. Frequently a sudden tropical storm would strike. Then we would scramble quickly to spread our canvas bedroll covers over everything, including our clothes. We would pull our heads under, turtle fashion, and emerge after the downpour was ended.

Coyne, who continued to sweat it out with the hold sleepers, described it thus,

"That guy below me twists and turns constantly, and has knees four feet high. They jab me every few minutes. And his arms... they're six feet long. They're always flying around and hitting me, or grabbing at me.

"And most of the fellows sleep with nothing on. Everywhere I look in the morning I see a lily-white fanny. I get up and stoop over to put on my shoes. Someone comes down the narrow aisle, trips over another person and whams into me.

"I lurched forward, catching myself with my hands just in time to keep my nose from rooting the deck. I look up, and four inches in front of my face is another of those fannies—one just swinging out of the bunk above me.

I pivot, but fast, straighten up and stand on one foot, trying to lace my other shoe. The ship lurches and I crash against the bunks. The aisle is just big enough for one person, but two yokels crowd past me at once, on opposite sides, going in opposite directions. They spin me around just as the ship rocks the other way.

"This time my head crashes against a steel pipe which is framework for another bunk. Like a whipped cur I slink back into my sack, and furtively wait for the traffic to clear."

"And mind you, dey don't even give de Poiple Heart for dat," he concluded, Going into his shanty Irish brogue which he could use or leave alone at will.

Our outfit was divided into six sections for daily muster and for work detail assignments. Dick and Stevens and I all were placed in section six, under our NCO in charge, Morris Fry.

Now Marines dote on rhymed phrases. There was a current list, to which we kept adding more. Some of them were:

Are you nervous in the service?
Do you have hysterics in the barracks?
Are you fed-up with the set-up?
Have you lost your zeal for the deal?
Can you still gloat in a boat?
Have you a disconnection from the ocean?
Are you bored in the ward? (hospital ward.)
Do you give a rip for the ship?
Remember, keep within Nimits limits!

At our first daily muster, MT Sergeant Fry told us we would muster with him each morning at 9 o'clock. Quipped Koch-Church:

"Reville with Beverly; muster with buster, and now cry with Fry."

Following our daily morning muster, we had calisthenics, also known as combat conditioning. Major Michael Lombardo, 35, of Newark, N.J., former physical director and an amateur boxer of some note, usually led the exercises. A graduate of University of Maryland, he was our ground defense officer.

When he was not available, our squadron commanding officer himself led us. He was Major William F. Feasley, 26, of Palo Alto, California, a graduate of University of Oregon.

Because of its technical nature and great variety of assignments, Marine Aviation is more informal and less G.I. than Marine Infantry.

Before we left the United States our officers told us we were a squadron of "hand-picked men." (We kidded about it, but of course all were forced to admit that we were pretty good men…knew our stuff.) Instead of driving us, our officers led us and gave us breaks when possible. The results were good morale and increased efficiency.

It was good psychology for our officers to lead us in calisthenics. Everyone followed willingly.

But by all odds the most imposing combat conditioning leader I ever have seen was Tech Sergeant W.C. "Moose" Matthews of Birmingham, Alabama, former Golden Gloves heavyweight boxing champion of his state. He was in the other Marine headquarters squadron on board.

This blonde giant was six feet, two inches tall, and not an ounce of fat showed on his 215-pound frame. He was the most rugged looking Leatherneck I've ever seen.

Exceptionally broad of shoulder, he tapered down sharply to the hips. Muscles rippled all over his huge frame—the supple, lightning-like muscles of a panther. His build was reminiscent of a buffalo-a massive neck, a barrel chest and arms as big and powerful as a boa constrictor, yet fast and lethal as a cobra.

In the evenings he and several of his buddies took strenuous boxing workouts on the forecastle, winding up with shadow boxing and open-handed sparring. Any time of the day they were likely to be sparring on slightest provocation.

When Tech Sergeant Matthews led combat conditioning drill for his section, the other soldiers, sailors and Marines watched with fascinated awe. It was a fearsome sight when the Moose led the breathing exercise—filling his huge lungs and then beating his chest with his fists while holding his breath.

His cohort and frequent sparring partner was Sam Cavelli, 24, a master tech sergeant from Bellingham, Wash., and an ex-blocking back for the University of Portland football team in Portland, Oregon, where I lived from 1934 to 1940. Sam plans to return and finish college.

After our first morning muster, several of us were discussing the forthcoming Okinawa invasion.

Buck private Joseph Vance, a tall tow-headed, shy lad of 18 from New Orleans, La., said he didn't like the thought of the poisonous snakes where we were going. He didn't know the name of the island at that time.

"Oh, those 21 step snakes are deadly," said one of the Navy corpsmen assigned to our squadron. Pharmacist's Mate 2/c Raymond Michael Flaherty of Long Beach, Calif., was a short, mischievous Irish youth, full of blarney.

"Twenty-one-step snakes?" asked Vance, his eyes popping with excitement. "What are they?"

Flaherty replied: "They bite and you take only 21 steps before you die."

"Oh, that's horrible," said Vance. "Is that so, Jim?" he asked me.

For some reason I was one of his favorites, perhaps because I was one of the first of the older fellows who took the trouble to notice him and talk to him.

"Yes, Joe," I replied tragically. "The venom is so deadly that frequently older men, or dope-offs can take only 17 to 19 steps. Occasionally real energetic young men can take 23 steps, and a few have been known to take 25."

"My goodness, that's terrible," said Vance, a devout Roman Catholic youth who seldom swore.

"Yes, it's going to be rough," said Flaherty, shaking his chubby head sadly.

"Furthermore, they're very fast," I added. "And they strike just like that!" My right hand suddenly lashed out and 'hit' Vance on the left shoulder. I thought the lad would faint.

In the mess hall a few days later, one of the fellows told me we had Vance thoroughly "snowed" with our 21-step snakes. "Snow job" is Marine lingo for a line.

"Have you heard what those fiendish Japs have done now on this island where we're going?" I asked testily. Vance was opposite me, but I was looking at the other fellows. Without interruption, I answered my own question.

"They have set up breeding grounds—hot houses—for those 21 step snake, and have tripled the number of them. And now they're releasing them in the areas where they expect us to make our beachheads."

I have seen frightened faces before. But Vance's look of stupefied horror is something I can't forget. He paled, his eyes looked glassy and his lips quivered. His face faded to a chalky white. I relented and began laughing, and everyone exploded. A relieved expression came over his face.

But he still feared "Habu," the most venomous of those Oriental serpents on Okinawa. Only after a medical officer, giving us a health lecture, said the bite prove fatal only about 14 per cent of the time, did Vance have surcease from his fears.

Vance also provided merriment aplenty the first morning we went to the ship's library.

"Jim, what shall I read?" he asked.

My eyes chanced on a book entitled "Joseph Vance."

"Here's your book," I exclaimed, pulling it from the shelf and thrusting it before his bewildered eyes.

But the real fun started when Joe was checking the book out.

"Name of the book?" asked the Liberian.

"Joseph Vance," replied the youthful Marine.

"Your name?"

"Joseph Vance."

"No," said the Liberian. I mean your name."

"But—but it is Joseph Vance," he stammered.

"Now look here, Mac," the Liberian said sharply. "I'm busy. There's a long line of fellows waiting to check out books, and I don't have time to joke. Now, what is your name?"

"The same as the book. My name is Joseph Vance too." Joe replied meekly. The librarian still seemed skeptical as Vance left with the book.

Except when anchored, we were required to wear life belts constantly. Made of rubber-coated canvas, they are inflated by CO_2 bullets, or by blowing into air inlet tubes. Troops wore the belts, but most of the ship's crew wore or carried bulky, sleeveless Kapok life jackets.

"I prefer our belts," said Tech Sergeant Herbert O. Pedersen of Lynbrook, N.Y. whom we nicknamed "Lutefisk" because of his Danish ancestry.

"When we reached the United States after our previous tour of duty, one of the crew members celebrated by tossing his life jacket overboard. And right before our eyes, it sank!"

Obviously that life jacket wasn't a Kapok, for they really keep you afloat.

Incidentally, the Lutefisk was a red hot crap shooter. He sent $100 home from Ewa during the three weeks we were there. Frequently he would run five or seven passes, with only one or two craps in between. Of course we had to be secretive about or crap games and other gambling, because our officers were strict about the "no gambling" rules. We had to know when to play, and then establish "security on the dope off" by posting sentinels. Being a PFC, I didn't have much to lose, but "lots to win," as the saying goes. I picked up $17 the first payday, and then dropped seven dollars the next. But I sent $10 home to my wife.

Craps is a noisy game, particularly the way it's played by servicemen. And it always has been played in the service, and probably always will be. Back in 1920 when I was a lad of 10 years, I sold newspapers at Municipal pier in San Diego, Calif. Most of my customers were sailors. Every payday, as soon as the Skipper went ashore, the bones would rattle on the oaken decks of sub-chasers lying there. I particularly remember sub-chaser number 77, and also an oil barge with its bull dog named Chief. Old Chief never lost a fight in his life. I saw him whale the tar out of a young, giant bulldog from a destroyer one day. Chief got his adversary's tongue in a vice-like grip, and it took 15 minutes to pry him loose.

Servicemen huddle on their knees or stand in a circle shooting craps, while the galloping dominoes ricochet from a locker box or bounce back from the wall in the head after lights are out elsewhere in the barracks. And the tall, 20-year-old Lutefisk Pedersen, who had a glistening, boyish complexion, used leather lungs to perfection in calling for his sevens or elevens.

But the most talkative gambler we had-in fact the most loquacious Leatherneck who ever breathed—was Staff Sergeant William H. Cole. His poker playing had all the boys moaning.

"Why you might just as well make out a monthly allotment check to me," he told Master Tech Sergeant Carl L. "Red" Hamilton of Plano, Tex., a little town near Dallas. "I'm going to get it anyway. Hah, hah, hah, hah, hah!"

His raucous laugh was enough to make even a lugubrious Ned Sparks smile broadly. There are infectious laughs, and contagious laughs. Cole's was compelling, overwhelming. It sounded like an evil witch cackling at some sinister crime she had just committed, yet it had a touch of genuine merriment.

Noisy as a flock of cawing crows, Cole was always talking about his "women," (he said he has been married three times) joking, and laughing loudly at his own jokes and anecdotes. And everyone else laughed, too.

He said he picked up more than $500 with the cards from the time we arrived at Miramar until we left Ewa. Then the poker and other games of skill ceased. Our officers were strict against gambling on ship, and I saw very little of it. Besides, we were permitted to bring only $15 apiece on board ship with us, and were told we could take only $15 off.

"That's going to be rather tough on some of you lucky boys," said Major Feasley, our C.O., when he gave us the word at Ewa.

At Ewa our most successful poker player was not Cole, who claimed to have dealt for the "house" at a card room in Charleston, W. Va., but Cliff Coleman, a soft-spoken sergeant from Carmel, Calif. He showed me money order receipts for $850 he sent home after the first pay day at Ewa.

Marines—and I believe this goes for all servicemen—are the best losers at gambling I ever have seen. To those who play, money doesn't mean much, and they figure they can afford to lose. To them, life itself is a gamble—an all encompassing lottery, with lucky numbers for some, and unlucky numbers for others.

Very few go into debt. All who gamble seriously hope to hit a hot streak, ride their luck and win a big roll to salt away or send home. And quite a few do just that.

Why, I know a prominent Seattle manufacturer who went into business after the last war with his poker winnings. Thereafter he quit gambling, and never resumed.

With gambling taboo on the S.S. Allendale, all other manner of card games were almost constantly in progress as troops and ship's crew whiled away monotonous hours. Of course ship's crew had less leisure. They were kept pretty busy.

There was pinochle, 500, hearts, casino, cribbage, even bridge. Others played dominoes, checkers, acey-ducey, chess. Some lolled in the sun. Others argued constantly—little matter the topic.

Seen on every hand in uncomfortable clusters, the players usually found themselves seated on the deck. There were absolutely no chairs available to enlisted men, and unlike some other troop ships, not even any benches. (At the moment this is being written, I'm sitting on an upturned supply box with my typewriter field desk in front of me.)

Nor is the mess hall any exception, as far as comfort is concerned. The theory is that we eat and move along faster when standing, so the benches which were there had been folded and stacked, tantalizingly, at the sides of the compartment. As Shamrock expressed it:

"There's a general regulation against an enlisted man being comfortable on the Allendale."

As the trip wore on, a few of the more enterprising individuals were seen perched on empty boxes or empty 10-gallon cans of the square variety. When their card games were over, they would carry their precious pedestals to their sleeping compartments and hide them, bringing them out only for their games, or for the movies which were presented when we were spending a night or two at some way point anchorage.

Early on the trip, Koch-Church, Carver and Staff Sergeant Lavern Van Ochten of Bay City, Michigan, sought a place to play 500 rummy. The top of the number two cargo hatch, our main assembling piazza, was completely buried with humanity. It was elevated about two feet above the deck, and on all four sides troops sat with their feet outward and their backs toward the center.

Inside this human corral some sprawled full length, on their stomachs or backs or on their sides, while others sat with their feet straight out in front of them. ... Or with their knees doubled up ... or their knees crossed in front of them, Oriental style.

They read, played cards, shot the bull, argued or just crapped out in the sun. Most were stripped to the waist, and many bobbed their khaki or dungaree trousers into shorts.

The deck around the cargo hatch cover also was completely littered with Leathernecks and dog faces, as Marines call soldiers. So Bill, Dick and Van plopped their fannies on an intriguing seat on one of the crane winches. But before the first hand was played, the troop guard with S.P. (shore patrol) on the brassard on his left arm, informed them that all troops must stay clear of the winches.

They crossed to the other side of the main deck, and perched on a paravane, a huge iron gadget looking like an abbreviated torpedo, which was for mine-sweeping operations. But the cards weren't even shuffled when the same guard told them that sitting on the paravanes also was taboo.

With dogged determination the players went back to the fan tail at the ship's stern. Like gold rushers, they avidly staked claim on a tiny portion of bare deck, and for the third time launched into their game.

Things went better this time, but they weren't half through their game when a Naval officer cleared everyone from the fantail for a gunnery lecture and drill.

"How do you like that?" Said Koch-Church.

"Well kiss my ankle," Said Bill Carver.

"We can't stop now," Said Van, who was ahead. "Let's take another look up front."

Luckily a game was just breaking up, so they swooped like SBD dive bombers onto a tiny patch of open deck right under the ladder leading up to the main deck. Under the blazing, early-morning sun they resumed their game.

Things went better for awhile. Bill and Van rested their weary backs against the bulkhead, and Dick sat facing them with his long, sturdy legs crossed under him like a Hindu fakir.

They were progressing nicely, when the Skipper's voice sounded from the speakers:

"Now hear this. Troop sweepers, man your brooms. Clean sweep down, fore and aft."

The trio mechanically picked up their cards and stood aside until the cigarette butts, candy wrappers, discarded comic books, orange peelings and other trash were swept into a pile and transferred to a G.I. can.

No sooner had the game resumed than the Skipper's voice sounded again:

"Now hear this. Wash-scrub down all decks."

But Bill, Van and Dick didn't hear it. In fact, they were oblivious to it until a deluge of salt water cascaded down upon them from the main deck, soaking them and their cards.

"Well kiss my ankle," growled Carver.

Shortly afterward it was time for muster, and then Van had some work to do, so they couldn't finish. But in the evening they again found two square yards of unoccupied deck on the fantail and resumed their game of 500 rummy.

"What are they playing?" asked PFC Walter R. "Mike" Dolan of Los Angeles, Calif., another of our Marines of Irish descent.

"They're playing 'Hell no; toilet face,'" replied Shamrock Coyne, who was draped against a huge anchor post watching the game.

"Naw, dis is 500 rummy," said Carver, who for the moment thoughtlessly reverted to his Bronx accent which he usually concealed. "Wot d'ya mean, Hell no?"

To which Shamrock replied: "Well, a player draws a card, and the others say 'is that it?' The player throws it down and says Hell no! Then the next player takes a card, looks at it, and discards it, saying Hell no! That's all you hear is Hell no, Hell no!"

Then, hunching his head sideways, Coyne assumed the glassy-eyed, dead-pan expression of an imbecile and gurgled in a nasal falsetto voice;

"Uh, huh. Dat's wot it is, Bill. . . Hell no!"

Everyone on the fantail roared with laughter. Just then Carver, who was holding four cards, drew one. Koch-Church asked him if it was "the" card.

"Hell yes!" said Carver, laying down three kings and discarding a seven, winning that hand.

Just about every branch of the service was represented on our crowded ship. There were sailors, soldiers, Marines and even a few Seabees, who were with us to operate unloading cranes.

About 100 of the soldiers were Puerto Ricans, who jabbered constantly in their Spanish tongue. In their public schools they speak English, but everywhere else it is Spanish.

I studied Spanish two years in high school, and two more in college, and was fairly proficient at reading and translating. But that was many years ago. Now, for the first time, I tried to converse in the language.

Their faces lighted eagerly as I spoke a few words in their native tongue, and they answered rapidly and excitedly. I always had to slow them down to understand what they were saying. They were jolly and had a fine sense of humor.

As we neared Eniwetok, our first stopping place west of Hawaii, I pointed excitedly to three ships and said to a couple of Puerto Ricans:

"Miren! Miren! Barcos Japanese alli." (Look, look! Japanese ships there.) They looked in alarm for an instant, then one replied:

"No barcos Japanese. Son Americana," His white teeth flashed in a broad smile.

One day I said to one: "Le gusta mata Japanese?" (Would you like to kill Japs?)

"No. No me gusta mata Japanese," he replied.

"Why," I asked in Spanish.

"I don't like to fight wars," he said.

"But the Japanese would be pleased to kill you," I persisted.

"Oh?" he replied. "Then I'll kill Japs!"

Before long the majority were responding that they would like to kill Japs.

George, one of my Puerto Rican amigos I met the first morning out of Pearl Harbor, said to me in English:

"Japanese bad!"

"Si, si," I replied.

These brown-skinned draftees from our island possession in the West Indies were meticulously clean in their personal health habits. They showered several times a day, first wetting their bodies, then standing aside and soaping vigorously while others stood under the shower and rinsed. This soaping process usually took at least five minutes.

They were in a compartment two decks, below us, and came up to use the head and shower as we did. It always was packed with their glistening, ebony or brown bodies. Negroid strains were blended frequently with Spanish and Indian among these soldiers who were headed halfway around the world from their native Island.

Most of them were in quartermaster or chemical warfare. There were several college men among their ranks, and their two officers were well-educated, personable senores.

Only for three hours a day was the fresh water turned on in our showers and wash basins. The salt water showers always were available, but little used. It's a big job manufacturing enough fresh water aboard ship.

Our head always was congested with black, white, and brown humanity. It was so hot and stuffy that after a shower and dry down we would be dripping with sweat before we got outside again. But it does help to start again with clean sweat.

For the first couple of weeks we extended our fresh-water hours by slightly turning the faucet keys which were chained and locked, but not chained too tightly.

Then the engineering officer began an investigation to find the "Leak." We went back to the schedule of three hours a day.

The Puerto Ricans reacted quickly to anyone who would speak Spanish. Most of the time they congregated on the well deck, which dipped down and was open between the elevated forecastle and the main deck amidships.

One day while I was on guard duty at a post in that area, one of their groups was walking back and forth, arguing and gesticulating vehemently. A jargon of Spanish words rolled rapidly from his lips. I marched up and exclaimed loudly:

"Habla mucho coma vieja!' (You talk as much as an old woman!)

His countrymen howled with laughter. He grinned good-naturedly, then resumed his earnest harangue.

Mike Dolan used to talk to them frequently too, but his Latin-American vocabulary was mostly of the skid row variety which he learned in southern California.

Most of the brown men carried "dagas," and sometimes whipped them out in mock threats to each other. Some would lay their long, sharp knives on their playing cards to keep them from blowing away. One had printed on his dagger scabbard:

"For a Jap only."

But they were a peaceable lot.

Men of our outfit bitched about having our head and showers constantly jammed with Puerto Ricans, but we respected their cleanliness.

By the second week out, the tropical sun had tanned Tech Sergeant Bill Carver to a chestnut brown. Mistaking him for a fellow countryman, one of the Puerto Ricans began talking to him in native tongue in the mess hall one noon.

It amused us a little, and immediately Carver's nickname became "Pancho." Shamrock Coyne also gave Carver another moniker, blackout!

Yes, our ship teemed with humanity. One afternoon our section mustered on number two hatch for a health lecture. There was no room there, so Tech Sergeant Fry led us to the fantail. A Navy lecture was in progress on the starboard side of the fantail, so we retraced our steps back around the poop deck and approached the fantail from the port side.

Then the doctor decided it wasn't a very good place, so we went forward a short ways and seated or draped ourselves under two huge landing boats.

As the lecture started, some of the nearby Puerto Ricans reached a heated point in their discussion, and voices reached a high crescendo. The medical officer glanced grimly in their direction, then raised his voices and continued.

Then some sailors began pounding on the metal decks of a huge landing boat above us. We moved again.

For the third time we followed the medical officer back to the fantail. Then he gave the lecture without further interruption.

Oh, we had a few discomforts. But, we knew our quarters and food weren't half bad. However, when civilians go to war, they retain the right of freedom of speech at least to the extent that they can do a bit of private bitching. It seems to make you feel better to bitch a bit and get it off your chest. Just like taking a bath.

At the request of Lieutenant H.L. "Jack" Ogden, the ship's personable chaplain, I began daily newscasts, which I read to the fellows over a public address system. Brief items of world news from the Associated Press were received by radio, and transcribed from Morse code by ship's radio service section.

These reports I re-wrote into broadcast style, and presented each morning at 10:30 o'clock and again at 6 p.m. There was intense interest in the news, but the public address system broke down in about 10 days and the newscasts were temporarily discontinued.

This had been taking from three to four hours a day of my time. I was standing eight hours of guard duty every other day, and sometimes every day. So I welcomed a bit of rest. But every day thereafter, anywhere from a dozen to a hundred fellows asked when the newscasts would be resumed.

Virtually no provision was made for letting the men read any news about the world in which they were fighting. The news reports which came by radio were mimeographed and distributed to officers on the ship's wardroom. One copy was posted on the bulletin board in each troop compartment, but you were lucky to see it before it got torn down.

When we were near radio stations, we got news broadcasts from servicemen's stations. But there were no speakers available for the troops, except one in the mess hall, which was so hot that you dashed away quickly as possible.

The men seemed almost starved for news, but for the most part they went hungry.

About the fifth night out, Dick Koch-Church conducted a quiz program. The ship's chaplain led a sing song, and Pharmacist's Mate 3/c Jeff Van Pelt, 22, of Little Rock, Ark., sang a couple of songs, accompanied by guitar-playing Mike Dolan. Van Pelt was plenty good, having had long training for classical singing, and later being vocalist for the Rhythm Doctors, a band at the Oakland, Calif., Naval Hospital.

Dick opened with a well-received monologue which went something like this:

"Howdy fellows. It's great to be here on the USS Allendale. (grimace from him, cat calls and laughter from the audience.)

"Yes, this is a fine ship. And that food. I can't get over that food; but it gets all over me. First I manage to get the food down, an then it gets me down.

"I'm writing a book entitled: "Boy, was I seasick—or, You Can't Take it With You.

"I see quite a few of you fellows still are traveling by rail—ship's rail."

The quiz show went smoothly, once the contestants were inveigled onto the rustic stage. They could choose their question topics from the fields of music, sports or war and current events.

When Staff Sergeant Cole strode up to the microphone, Dick asked him what he wished to talk about.

"Me," said the cocky Cole. Then he tilted his head backward and cackled wildly. It brought a tremendous roar from the audience.

The chaplain, Lieutenant Ogden, wound up the show by saying the "female guests" for the evening's entertainment was to have been Mrs. Roosevelt. However, he added, she was unable to fly out from Pearl Harbor because of priority for a 250-pound bull mastiff.

"And that's a lot of bull," he concluded.

One morning we were surprised, to say the least, when the Skipper announced over the public address system:

"A Fire on number three hatch."

I looked back, and it wasn't just a drill. Smoke and flames were coming up from diesel oil spilled while fueling one of our landing boats. A fire crew of sailors were there in about 15 seconds, and five minutes later had it under control.

Later we heard many reports like that over the speakers, but they were drills. One evening during general quarters alert the Skipper, Captain John J. Twomey of New Rochelle, N.Y., said:

"Plane crash on number two hatch. ... Starboard fire party take control." Plane crashed on number four hatch ... port fire party take control."

It was a drill, and really gave the men a workout. Part of the crew grabbed heavy fire extinguisher equipment, while other manned gushing fire hoses. However, they played their streams over the side.

An interesting mid-pacific drama occurred on the first leg of our journey. Our destroyer escort, the USS Varmen, pulled up close to us, and one of our flat-bottomed landing boats went alongside it.

We saw a stretcher being lowered on ropes. The seas were rather rough, with large swells running. But he coxswain knew his stuff. The D-E was rolling and pitching madly. The little landing boat, rocking and dipping wildly and bobbing crazily on the churning waves, rode a big swell right up under the poised stretcher. Four pairs of strong arms grabbed its corners and landed it safely.

The landing boat returned to the Allendale and was hoisted to main deck level on its davits. It then was simple to move the patient, Electrician's Mate 3/c Kenneth Powell, 30, of Jamestown, Tenn., to the ship's hospital.

He was suffering an acute attack of appendicitis. The little D-E had only two medical corpsmen, but no doctor aboard. Furthermore, one of those tiny, bobbing ships is no place to be when ill.

As he was being carried to the hospital, the Varmen steamed close alongside and the Skipper, Commander L. M. King of Redlands, Calif., said over his ship's speakers:

"Well done, men. Thanks."

Powell had been sick 15 hours, and was running a temperature. Two hours after coming aboard he went under the expert knife of Lieutenant Commander Fred A. Hasney of West Orange, N.J. Also in the operating room was our ship's other medical officer, Lieutenant (j.g.) Irving K. Neece of Decatur, Ill.

"I remember some pain when we were bumping over the waves in that landing boat," Powell said later. He debarked a few weeks later at Leyte, Philippine Islands to recuperate and then rejoin his ship.

Duty aboard the Varmen appeared to be rough, because two other patients came to us from her.

Lieutenant Karl H. Klein, 30, the assistant gunnery officer, sustained bad lacerations around his right eye when a hatch broke loose and fell on his head, smashing his sunglasses. The corpsmen didn't wish to take stitches so close to the eye, or run the risk of infection. Luckily none of the glass penetrated his eyeball. He returned to the Varmen when we reached Leyte.

Formerly of La Crosse, Wis., Lieutenant Klein worked for the Continental Illinois Trust & Saving Bank at Chicago, Ill., before entering the Navy.

The other patient was Seaman 1/c Victor Gontis, 23, of Johnston, Pa., whose leg was broken when caught in a gun mount. To Gontis went the honor of being the first "splint" patient on the Allendale. He and Lieutenant Klein were transferred by stretcher in a tiny whale boat from Varmen to another destroyer outside the Eniwetok anchorage and thence to the Allendale, while the Varmen hurried on westward with a new convoy.

The patients made an interesting trio in the Allendale hospital ward, telling anyone who would listen that the Varmen "is a fine ship," and she has a "swell crew, with many unusual characters."

Yes, there are interesting events, and characters galore on our nation's floating cities—those skyscrapers of the deep. . . Teeming with humanity.

Chapter 4

Mid-Pacific Holiday

Silver fingers of dawn streaked across the skies. Lined on the gray horizon, were three tiny towers, resembling distant oil derricks. They were the first ships we had sighted since leaving Pearl Harbor.

Like our convoy, they were headed westward toward Eniwetok Atoll, in the Marshall Islands, but from a more northerly angle.

In mid-morning a Marine plane, an SBD dive bomber, gave us a welcoming "buzz." He roared past at deck level, skimming the waves gracefully. Soon we sighted the first of the circle of tropical islets forming Eniwetok Atoll. Then we saw other small islands, more planes and many ships. Signal lights blinked out Morse code messages on every hand.

Rising no more than 13 feet above sea level, these dusty brown pancakes of the Pacific looked like buffalo chips on the American prairies... like camel chips on the Sahara.

Towering several times as high as the tiny atoll were the masts of many ships. On the far sides of the island we could see other ships—their masts and even their gunwales silhouetted in bold relief.

As we steamed into the Eniwetok anchorage—a typical mid-Pacific bay encircled by tiny coral islands and strands of coral reefs barely awash—we saw only a few coconut trees. And some were beheaded of their top notches of fronds.

Little vegetation remained on those lonely, dismal islands after the 22nd Marines and the 106th infantry, commanded by Marine Brigadier General T.E. Watson, blasted the Jap garrison into oblivion there in February 1944.

The attackers opened their lightening beachhead offensive on February 17, and eight days later all the islands in the Atoll had been secured.

Eniwetok Atol, lying at 10 degrees latitude—only 600 miles from the equator—is 2300 miles west-southwest of the Hawaiian Islands. Following World War I, this strategic mid-Pacific atoll was mandated to the Japanese government.

And it was from Eniwetok Atoll that the Japs launched their carrier task force which struck Pear Harbor December 7, 1941.

The Jap warlords had been planning just such a move for a long time—even before the last World War. That is one of the main reasons they joined the Allies at that time—to garner spoils in the form of strategic island bases all over the Pacific. From these bases the Japs launched their conquest designed to bring the entire Pacific under their control.

They calculated correctly that the United States, a peaceful, non-imperialistic nation, would be dominated by isolationists and idealists, and thus not be prepared. Our misguided isolationists, abhorring war, closed their eyes to a changing world being revolutionized by the airplane.

Isolationism and the Monroe Doctrine were true guiding beacons for our nation when oceans were spanned only by the steamship. As science changes our world, our governmental officials and our people must continue to change their philosophies of international relations.

These thoughts ran through my mind as I looked at Eniwetok Atoll. There it lies, some 4300 miles and 12 days by steamship from California, but less than 24 hours from California by a transport plane or a bomber cruising 200 miles an hour. And many of our new transports and bombers cruise much faster than that.

Land was a welcome sight to all of us—the sails as well as the troops. We had seen nothing but water—blue, salt water—for days. Dick and I had longed to dive overboard and swim in the inviting waters. At Eniwetok we snapped quickly out of our listlessness, and eagerly ogled our new surroundings.

Many of us were humming or singing: "Oh, give me land, lots of land under starry skies above, don't fence me in."

Shamrock Coyne was putting on a terrific show—just going nuts over the sight of tierra firma. He blew kisses at the atoll, then hunched his shoulders forward like a gorilla and paced back and forth excitedly, snorting and raging like an anthropoid seeking to escape his cage and go ashore.

Then Shamrock spied Scotty McTavish, the ship's pedigreed Scotty dog. Seizing the ebony canine, Coyne cried:

"Look, Sandy. Trees! Real trees! Not just steel mast poles!"

Sandy perked up his ears... a cunning light shone in his eyes... he whined and barked excitedly. I swear he must have understood.

Sandy was as much a part of the Allendale as the big St. Bernard dogs—Breuhl and Lady—were of Timberline Lodge, the mile-high ski and summer resort on Mount Hood near Portland, Oregon, where I was advertising and promotion manager for two years.

A Los Angeles minister presented Scotty to the Allendale, and the bony, black beastie was much in evidence when the ship was commissioned November 22, 1944.

Not contented with the usual champagne christening on the bow of the ship, Scotty, the young, excitable pup, added some canine "spirits." The spot of his ceremony was the canvas cover of the number two hatch, amid pompous ceremonies being observed by high-ranking naval officers whose Navy blue uniforms glittered with scrambled egg trim.

Scotty loved the sailors, but was a poor host. His usual greetings to the troops were loud barking and angry snapping.

One morning Scotty was exceedingly irate at soldiers doing calisthenics on the number two hatch. One exercise was with the men—down on all fours—alternatively kicking sidewise to the left and right while the leader counted.

Sandy, who had been camped out comfortably beneath a landing boat, suddenly awakened and saw this strange sight of bipeds not only transformed into quadrupeds, but going through the canine capers of hoisting first one leg and then the other.

The enraged Scotty sailed forth like Scots of old, to do battle with these mocking mongrels of men.

I'll never forget that sight—the dismayed Scotty barking at first one and then another—snapping menacingly, but being discreet enough not to bite. For after all, a pedigree dog should disport himself as a gentleman at all times.

The Allendale's massive anchor descended from the bow of the ship, split the pasture-green waters of Eniwetok lagoon, and came to a heavy rest on the coral and coral sand bottom.

Bill Carver, Dick Koch-Church and I were in shorts, sunning ourselves on the number two hatch.

"Let's start some scuttlebutt," said Dick, "and see how long it takes to get back to us."

So we sauntered over to the rail near some soldiers.

"What are we wearing on liberty tomorrow?" asked Dick innocently.

"Either full khaki or full dungarees," replied Bill. "There's no mixing of uniforms."

"Let's see, what time does our liberty start?" I asked.

"At 0800 (8 a.m.) tomorrow," answered Dick.

Oh, the rumor spread rapidly. And, to our delight, it proved true.

The following morning we prepared for a "beach party." But Dick was unhappy. He had guard duty.

"How do you like that?" he demanded hotly. "That really dusts me off... having guard duty and getting rocked out of shore liberty."

Dick really blows his cork at times. This is when I delight in "consoling and cheering" him, knowing full well that he doesn't want to be cheered. No sir! When Dick gets a big peeve on, he doesn't want to be kidded or reasoned out of it. He doesn't want to laugh, or smile. He just wants to stay sore awhile and enjoy a good mad.

What made it all the funnier was that the sergeant of the guard permitted the men on Dick's guard relief to go ashore, and report for guard duty just as soon as they got back. So, after crying before he was hurt, Dick went ashore after all.

Eagerly we swarmed over the rail and down the debarkation net into a flat-bottomed LCT landing boat—soldiers, sailors, and marines. The LCT bobbed like a cork. Huge fountains of water welled up between it and our ship, and sprayed over us. Many were drenched, and everyone laughed uproariously. We were in a festive mood, for beer and coca cola awaited us on the shore. Suddenly Shamrock pointed to the debarkation net.

"Hey, pipe O'Donnel," he ejaculated. "Looks like an elephant walking a tight rope in a circus."

And so it did. Sergeant Joe O'Donnel, a soldier from Trenton, N.J., was only five feet, seven inches tall, but his puffing paunch, his baggy chests and prodigious posterior all added up to 245 pounds.

There he was, his huge hulk swaying back and forth as the LCT drifted farther out or suddenly came in close. But O'Donnel made it all right, albeit at a ponderous pace.

When we got underway, Pancho Carver mounted the snub-nosed bow of the landing boat for a good view of the islands, the ships and the water. He got an eye full of the latter when our craft hit the first big swell. It seemed like half the water in the bay came up like a tidal wave. It almost knocked Bill down. After that we shied discreetly from the fore part of the boat.

We headed squarely in for the beach of Parry Island, and our boat's rugged bottom slid up the sand with a crunch. The front gate swung downward, and one long step put us on dry sand as we swarmed out.

At first the ground felt funny. It seemed to rock and pitch under our "sea legs." Shamrock dropped to his knees, salaamed and kissed the ground, saying:

"Oh, land! Wonderful land. But why do you keep rocking like this?"

We forgot that sensation, however, as we marched briskly up the beach like militant pickets, and then swung down an oiled roadway toward the recreation area. I picked up a couple of souvenirs of unusual coral formation. We passed a grass shack chapel.

Huge bomb craters and pillbox excavations were on every hand. The Marines had taken this island in only four days. A few, scattered coconut trees had lived through that withering blast of Naval and Marine gunfire. Some of the jagged, be-headed snags still remained upright.

This island was mostly sand and coral. A brisk breeze propelled a number of small, home-made windmills which operated plungers in barrels, making inexpensive washing machines.

Our beer parlor was rustic. Atop pillars of coconut tree logs, had been nailed a roof of rough, off-cast lumber. Over this were stretched canvas tarpaulins. The sides were open, permitting the breeze to fan us as we sat at picnic-style tables and benches.

Having paid 50¢ each, we lined up and received three cans of cold beer and one coca cola.

Joe Vance, the lad who feared the "21-step snakes," was a teetotaler, so I looked for him. Not finding him immediately, I shouted his name loudly. Koch-Churchill whom Coyne was nicknamed "Lunchface" because of his determination that none would get more extra desserts or other goodies than he—heard me calling Vance and knew at once what I had in mind.

Dick and Pancho dashed over just as I found Vance and was asking him for his extra beers. They tried to horn in, and poor Joe blushed paint-red.

Finally I persuaded Koch-Church and Carver to leave. Then I consummated the deal. I borrowed .50 cents from Carver to pay for Vance's drinks. He drank the coke, and I divided the three beers between Dick, Bill and myself.

Bill also fell heir to several other beers—I believe he had six cans—but he still looked and acted parched.

Dick and I stripped to our shorts and swam on a beautiful beach with a necklace of white, coral sand. The water was warm and pleasant, and not too restless. A beautiful bird winged past, a dazzling white dove—streamlined, small, sylphlike.

Lieutenant Ogden, the chaplain, was knifing through the water with the agility of a shark.

"Come on, let's play 'King of the Barrel,'" he shouted.

There was a 50-gallon oil drum, filled with sand and set upright, with its top a foot under the water's surface. Half a dozen of us fought for standing room atop this submerged pedestal. When one got on top he would shout:

"King of the Barrel," and beat his chest.

The others would swim up quickly and dethrone him, and usually hold him under water awhile for good measure. Lieutenant Ogden was good at this game, what with his big six-foot Irish frame.

More servicemen, including a flock of Seabees from another ship in our convoy, flocked ashore on Parry Island and lined up thirstily for beer.

One of the Seabees. Who had been overseas a long time, offered MT Sergeant Fry $5.00 for the three cans of beer. Fry refused, so the Seabee made the same offer to a sailor.

The sailor, sitting on an empty beer case in the tropical sun, looked at the crisp chunk of cabbage on the Seabee's hand, and at the cans of beer. His toe dug meditatively into the sand. Impulses and doubts were mirrored in his face as he pondered the question. Finally he took the five dollars, and the jubilant Seabee whipped out a long, heavy hunting knife and stabbed open the cans of beer; then drank lustily.

In a couple of hours we returned, refreshed from our holiday. A bit of typical servicemen's horseplay was in progress as we headed homeward. Private First Class Jim Klochko of Hillsboro, Ore., had an inverted L-shaped tear in the seat of his khaki trousers, on the right side.

He was laughing about it, sparring with Moose Matthews, and being pushed from one side of a tiny circle of humanity to the other. It was providing great merriment for all, so I stepped indiscreetly forward to join in the pushing.

Then I began to mimic Klochko, echoing each word he said and emulating every gesture. Just to make the act more realistic, one of those ever-present knife-carrying commandos cut my pants in the rear, and ripped them wide open. Then ensued a general pants-ripping orgy, with Jim and myself the victims. We were lucky to escape with our shirts!

I didn't mind too much, because I happened to be wearing an enormous, tent-like pair of khaki pants which the wily Koch-Church got back by mistake in his laundry at the El Centro and traded to me, saying:

"Jim, they're just a little loose on me and should fit you perfectly!" They would have fit us both—at once! So I figured those pants were expendable.

It had been crowded on our boat, so only a few of the passengers saw our little strip tease sideshow. But I happened to be one of the few going up the debarkation net, and suddenly there was a roar from the fellows below as they saw my unfrocked fanny wriggling up the ladder.

I stopped, turned and waved, and with a big, silly grin made a remark which is best not printed.

Then I set an all-time record going the rest of the way up the net. Sergeant Major Wray was on the deck handing out cigars to the men from our outfit. I grabbed mine and darted quickly into the hold to change pants.

On the main island of Eniwetok was the handiwork of a sailor who retained his sense of humor through long, monotonous days of desolate island duty. At the rustic ship's service store was a sign, in beautiful hand lettering, saying:

"IT'S SMART TO TRADE AT ENIWETOK."

And another sign read:

"Quality – CLOTHES OF DISTINCTION – Service." Inserted in small letters in the upper left-hand corner was: Government approved."

We had movies at night at Eniwetok, a usual practice in port.

After the first night's show, big 225-pound John Thomaselli of Follansbee, W. Va., and the cackling Cole remained on the darkened number two hatch singing:

"Off we go, into the wild blue yonder—CRASH!

"Nothing can stop the Army Air Corps—except the Marines,

"Nothing can stop the Army Air Corps—except the Waves,

"Nothing can stop the Army Air Corps—except the Wacs."

Then Cole would cackle: "Hah, hah, hah, hah, hah! His snow jobs formed the biggest blizzard which ever hit the western Pacific.

But it was the next day on a second beach party that Thomaselli and the ever-talking Staff Sergeant Cole panicked everyone. It seems the beer flowed more freely that day, and several fellows acquired a pleasant glow. It was our last beer before our invasion—some might never have a chance for another.

It was like herding wild zebras to get all the men back on the LCT. While they were milling around, Cole and Thomaselli walked right out into the surf with their clothes on.

At armpit level, Thomaselli picked up Cole like a babe-in-arms and doused him under the waves. As Cole's dripping head emerged, his choppers were open wide and his noisy cackle sounded:

"Hah, hah, hah, hah, hah!"

Then Thomaselli submitted to a dunking by Cole, after which they waded ashore like conquering generals, with gestures of triumph. Their pantomime was majestic.

The mellow marines, soldiers and sailors on shore howled and doubled over with laughter.

The next morning the waters of Eniwetok lagoon seemed more restless. Soon we were turning, and leading a parade of a large number of transports and oilers out through the submarine net which net minders pulled aside for us.

Ahead of us steamed numerous destroyers, and one destroyer escort, also in single file until they cleared the entrance to the anchorage. Then they fanned out in all directions—protection for our growing convey.

By the number of escorting destroyers, and by our maps, we knew that we were going closer to possible enemy interception.

Westward we steamed—plodding steadily westward—day and night.

Chapter 5

Through Perilous Waters

Our convoy steamed westward from Eniwetok, ploughing furrows of lacy snow which danced and glistened in dazzling sunlight. Then night fell... Dark and ominous.

Between Pearl Harbor and Eniwetok, bright moonlight shone serenely on our convoy. But now the moon had changed. When it belatedly appeared in the wee hours of the morning, only an uncertain silver remained.

As we knifed through inky waters, we passed within a few hundred miles of Japan's great mid-Pacific stronghold of Truk, which was by-passed in our island-hopping offensive back across the Pacific.

Constant bombings kept Truk pretty well neutralized, but we knew there still were a few fighter and bomber planes there. Also, it probably still harbored Jap submarines.

Disaster leered at us that first night out of Eniwetok, but in an unexpected form. Phosphorescent lights twinkled in our frothy furrows, a phenomenon probably caused from a combination of static electricity and chemical content of the water, or from some form of marine life in it.

Tiny sparklets of light flashed and bubbled in the disturbed waters like sparks from an emery wheel. Save for that, there was all-encompassing blackness 'neath cloudy skies. The forms of other ships near us were barely visible, and our escorting destroyers were unseen ghosts, except for isolated blinker signals.

Dick Koch-Church and I got off guard duty at 10 p.m., and sacked down beside Pancho Carver on the number two hatch. About two hours later we were virtually dynamited from our slumbers by a deep-throated blast of our ship's whistle. It was a fearsome, 15-second blast which sounded like a mad bull elephant trumpeting a warning to his herd.

Dick and I sat upright, and Carver leaped to his feet.

"Well, kiss my ankle," said Pancho.

Then the Allendale whistle sounded a short, angry blast. It was answered in a few seconds by a squealing snort from the ship on our right.

"Son of a bitch!" said Pancho. "There's going to be a collision."

Blinker lights flashed feverishly.

"What is it, Bill?" asked Dick sleepily. He had sunk back into his sack.

We're jamming up here," Bill declared. "We're going to ram that ship on our starboard side."

"Oh, no," I said optimistically. "They know what they're doing on the bridge."

But I wondered. I heard crew members shouting back and forth excitedly from the main deck to the hurricane deck, and to the bridge. Now I too was on my feet. I'm a sucker for excitement.

"Well, kiss my ankle," said Bill again. "We're going to ram him sure."

"No we're not," I said.

But there the tanker was, creeping right in our path, with our bow aimed amidships. We learned a bit later that the troop ship on our port—the 203—was all but ramming our stern, so we were trying to elude it.

We bore down on the tanker to our right at full speed... closer and closer. Now I began to think we would hit. We were within 300 feet...200 feet...100 feet!

Then suddenly swung left, and missed the tanker by about 75 feet. The other ship, the 203, came even closer to us, missing by a scant 15 feet. It had given us a couple of bad times previously, but nothing like this.

"Gosh, we almost collided," muttered Bill.

"That was a bit close," I admitted.

"Well, I'll be a sad sack," said Dick, now wide-awake. "There we were, running a straight course and minding our own business when that 203 tries to ram us."

Only skillful work on our bridge saved us in that mid-Pacific squeeze play.

We sank back to our sacks, about as sleepy as a bald-head in the front row at a burlesque show.

Finally we fell asleep, only to be awakened again by a short angry blast from our ship's whistle. It was a signal for our convoy to change directions. We swung onto a west-northwest course.

Sleep came again, finally, and then came rain. Quickly we scrambled to get our canvas covers over everything. Wind and rough waters accompanied the rain... It denied us sleep.

Later the elements relented, but then my wool blanket began scratching. (Only the officers were issued sheets on ship.) Reveille found us all a bit bleary-eyed.

I'm glad we're on our way again," Joe Vance told me the morning after we left Eniwetok. "I'm anxious for us to get this war over and get back."

Most of the other men felt the same way about it. We always were more contented when moving, and definitely restless while anchored and waiting.

In a few days we reached another anchorage, and saw a gigantic assemblage of Uncle Sam's naval might. There were scores of warships—carriers, battleships, cruisers, destroyers, and all manner of smaller craft. We gazed in wonderment. Probably all this striking force and more too would be in on our invasion.

"Shore party at 4 p.m. for Gunner Harris to pick up some native recipes," announced Shamrock Coyne.

"Yes, we can always use new recipes," laughed Warrant Officer Raymond C. Harris of Portsmouth, Ore., our mess officer for Marine Aircraft Group 43.

But none of us went ashore. We moved on quickly from that anchorage, and without another beer party. Nor had we received any mail since leaving Pearl Harbor.

However, before we left, there was a momentous decision for Koch-Church to make. We were in the chow line leaning against the rail...waiting, of course.

"Gee, I'd like to dive off and go swimming here," he said.

"I'll give you $50 if you do," said Carver.

"It's a deal," said Dick. "Right after chow I'll get on my swimming trunks and do it. But...gee! What would they do to me for diving in without permission? I guess I won't do it. But I would for $100."

"I'll make it $100," said Pancho, pounding the rail with his fist for emphasis.

"Cash?"

"My word is as good as cash!"

"Will you sign an agreement?" said Dick.

"Sure!"

Excitedly Dick wrote out an agreement, which Carver signed. Then Dick had Van Ochten and Shamrock co-sign it.

"I'll tell you what I'll do," said Dick. "I'll have the chaplain get me permission, and I'll donate $50 to the ship's recreation fund and keep $50,"

"Oh, no," cut in Shamrock. "It's only $100 if you make an unauthorized jump. And I can just hear the Captain announcing:

"Disciplinary action had been taken against a troop member for making an unauthorized jump into the water. There will be no more of that!"

I suggested that Dick might lose his lonely little PFC stripe. Carver just grinned and said:

"Yep, $100 for an unauthorized dive or jump."

Dick's mind was a turmoil. After chow he put on his swimming trunks, but for comfort's sake only. Instead of diving overboard, he played "Hell no" with Pancho and Van. I guess you know, we razzed him for days... "Oh, you high diver!"

Flocks of flying fishes skimmed over the waters, splashing suddenly out of sight in a high wave, as we continued westward. Occasionally we saw porpoises swishing and bouncing playfully.

The nights remained dark, but we weren't quite so concerned about ramming or being rammed. For our convoy had dwindled to the original three APAs, plus three destroyer escorts.

On those dark decks we soon developed "Allendale shins." Coming from a lighted hold, it required five or 10 minutes to accustom our eyes to the darkness. So it was quicker to proceed by feel and memory of obstacles, but half a dozen times I paid for my haste with bloody shins.

While standing guard duty, I would guide nocturnal deck roamers, especially the bakers from our group who covertly kept a few of us supplied with hot bread or rolls each night. Soon I began to feel like a seeing-eye dog, and couldn't help barking a bit while escorting one of my human convoys. Daffy, wot?

Despite the darkness, we usually gathered on the forecastle after general quarters for songfests. There were just a few of us—Mike Dolan with guitar, usually the chaplain, Sergeant Fred Reed of Beckley W.Va., a tall youth with a fine bass voice, Sergeant Frank Treuting, tall, slender piano pounding expert from New Orleans, Shamrock, Carver, Koch-Church and I.

In moonlight or darkness, we met there whenever enough of us were off guard duty, which now came only every third day. To our delight they had started giving sergeants guard duty, instead of just the corporals and privates. Not such a bad war, after all.

Guiding us ever was Venus, the evening star, in the West. On moonless nights its brilliant light cast shadows across our deck, and mirrored a silver sheen on the surf.

Soon we formed a jazz band by adding the chaplain's portable church organ, and then some horns and other guitars, and began practicing for a ship's show. Frank Treuting got an unbelievable quantity of hot music from that tiny sound box.

In a few days our convoy reached one of our most unusual Pacific anchorages—Babelthaup in the Palau Islands chain. When the Marines captured Peleliu, they by-passed the sister island of Babelthaup, some 35 miles distant, but kept pounding it by air.

With 30,000 Japs besieged prisoners of war on their own islands, we proceeded to use the Babelthaup anchorage. The closest ships lay some five miles offshore, while we tantalizingly made ourselves at home a little farther away. But a strange, eerie feeling shadowed us, sleeping with our ship in sight of 30,000 Jap soldiers.

Both of the nights we were there we had sentries posted with Thompson submachine guns, because the Japs had on occasion tried to swim out to ships on small flotation bladders or on rafts to throw hand grenades aboard or guide floating mines against our ships.

The sentries cut loose at anything afloat, and several times we deck sleepers were awakened by the chattering guns, fired at floating boxes and debris.

One day after we departed, Marine pilots bombed Babelthaup again, and hit an ammunition dump which burned for 16 hours. But we missed the show.

In the late stages of the Peleliu campaign, 150 Japs escaped that island on rafts and fled to Babelthaup. But there were penned up as "traitors." Soon food supplies ran low, so they were freed and told to go back to Peleliu and fight like true "Sons of Heaven."

Their hands were reaching toward heaven when they returned to become voluntary prisoners with good food and good living conditions, and with their salaries paid by the United States government, according to international law. Occasionally others fled and surrendered, wanting no more of starvation rations and regular bombings.

When we left Babelthaup, the blues sailed with us, clouding many a soul. The reason...no mail. With a much larger convoy, including LST and LCI landing boats, mine sweepers, destroyers, APAs, tankers and freighters, we moved slower. Another black first night... then the executive officer's voice in early morning over the speakers:

"Now all hands hear this. Two floating mines have been sighted in the convoy this morning. All troops personnel will help keep a lookout for mines."

Shamrock pointed one out to me half an hour later. It was a huge, brown, pear-shaped monstrosity which bobbed in and out of view, on each swell and dip. That day we saw eight of the formerly submerged mines which had broken from their moorings and surfaced. The closest ships would puncture them with bullets, and down they would go.

We still traversed mine-infested waters that night, and it was so black that they couldn't possibly be seen more than 50 feet away. It seemed miraculous to me that our entire convoy ploughed through unscathed.

As we watched for mines, a Marine told us of a friend in the service who angled successfully for statewide duty for the duration.

"I wouldn't mind a deal like that," said a member of our group.

"Damn it man, didn't you want to come on this invasion?" demanded Shamrock hotly.

"I wanted to, but now that I know what the deal is "I'd rather be back," he replied.

Shamrock exploded: "For God's sake, man, you got any red blood or manhood about you? Too damn many people are selfish about this war. They want to stay home and let someone else have the crap detail and risk his life. I've got plenty of reason to want to stay home, but you couldn't keep me there!"

That was my first glimpse of Shamrock's Irish temper, and a fine glimpse of the character of this typical Leatherneck. He had been out before, and knew this campaign might be rougher than his previous ones.

But there is a wonderful tradition in the Corps that no Marine will let another Marine down. And they won't let their loved one back home down, either.

Most of us received our inoculations and vaccinations stateside. For those who didn't, there were almost daily processions to sick bay. Aboard ship all of us got a booster shot against tetanus, and it left our arms stiff and sore for days.

Now we all began taking one atabrin pill a day to safeguard ourselves against malaria. Our section leader, MT Sergeant Fry, hounded us with motherly instinct to take our pills daily, so we nicknamed him the "yellow peril."

After taking all the prescribed immunizations, we felt like walking drug stores. They included shots or vaccinations for cowpox, typhoid, tetanus, yellow fever, typhus, cholera and plague. And most of these require two shots... a regular one, and then a few days later a double booster shot which sometimes loops one a bit.

Despite tropical heat—we were less than 500 miles from the equator at Babelthuap—everyone remained healthy. However, one poor fellow couldn't make his bowels move while aboard ship. He found relief at Eniwetok, and then finally conquered his difficulty aboard ship 10 days west of Eniwetok.

Unusual characters abound on troopships. There was guitar-playing Mike Dolan, who had been a race car owner and driver, a commercial pilot, a mechanic, a successful super-service station operator in Los Angeles. Of all things, he had a pet rattlesnake.

"He liked me," said Dolan. "I'd pick him up and play with him. He'd never bite me. Maybe it's the Irish in me."

But the real snake fancier of MAG 43 was Staff Sergeant Lorenzo C. Herbs of Canaan, N.Y., who trapped rattlesnakes, moccasin snakes and coral snakes—all poisonous—for a living. He sold some to the famous Silver Springs reptile farm in Florida, where he did the serpent sleuthing.

"You must get acquainted with snakes slowly, hold them gently and don't scare them," he explained. "Get them first with a forked stick—the longer the better."

He never was bitten by a snake, but did have a four-foot alligator take a chunk out of his finger. Herb's partner dived into the swamp and hurled the gaiter into their boat. While they were putting him into a strong canvas bag both were bitten.

"The only scare I ever had," said Herbs, "was while driving from Florida to New York in a Ford V-S coupe. I had my mother, my cousin, 19 snakes, two cats and the alligator jammed into the car and was driving along when hold up men in two cars tried to box me and stop me.

"I passed the front car on the wrong side, and drove wide-open, 60 miles, into Richmond, Va. Most of the time we traveled more than 90 miles an hour."

"I don't know about that fellow Herbs. We're going to have to watch him to see that he doesn't fill our camp on Okinawa with "Habu," the deadly Oriental snake which abounds on the island."

Buck Private Chuck Poling, 24, of Kansas City, Mo., got homesick when he saw circus nets on a movie aboard ship. Formerly he was a trapeze aerialist with a number of circuses, and also was a clown acrobat in night clubs in the winter. He did the double flips and twist flips without nets below. As a lad of 16 he had been a race truck jockey at the state fair at Syracuse, N.Y.

Poling bemoaned the fact that he wasn't home to start teaching acrobatics to his two-year-olds son and his nine-month-old daughter.

A former circus and carnival fire eater was PFC Edward Gosnell, a soldier from Spartanburg, S.C. But he made more money with a medicine show demonstrating salve for burns. Of course before submitting to the "burns" which were "healed" by the "cure-all," he coated his hands with a special preparation known to fire eaters.

"Actually it was pretty fair salve, but not that good," he chuckled. "We sold it like hot cakes at a dollar a throw."

Then there was Staff Sergeant Frank G. Prattis, a 20-year-old Leatherneck of Greek parentage, who hailed from Atlanta, Ga., and Chicago. We named him the honorary president of the "Horn In Club," a discussion—or should we say argument—group which derived its unusual moniker from the fact that anyone could horn in on any argument at any time.

"I don't horn in," said Prattis. "I start the arguments. Anyone is welcome to horn in, but it's a rough league."

Although he didn't finish high school before entering the Marine Corps, Prattis was one of he best educated fellows in MAG 43. He had a long, thin face with a large, bulbous nose protruding over a handlebar moustache which sagged wearily at the sides, giving him the appearance of a villain in a Gay Nineties play.

Of his own volition he read widely of biology, history mathematics, geology and current events. Also, he listened to records of symphonic music by the hour. We were very fond of him.

Hour after hour, day after day, the "Horn In Club" would discuss or argue anything and everything, babes"...when will the war end?...electrons, molecules, atoms and sound... trial marriage...guns and planes...politics...religion..."babes!"

Tech Sergeant Mounger usually sounded off, and so did MT Sergeant Tubby Poorman. Mounger and Prattis would discuss questions, whereas Poorman seemed more interested just in arguing. He would take either side of any question and toss high sounding words into those pools of fellowship, just to hear them splash!

MT Sergeant Bob Laurent of Detroit, Mich., the scholarly NCO in charge of communications, would add scientific data to the discussions.

When the topic turned to women, Staff Sergeant Cole always moved in. He said he had been married three times, but he talked in lurid detail of many other "shack up jobs." He had been a night taxicab driver and a gambler. His stories amused us by the hour. And, of course, they amused him, for they always were punctuated with his cackling laugh.

Most sailors are glad they're in the Navy, the Army Air Corps men "look down" on Army infantry or artillery and we Leathernecks would have nothing but the Marine Corps. Certainly it's for the best that each branch of the service has self-pride. This is a war of specialists, and all branches worked harmoniously on our operation.

Oddly, I found only one sailor who didn't prefer land station duty to sea duty. Yet the sailors preferred their job of putting Marines and Soldiers ashore to do the in-fighting, while they laid offshore and fired their big guns, or steamed away.

One exception to the rule that sailors preferred land duty was Chief Steward Julian Carvera, 49-year-old Filipino who insisted on nothing but active duty on the high seas until every Jap was vanquished.

He hadn't heard from his three sisters and brother in Leyte, Philippine Islands, since the Japs invaded. Probably we were close to them while our convoy lay anchored at Leyte, but it was not possible for Chief Carvera to go ashore and seek them.

"Couldn't you retire with your record of 26 years of service?" I inquired.

"Yes, but I won't quit until after the war," he replied with feeling. "I hate the Japs. It was bad for them to kill women and children in Manila. We will never forget. Our guerrillas will chase them into the mountains and kill them!"

Chief Carvera's quiet, Oriental philosophy made him many friends. One day he said to an irate bos'n's mate, who was cursing fouled up rigging:

"Before you get mad, think how you will feel about it day after tomorrow."

Taking some side glances around our troopship one day, I noted the following:

Two Marines and a sailor sharpening bowie knives... sailors learning to field strip Springfield rifles...soldiers firing .50 caliber machine guns...swabbies at a first aid class...Leathernecks getting a health lecture on diseases and snakes of Okinawa...many fellows proudly showing pictures of pretty girl friends... a plane recognition school in the steamy mess hall... troops doing laundry in wash bowls in the heads...sailors washing their clothes in the surf with long drag ropes...

A dozen styles of beards on Marines, soldiers and sailors...a black beard making Army Staff Sergeant Jack Merritt of West Harrington,

R.I., look exactly like Abraham Lincoln...three different troop study classes in progress side by side in a low-roofed cargo hold...two swabbies on the fantail practicing knot tying...sailors splicing ropes and putting graphics and tar on winch cables...card players huddling under landing boats during sudden rain squalls...

A lucky chow hound devouring three pieces of pie stacked like a Denver sandwich...Tech Sergeant Don Houseman of Jerseyville, Ill., and Lutefisk Pedersen writing poems... Staff Sergeant Prattis reading a dictionary...Marines and sailors studying correspondence courses for high school credits, or business background...a sailor plumber swinging a toilet plunger like a baseball bat and saying:

"I wonder if I'll be too old to make the grade in baseball when I get back?"

Yes, the Allendale was a teeming cauldron of interesting personalities.

Chapter 6

Mighty Armada

Scores of ships loomed on the distant horizon, heralding our approach to the Philippine Islands. The tropical sun burned wrathfully in a pale blue sky. Heat waves radiated from the Allendale's steel decks, scorching our feet through thick leather soles.

Then the hills of Leyte and Samar appeared dimly through distant haze. Land is a welcome sight to seafaring troops, and every hand not on duty below went topside. Spirits rose...the hills drew closer.

Ships were funneling into San Pedro Bay from all over the Pacific, and even some from the Atlantic to form a mighty armada, and we were part of it. Other convoys had arrived before ours, and more followed. Being flagship of our convoy, the Allendale led the procession of broad-beamed freighters, tankers and personnel assault ships into the mammoth anchorage.

In single file our bobbing behemoths penetrated a mighty crescent of anchored ships in the outer harbor, and steamed slowly toward our mooring area.

Parallel to us, the LCT and LST landing boats lanced through the harbor in long procession, to anchor with other landing boats.

As I gazed at hundreds of ships gathering for the Okinawa invasion, I suddenly had a strange, detached sensation... a feeling that I was witnessing the birth of a significant historical event... the first invasion of a Jap island thickly populated with unfriendly, Empirical subjects... the starting of an event which might be the turning point of the Pacific war.

It was as though I had been catapulted 25 years into the future and were looking back at animated archives of destiny. I felt like a tiny grain of sand in the hour-glass of the ages... like a tiny cog in a tremendous amphibious war machine combing hard-striking forces of the Army, the Navy, the Marine Corps and the Seabees.

A British cruiser crossed our path... the British were assembling a carrier task force to make supporting strikes in the gigantic operation. Two Spitfires and a mosquito bomber arched gracefully overhead.

Then across the bay the brisk breeze pushed a tiny, bobbing sail banca with outrigger floats on either side, and with one Filipino at the rudder and another tacking the sail. How that tiny canoe kept atop the churlish surf, I'll never know. But the Filipinos are second to none as fishermen and sailors.

"Three months ago it wouldn't have been very healthy steaming in this way," said Major Donald C. Shultis of Milwaukee, Wis., assistant operations officer for the Tactical Air Force of fighter, bomber and air warning squadrons, which were to move onto Okinawa air fields as quickly as they were captured. Brilliant young Major Shultis, a four-engine bomber pilot, was a walking encyclopedia of military tactics, supplies and intelligence information.

American warships had steamed into San Pedro Bay and shelled the shoreline some three months earlier, and then amphibious forces stormed ashore and secured the beaches.

Making a strong counter-attack, the Japs attempted to reinforce their belabored and retreating shore garrisons, and lost 40,000 troops in the operation—the worst carnage of the entire Pacific war to that date.

We glided serenely over sunken Jap ships, barges and dead bodies, coming to anchor in close view of the Leyte shoreline. Occasionally the stench of dead Japs blew our way.

The thick growth of trees lining the shoreline was decimated and shredded by heavy shellfire and bombings by our assaulting units. Jap snipers, cut off from their units, still took a toll of lives ashore with sporadic outbursts.

Quickly this former Jap stronghold had been transformed into the spawning grounds for our avenging crusade. With most of the Philippine Islands already recaptured, we were preparing to move ahead and permanently secure the right to freedom for the ravished natives.

The quick, efficient conquest of the Philippines by General Douglas MacArthur's combined Army, Navy and Marine units was of tremendous strategic importance to our forthcoming operation. It gave us bases on Luzon for air support for the Okinawa campaign.

Already bombers of the Far Eastern Air Force commanded by Lieutenant General Kenny were striking sledge hammer blows against the Japs from the Ryukyu islands to Borneo, aiming principally at Jap air fields and planes. Oil supplies and airfields of Japan's mighty Formosan bases were blasted heavily, and other bomber planes made the China Sea virtually untenable for Jap ships and barges.

Gull-winged Corsair fighters, Hellcat night-fighters and old faithful SBD Douglas dive bombers of the First Marine Air Wing played key roles in the Philippine campaign.

Colonel Jerome was in command of Marine Aircraft Groups 24 and 32 when they struck Lingayen Gulf with pin-point precision bombing, knocking out enemy hot spots. Lieutenant Colonel John Smith, Marine Ace and Congressional Medal of Honor recipient was executive officer of Mag 32.

Mag 14, under Colonel Hopkins, helped on the Samar invasion, and Mag 12 with four Corsair day fighter squadrons and one Grumman Hellcat night fighter squadron, shot many a Jap airman from skies.

To the end of January, 1945, Marine airmen had downed between 45 and 50 Jap planes, 12 of which were by the Bat Eye Night Fighter Squadron. Other fighter squadrons were the Flying Hell-ions, Joe's Jokers (formerly headed by Major Joe Foss, top Marine Ace,) the Lily Packin' Hell birds and the Wake Island Avengers.

Marine dive-bomber planes also helped run interference for the Mindoro, Panay and Cebu invasions.

Our convoy took on oil, foodstuffs and other cargo during a week of waiting at Leyte for the signal to move against our target, 1000 miles to the north. Supply is a tremendous problem. Already we had travelled 7000 miles... seeing a lot of water. Now huge landing boats pulled alongside and transferred trucks, tractors, cranes and hundreds of boxes of supplies onto our ship. Troop working parties of Soldiers, Seabees, Sailors, and Marines aboard helped stow the supplies, but the busy bees were the ship's crews. They worked almost around the clock replacing slightly frazzled ropes... painting here... greasing there... launching landing boats... working ever on the double.

A movie was in store for us the first night at the Philippine Islands, and of course only half of the ship's population could be jammed into the open-air theater on hatch number two.

It was the turn for the ship's company and MAG 43 to see the show. Many of us grabbed choice seats (on the deck) right after chow. But just before show time, all Mag 43 personnel were ordered off the hatch. That was so other troops not, entitled to see the show that night could be turned back, and then we were re-admitted. Naturally, as soon as we were herded out, the sailors moved into the choice spots.

We were re-admitted shortly, and there still were a few fair seats. But for some reason we were chased off again... this time really angry and muttering. We all laughed, however, as rain drenched the sailors while we huddled under cover. Finally rain became a downpour and the show was cancelled.

"That was really funny," said Dick Koch-Church. "Those sailors sitting out there in the rain waiting to see the picture entitled "Salute to the Marines."

Soon the rain abated and persistent picture fans hooted, whistled and howled,

"We want a movie. We want a movie."

Curtly the word came again over the speakers:

"There will be no movie tonight!"

A few nights later there was another fouled-up movie. Right in the middle of the picture there suddenly appeared on the screen a busy little man weather-stripping a house while a commercial announcement blared from the sound track. Then the feature flashed back on. Now who in the hell spliced that film?

Usually we had four or five interruptions when the ageing film would break and have to be re-spliced. We had our usual quota of breaks that night, but accepted them patiently, even understandingly.

The picture starred Red Skelton and Ann Southern in "Maisie Get's Her Man." But if she got her man, or how she got him, we didn't find out. Because the last reel had been lost, our operator discovered in mid-performance.

Our pictures were mostly of rather ancient vintage, but that didn't bother Tech Sergeant John Runciman, who had been overseas before. During the six months he was back stateside he refused to go to a single movie, just so he would enjoy "first runs" on his next tour of overseas duty.

Tall, handsome Runciman explained it this way:

"I found more interesting recreation at El Centro."

March 16, 1945, Leyte was a welcome haven to Tech Sergeant Jim Lenk of Detroit, Mich., a veteran of the Bougainville campaign. Shortly after we left Pearl Harbor his bridge broke, depriving him of services of six front choppers, top side, for three weeks. At Leyte he was taken to another ship which had more adequate dental facilities than the Allendale, and there got a new span of incisors and eye teeth. But he didn't get it in time to play saxophone in the ship's orchestra for the "Fubar Follies."

At request of the Ship's Chaplain, Dick and I produced a vaudeville show which we entitled the Fubar Follies. (Fubar means "fouled up beyond all repair.")

The ship's orchestra, Frank Trouting's Troubadours, went over big with old jazz tunes and new... hot music and sweet music. And the fellows thoroughly enjoyed a sing along with Chaplain Ogden as leader.

It fell my lot to be a master of ceremonies. Now everyone has something to bitch about after being on a troop ship a month, so my opening monologue went something like this:

"Good evening ladies and gentleman... Oh, excuse me... those aren't ladies. You fat men who don't wear shirts!... don't you know it's vulgar to point?"

"Well, fellows, it's great to be here in the Philippine Islands on the good old Allendale. (grimace) We've got a swell bunch of men, and wonderful officers.

"Now take Captain Twomey. They laughed when Skipper Twomey came out on the dock wearing shorts... but when he bent over, they split!

"And Lieutenant Colonel R. O. Bisson, the commanding officer of MAG 43. Now there's a sharp Marine and a fine pilot. He came up fast in the Marine Corps. Why he became a lieutenant colonel one day, and a full colonel that night drinking at the officer's club."

"Ah, yes. We have swell officers. We can thank them for our fine food, our fine quarters, wonderful recreational facilities and for our shore liberty here. (We didn't get any.) And those natives are so friendly. Why, one pretty native girl wanted to learn more about sailors... so, she put out to sea!

"Really, though, I don't mind not getting shore liberty, but I certainly feel sorry for the ship's dog, Scotty McTavish. He's going crazy looking over at all those trees, and not being able to get ashore. Why he just sits up there on the officer's promenade deck and howls!"

The audience roared at a crack I took at the APA 203, which carried a big load of explosives and seemed constantly on the verge of ramming us. The lines were:

"After making our 7000-mile oceanic pilgrimage, I can appreciate more fully what old Christopher Columbus did when he sailed to America. We don't give Columbus enough credit. Think of his hardships and dangers... but of course he didn't have that damned 203 trying to ram him every night."

Bill Carver and I popped some corn in a couple of dialogue routines, and he got a big hand. One of the biggest "yak Yaks" was when Dick Koch-Church made an announcement—a takeoff on the usual ship's announcement of "dinner is now being served for the First sitting officers;" later for the second, and then the third. Dick, the man with the many radio voices, said in honey-sweet tones:

"Dinner is now being served for the 19th STANDING of troops. Holders of pink cards and lavender cards will fall in on the starboard side... and holders of Chartreuse and robin's egg blue cards will fall in on the port side."

The roar of laughter was tremendous. Then followed a dialogue in which I asked Dick if along with his acting and radio broadcasting in New York, he also sang.

"No, but I did write a song," he replied.

"Fine, fine," I said. "What is the name of the song you wrote?"

"Don't Fence Me In."

"Ah, that's one of my favorites. Frank Treuting, will you and the boys play 'Don't Fence Me In?"

The music started and Dick threw out his chest, smiling smugly, while fellows cat-called. Suddenly he looked angry, pointed at three Marines and shouted:

"Stop the music! Stop it! I actually believe those fellows down there don't believe I wrote 'Don't Fence Me In.' Really I did, so help me. If I didn't, may something awful happen to me."

Something awful did happen. Suddenly a stream of water ran down his left pant leg, and the audience went into stitches. (A syringe bulb from sick bay did the trick, Dick says.)

Talkative Staff Sergeant Cole came up for a "Vox Pop" interview. (I'm sure my good friends Parks Johnsen and Warren Hull will okay my use of the name of their fine Monday night radio show.) I asked Cole if he went to church regularly.

"Nope," he replied. "My mother took me to church when I was five years old. I got tired and went to sleep and a man passing the collection plate took a dime out of my hand.

"I woke up and shouted: 'Hey, you son of a bitch, gimme back my dime." Mother never took me again."

Then Cole tossed his head back and cackled loudly, and so did the crowd. Another of his remarks was:

"I've been married three times. Two weeks after one of my marriages, I found out I was going to become a father four months later. Oh, those sailors!"

But the climax of the show—one of the funniest acts I've ever seen—was when I announced we had a great mind reader on the program, "from San Francisco, that wild, impetuous, clairvoyant Irishman, SHAMROCK COYNE!"

"And his assistant, from Washington, D.C., at great inconvenience, the one and only Tech Sergeant Johnny Martin—the human CRYSTAL BALL!"

Cisco Martin was taken totally by surprise. That was part of the act. Before he could catch his breath, he was whisked bodily onto the stage behind the mike by a pair of six-foot, two-inch Marines, Tech Sergeants Victory J. Thomas of Birmingham, Ala., and Allan (I'm really handsome) Knight of Syracuse, N.Y.

Grimacing zanily, Coyne slinked across the stage like a sedulous simian and went into spasms of joy at finding the CRYSTAL BALL—Martin's bald head. The ship shook with laughter.

Shamrock the "psychic" intoned in a low, hollow voice:

"As I look into this crystal ball I can foresee the future—less and less hair here!"

Martin writhed, bit and kicked frantically, but to no avail. Thomas and Knight held him vice-like, half a foot off the deck, and his short legs pumped like a six-day bicycle rider. His head was a red toy balloon with embarrassment.

Then Shamrock began singing, in high falsetto, "Oh, Johnnie, Oh, Johnnie, how you can love."

When the song was finished Martin was released. Like a true showman, he clasped his hands above his head, wrestler style, then strode over and shook hands with me. The crowd gave him a tremendous hand.

We threw many barbs at the officers, and they took them in wonderful style, laughing at their ribbing even more than the men. Along with some corn, and a few racy jokes which rather embarrassed the chaplain, I leveled some sardonic quips at the non-commissioned offers, our chief petty officers and master tech sergeants, saying:

"I have been requested to announce that a new mutual admiration society is being formed aboard the Allendale by CPO's, BTO's (big time operators), MTS's and BS's. It seems nobody else took them seriously enough, so they are organizing to pat themselves on the back... John L. Lewis hasn't muscled in yet for a share of the dues, but then it's a very new club... But really, they're fine NCO's. They wouldn't think of pulling their stripes on you... only a skunk would pull his stripe."

Well, the Fubar Follies backfired somewhat, and Dick and I found ourselves fouled up. For our Master Tech Sergeants didn't like the cracks. A few days later we got told off by our NCO in charge, Morrie

Fry, who it seems had his shoulder cried on by several of the other MTS's. So Morrie felt it his duty to give us the word.

However, Major Feasley, our commanding officer, complimented us on the show and so did the Ship's Captain.

We were scheduled to put on another show the following Sunday night, but we cancelled it. Scores of fellows asked us why the next show was not held, and we told them:

"We weren't scared out by the MTS's but we just want the word to get around that some crap washed back on us for a few of the joking remarks that we made about them on the last show."

A few days later Morrie Fry softened a bit and asked Dick and me if we would put on another show. We intended to do it, but got too busy, so we postponed it until some later time on shore.

Our first air raid alert sounded the second night we were at Leyte. Dick, Pancho and I were in a rear compartment, and fear was the thought farthest from us. We were curious, and wanted on deck to see the show. Fortunately, the plane was identified as friendly. But we were anchored little more than 50 miles north of Mindanao, where the Japs had 12 operational air fields.

Disappointment was keen when no mail awaited us at Leyte. There was some for the ship's crew, but none for the troops. The days dragged... hearts were melancholy... eyes misty at times.

Then on Friday, March 23, Brigadier General William J. Wallace, the commanding general of the Air Defense Command in charge of operation of fighter planes from Okinawa as soon as it was secured, flew in from Ewa and came aboard with mail for MAG 43.

But the real hero, as far as we were concerned, was the general's flag secretary, First Lieutenant W. O. Cain of Sumpter, S.C. It was he who cut red tape and got our mail from the Ewa post office by threatening to bring the general himself over to give the mail clerks word.

There was Christmas Eve excitement and expectancy as mail was being sorted. Then came the joyous deluge.

Dick received 47 letters—from his mother, his father, three sweethearts and two buddies in the service. Gleefully he would slash open an envelope with bowie knife, read it hastily, then hurry on to another. He bubbled with joy. After he finished, he went back and read all again, more leisurely.

From his dark, rosy-complexioned wife, Shamrock received the letters closest to his heart. It had been only some six months previously that he married the former Annabelle Troglia, a San Francisco beauty. Among Coyne's 30 letters was the disturbing word that his father's health had become poor.

Grim, tragic news came to PFC John Donovan of Oklahoma City. On February 24, his father had died, and it had taken until March 23 for the airmail letters with the news to reach him. He then was concerned about letting his folks know he finally had received the message, for we didn't know whether or not our letters would be released until after the Okinawa invasion.

Army Captain Geoffrey Willoughby, an overseas veteran from the last war, received letters from his home at Milwaukee, Wis., and from his son, Alan, 20, who was driving ambulance in Italy for the British. Because of a once-fractured elbow, Alan, a big six-footer, was classified as 4-F. Disappointed, he took the hazardous front-line job as ambulance driver, for he felt he should have an active part in this war.

Captain Willoughby, former newspaperman who attended the University of Wisconsin, was public relations officer for the Tenth Army's Tactical Air Force to operate from Okinawa.

Second Lieutenant Philip R. Hade of Bremerton, Wash., a leathery-faced old Devil Dog who came up through the ranks, beamed contentedly as he read letters from his wife at Bremerton and from their step-son, PFC Edward D. Simmons, who was in Europe with the Ninth Army.

Love letters from a comely Woman Marine at El Centro winged to Second Lieutenant Derald D. Underberg of Madison, Neb. The Women Marines at the El Centro Air Station considered him one of the most popular eligible bachelors... one of the best catches... in the matrimonial pool.

Tech Sergeant Richard "Stompy" Rosnik of Milwaukee, Wis., received word that for the fifth consecutive year he had been selected on the all-state, all-time wrestling team as middleweight. Since his junior year in high school, the short, powerful Marine had not lost a match, and had but one draw. That was in an exhibition match with the national amateur champion.

Joe Rosen, dark, handsome tech sergeant from Waco, Tex., received letters from seven different girls, all of whom he said he liked. But Joe declared he never told any of them he loved them. He was still waiting.

In contrast, Don "Lover Boy" Houseman of Jerseyville, Ill., received letters from 11 different girls and said:

"I REALLY love all of them."

The future son (?) of Corporal Daniel McCabe of Allentown, Pa., was in good condition and scheduled to be stork bombed into this world in June, 1945. Joyce McCabe, the corporal's pretty wife, entered the Marine Corps with him in November, 1943. A year later she left the service to begin raising a family.

And so the letters went. Handsome Lieutenant Colonel Radford C. West of New York City, whose black moustache gave him a striking resemblance to Douglas Fairbanks Sr., took all records for volume of mail, with 75 letters.

I received priceless treasures—letters from June, and our children, Barbara and Jerry. Also a letter from my brother, Earl, of Ashland, Ore., with one of the Armies in France, and a letter stating I had a new nephew, born to my sister, Wilma Marvin at Mineral Wells, Tex. Her husband, Corporal Max Marvin, former baseball pitcher at South Oregon Normal School, had been praying for a son—a future big leaguer. Roy Wayne Marvin should be a whiz at baseball, for his mother, my "kid sis," was by far the best girl baseball and basketball player I've ever seen.

Jerry, in the first grade, printed this letter:

"Dear Daddy

"When I was coming in the school a dog got his nose cot in the door and I laughed at it. I was glad to get your letter and the picture too. Last Sunday when we went to the show I found 5 dollars on the way there.

"We are having a paper drive at the school and we are going to have a movie. Write soon.

"Love, Jerry N."

Part of Barbara's letters—she is 10—informed me:

"At school Tuesday I played two duets (with her mother) at P.T.A. The chairman pinned a corsage on my dress. Today Mr. Reevs, the principal, said 'I think everyone enjoyed the duets.'"

Then she drew a valentine for me, with the heads of four horses in a heart. She loves horses. And she said she was getting along fine in the "Giggling Sprouts, as you call it." (I had kidded her about the Girl Scouts).

One of June's letters informed me she received a letter I wrote on the ship, and which was flown back from Eniwetok Atoll. I was glad to know she had received the letter and knew we were headed into combat.

But another letter she wrote the following day made me boiling mad. It said:

"My life certainly isn't getting any easier. Yesterday Barbara brought me a note stating that Jerry was not to come to the Day Center anymore because he had caused a little boy to get injured and that he wouldn't mind anyone.

"I was terribly upset. It seemed another little kid had his hand on an iron bar and Jerry pried him loose, making him fall. Jerry said the boy's nose bled.

"Jerry misses and needs you badly. So does Barbara, of course, but she has her music and scout work. But it seems strange to me that one little six-year-old boy could get a day supervisor so upset."

June taught piano lessons every afternoon to help support the family and keep up my insurance policies, so she needed Day Center privileges for Jerry. Furiously I pounded on a typewriter this reply:

"Jerry is an angel compared with myself at his age. I know he needs a dad's companionship, but fortunately you understand him pretty well."

"But you can tell those old bitches at the day center that if I'm out here in the combat zone, the least they could do should be to treat my son civilly and try to understand and lead him."

"They've never seen an enemy march past, burning churches, pillaging schools and murdering women and children like the Japs did at Manila. Tell them. Tell them I'm so mad I could almost spit in their faces!"

Many happy hours I had romped with Jerry, teaching him tumbling tricks which he performed with professional proficiency. Quick to learn, musically inclined and a splendid artist for his age, he always responded amazingly to anyone who was friendly and endeavored to lead him. On the other hand, Jerry has a stubborn streak if driven. He's a chip off the old block. I wouldn't want him any different than he is.

A few days before we left Leyte we drew what pay we needed, and then exchanged all our money for invasion currency. We were permitted to take only $15 ashore, all in the paper invasion currency. No

United States money was permitted. A Japanese yen is equal to our dime, and a sen is one-tenth of a cent. A few sharp deals were pulled by quick-change artists before everyone got hep to Mr. Yen and Mr. Sen. Poker playing seemed more fun with the new currency.

When paid, each of the Puerto Ricans voluntarily made a donation for clothing for Philippine civilians.

On Sunday, March 25, a tremendous procession of slow-moving LST, LCI and LSM landing boats, together with support and supply boats, left San Pedro Bay, target bound.

We were restless. We had practiced debarkation—swarming down the nets with full packs into landing boats in rather choppy water. Let's get going… get this thing started!

Fist fights began breaking out aboard ship. I saw two in one day, almost had one myself. Shamrock jumped in and stopped a fight between a Negro steward in MAG 43 and a Puerto Rican when three more Puerto Ricans impulsively joined the brawl. That big 200-pound Irishman's appearance brought a sudden cessation of hostilities.

In my little tiff I guess I bluffed the other fellow out, for I had determined to let him beat the tar out of me—if he could! I'm old enough to know better and regretted the incident later. But inactivity made us fidgety.

Fortunately, during the last few days we kept somewhat busy by feverishly writing "just one more letter" before leaving.

It was with pleasure for most of us that we left Leyte Tuesday, March 27—target bound for Okinawa.

Chapter 7

Target Run

The mighty Fifth U.S. Fleet, commanded by calculating, hard-hitting Admiral Raymond A. Spruance, swung a nifty Sunday punch at the Japs the day before our convoy steamed from Leyte.

It was Sunday, March 25 in the United States, but Monday in the Orient. Yes, the Fifth Fleet landed a pip of a punch.

The Japs, whose ships and boats in the China Sea were being relentlessly punched to pieces, ventured southward with a small convoy, hoping to bolster defenses and augment supplies on Okinawa.

Three large Jap cargo ships, two destroyers and three other escort ships were contacted some 100 miles north of Okinawa, just west of Amami Gunto, a small group of islands.

Suddenly angry U.S. Avenger torpedo bombers and Helldiver dive bombers from Fifth Fleet aircraft carriers roared out of the sky, escorted by Corsair and Hellcat fighter planes.

Aerial torpedoes splashed into the water...sizzled ship ward...crashed through the ship's sides and exploded. Bombs swished from bomb bays of the Curtis Helldivers... whistled earthward... exploded on decks and superstructures of Jap ships. Nip seamen raced madly to their anti-aircraft guns.

There were more planes...more bombs...more torpedoes...terrifying strafing runs. Then sleek, gull-winged Corsair and sturdy Hellcat fighters—scornful of frantic Jap ack-ack—raked the battered, smoking ships with .50 caliber machine gun bullets, hot tracers and armor-piercing, exploding 20 millimeter cannon shells.

Blasts rocked the convoy components... dead and dying Japs littered the flaming decks...salt water gushed into breached holds as the battle ended.

Tokyo was raided five times in 10 days...2000 tons of bombs rocked Nagoya...2500 tons of incendiaries turned industrial Kobe into a blast furnace.

Then fire bombs cascaded like molten lava from Mt. Fujiyama, onto five square miles of Nagoya and 10 square miles of Tokyo. Hell rained from the heavens...six pound incendiary bombs...two-thirds of a million of them! These clustered bomb packages of jelly-gasoline compound burned long and fiercely...ravished the flimsy Jap structures...started Tokyo radio screaming about "atrocities and barbarism." Flames scourged the 10 square miles of the Tokyo target area and spread to five more square miles, making a total of 15—approximately 9700 acres.

While Tokyo and Nagoya still smoked and sizzled, a star-spangled Eagle winged definitely over Japan's southern shores, clawing and mangling Jap airplanes, airfields and shipping.

Pacific Fleet Admiral Chester W. Nimits, who two months earlier had moved his headquarters some 3500 miles westward from Pearl Harbor to Guam, sent Admiral Spruance's Fifth Fleet, including the fast carrier task force of Vice Admiral Marc A. Mitscher, to smoke out the Jap fleet.

An armada of 1400 Navy and Marine Corsairs, Hellcats, Helldiver dive bombers and torpedo and bomb-carrying Avengers zoomed from the big, fast carriers and lashed thunderously at Kyushu, the large southern home island of Japan itself. The attacking planes struck at dawn, heavily pounding the many Jap airdromes, industrial targets and training and supply centers.

Then, with Japan's southern air defense crippled and bleeding, Admiral Mitscher unleashed the boldest stroke of all, hurling his speedy armada after the Jap fleet itself.

American planes roared over the terraced hillocks of the coast and across the Inland sea. For four days the Jap fleet was tortured, torn and finally shattered by bomb-dropping, torpedo-launching and rocket-firing bomber planes, accompanied by triple-threat Hellcat and Corsair fighters which bombed, rocketed and strafed the ships, splashing Jap planes all over the inland sea in lightning strikes and torrid dog fights.

Fourteen Jap warships were sunk or damaged, including three aircraft carriers, two light carriers, a 45,000-ton battleship, one heavy cruiser and four destroyers. Also hit were scores of merchant ships.

One of Japan's bitterest and most crippling losses was destruction of 731 planes. American losses were light—a small number of planes and serious damage to only one warship.

With the Japs reeling from this blow, the Fifth Fleet swung southward to the Ryukyus, and Philippines-based bombers struck Jap airdromes on Formosa and Borneo with increasing crescendo. But before swinging southward, Admiral Spruance sent his fast, contemptuous battleships in for point-blank shelling of the southern Jap coastal targets.

A surprise package in the massive Okinawa invasion operation was a bold strike by a British carrier task force which sped northward from a secret American base March 22, to join the American forces.

The day before our Okinawa invasion convoy steamed from Leyte, British carriers launched fighters and bombers which struck airfields of the Sakishima group of islands to the northwest of Formosa and between 125 and 200 miles from Okinawa. The Tommy pilots from the Illustrious and other carriers destroyed numerous fighters and bombers which otherwise soon would have been hurling their lethal loads at us. They destroyed 14 of 20 Jap aircraft which landed in the Sakishima's during those attacks and damaged six more. Then the British warships moved in and shelled the islands in their support assault for our gigantic operation.

Directed by Vice Admiral Sir Bernard Rawlings., the large British task force was the first element of the Royal Navy to strike offensive blows so closes to Japan in this war. It was a self-serving fleet force, using British made shells and bombs, and stocking much of its food and other supplies from Australia and New Zealand. Vice Admiral Rawlings flag flew from the H.M.S. King George V. the British battleship which helped sink the German Battleship Bismarck.

"When the hell are they going to start bombing and shelling Okinawa?" we all were asking on the Allendale. Iwo Jima had been bombed 75 consecutive days prior to the invasion there.

"The strategy is different this time," it had been explained by hefty Colonel Boeker C. Batterton of Tallula, Ill., veteran Marine pilot selected as operations officer for the Second Marine Wing Fighter Command to be based at Okinawa and of which our group., Marine Aircraft Group 43, was a part.

"The fleet will move in close about 10 days before D-Day and blast the daylights out of the island with shells and bombs." he continued. "So the Japs won't know for sure until the last 10 days whether we're going to invade Formosa, the China coast or Okinawa. And then it will be too late for them to bring reinforcements past our carrier planes."

Boy, they'd better blast it plenty hard," growled Technical Sergeant Pancho Carver. "I want to see a lot of dead Japs lying around when I go ashore."

"There'll be bombs and mortars falling when we go ashore, regardless of how hard they pound it in advance," predicted Tech Sergeant Shamrock Coyne. "But don't worry, our team's going to win."

Actually, the gigantic bombardment of Okinawa had started already. It took a while for news releases to reach us. But it was good news when it came.

On March 26 Admiral Spruance opened the assault on Okinawa itself, unleashing the full fury of his fast carrier task force planes against airfields and installations along the railroad running between Kadena airfield and Naha, Okinawa's principal city.

As dive bombers and torpedo bombers lashed at the waning Jap air strength on Okinawa, big battleships, cruisers and other fleet units moved up and shelled shore installations. It was one of the most concentrated bombardments of the Pacific campaign. The stunned Japs mustered a little aerial resistance, and one of our light naval units was damaged. Six enemy planes were shot down.

With the nip garrison under a devastating bombardment, doughboys of the Seventy-Seventh Army Division surged ashore on Okinawa's very doorstep. Kerama Retto, is a small group of islands lying in the China sea just off the southeast coast of the main island. Long-range artillery soon would pound Okinawa from Kerama Retto.

Major General Andrew D. Bruce's 77th, in this bold pre-invasion strike starting March 26, 1945, made short shrift of Jap defenders. Yank amphibious assault troops charged rapidly through sporadic resistance which was bitter in spots. By noon of the first day some of the islands were secured.

On Tokashiki, largest of the Kerama islands, sharp blasts of hand grenades and agonized wailing rent the air during the first eerie night. It was the overtone of a tragic, pitiable episode. The natives had heard and believed Jap propaganda about American barbarism. Consequently our invasion was the signal for the largest mass hari kari orgy of the Pacific campaign.

More than 150 frenzied natives killed themselves and each other. Daylight revealed the macabre scene of strangled, slashed and blasted bodies of dead and dying, old men, mothers, young children. American surgeons quickly went to work to save what mangled and wounded natives that were not already dead. Fear subsided, and remorse followed. An old man wept bitterly... he had killed his daughter.

Quickly the doughboys overran the islands, securing more by night-fall. They wound up the campaign by March 29, after killing 331 Japs, capturing 100 and sealing probably 150 more in caves. Then the assault troops returned to their ships, leaving a small garrison unit behind, and bevy's of 155 millimeter guns to bombard southern Okinawa.

One of the most important pre-invasion strokes at Kerama Retto and offshore Okinawa was capture and destruction by troops and naval units of more than 300 small Jap torpedo and suicide crash boats. Navy machine gunners patrolling at night in landing boats accounted for many of them. Powered by four-cylinder engines, the suicide boats were 18 feet long and were loaded with depth charges at the stern and "torpedo bombs" in the bow... a formidable weapon to crash full-speed into the side of a ship... in the dark of night.

The use of suicide crash boats was one of many desperate, fanatical schemes to which the Japs, with their distorted oriental philosophy, had planned to save face and delay our conquest.

Destruction of so many of these boats was good news to us on the Allendale, target bound and nearing our objective.

We were going into combat, open to enemy, bombs, shells and torpedoes. Those last few days before invasion are never-to-be forgotten. We discussed reports of enemy defenses...wondered how we would react under fire, (but kept these thoughts to ourselves)... weighed values...felt occasional catches in the pit of the stomach or the clutch at the heart as we apprehensively contemplated combat and the potential price. Moving in that close to Japan, we knew we would be prime targets of Jap bombers.

The sea was rough that first night after we headed northward from Leyte. Scuttlebutt said we were on the fringe of a possible typhoon. And that also arouses more, shall we say, curiosity? Long since, bedrolls had been taboo for sleeping on deck—too much of a fire hazard. But a ship is pretty dark at night, and Dick Koch-Church, Bill Carver and I consistently slipped past the SP's and nested under landing boats near the poop deck.

That night, and the next night, we were tossed and buffeted mercilessly by angry seas. The wind drove streams of rain onto our sacks. There was another flurry of seasickness, which caused nothing but merriment for Shamrock, Pancho, Dick and me, for fortunately we never were bothered. But the distress of some was contagious, spread by high winds which whipped streams of the lost victuals into faces of bystanders.

Shamrock tossed his head back and roared with laughter as one of the enfilade attacks sprayed half a dozen faces. Then a look of great dismay clouded his usual jovial countenance. The fiendish wind had whisked his beloved baseball cap overboard.

"Damn it. This is really a tough war, losing my cap," growled Shamrock.

He just wasn't the same for a couple of days. Then a buddy dug into his sea bag for an extra cap, which put Shamrock back in the groove. Most Marine pilots wear caps when they fly, so just about everyone else in Marine Aviation follows the style.

For 7000 miles fate had been kind to our convoy—no mishaps. But the third night north of Leyte the elements assailed us furiously. We rolled and pitched in seas lashed by a 55-mile-an hour gale. Sheets of spray whipped frequently over the deck. A few nights later we rode on even rougher seas. Our ship's bow would teater upward on a huge swell, then suddenly drop with a violent bump into the troughs or against the next swell coming toward us.

The seas were running high, and frequently the stern would be left far above the water line. Then the propeller would race madly, making the entire ship vibrate like an air hammer. A series of swells sacked us broadside, causing the ship to pitch, dip and roll in a crazy, eccentric pattern. Two big swells pounded against our starboard side, rocking us like a child's cradle. Then the angry water rushed up at us in tremendous swell. It broke against our starboard side while we already were rocking to port. The Allendale tipped crazily. The port deck almost became awash. The big broad-beamed APA lay on its side and shuddered. It hung there for a few breathless seconds. A seeming eternity. I guess just about everyone on board tried to help hold it up with his stomach. Then slowly it began to right itself, and rocked wildly to starboard like a huge pendulum.

The next night while I was standing guard duty, a youthful sailor came topside and sacked down on a spot only half sheltered from wind, rain and spray.

"It gives me the willies, trying to sleep down in the hold below-below the water line with submarines all around us," he confided. "We wouldn't have much chance down below if a torpedo crashed into our hold."

Jap submarines had been accosting us. One evening we saw our destroyers circling and hurling one depth charge after another which exploded into high fountains like spouting whales. And there were other contacts with Jap pig boats. Results of these duels are not announced until months later—let the enemy wonder and sweat as to the whereabouts of his slimy interceptors. Suffice it to say that none of our ships was hit by torpedoes, and so far as I know, our alert, fast-maneuvering destroyers didn't even give the submarines time to launch a single fish.

We developed gratified respect for our gallant escorts. And we also loved the comforting and assuring sight of Wildcat fighter planes from nearby but unseen aircraft carriers. Those nimble interceptors with their square wingtips hovered watchfully over our convoy, circling and ready.

You do lots of thinking, those last few days aboard ship. And I was curious to learn what thoughts throbbed in the minds of my buddies.

I have read of servicemen fighting and dying, and not knowing what they were fighting for. But I've talked to a lot of them, and have yet to find one who doesn't have a pretty good idea what World War II is about. Oh, I've found plenty who didn't want to be out here—who wanted someone else to face the enemy for them. And I found some who weren't too articulate in expressing their ideas of just what they were fighting for. But just a little interrogation—and not with leading questions at all—never failed to reveal that all had pretty much the same idea.

There was Buck Private Frank Bavetz, a 19-year-old Pittsburg Marine of Polish extraction. I wondered if he had an alien outlook.

"Say, we're a hell of a long ways from home." I said. "Just what are we fighting for? Just what does this war mean to you?"

"We didn't start it," he replied. "We're fighting for self-protection and freedom."

"What kind of government do you wish to see after the war?" I asked.

"Do you favor the system we now have, or would you prefer socialism or communism?"

"It's going along pretty well the way it is," he answered. "I hadn't thought much about it, but I'm not for any socialism. No sir! No G.I. civilian government for me!"

"I'm fighting a very selfish war," said PFC Richard P. Griffin of Denver, Colorado. Thirty years old, and father of two children, Griff signed form 219 for voluntary induction into the service.

"I feel that woman's primary purpose in life is to bear children, and man's duty is to provide and protect," he continued. "I hope that by fighting this war, we'll be able to help make the world a better place for your children and my children. I hope the world eventually will be able to work out its problems so we can live together in a peaceful manner.

"I wasn't interested in national or international affairs until a few years ago. But the magnitude of this war is such that it has affected more people than any other war or catastrophe."

Another question I asked repeatedly was:

"Do you believe we'll have peace for 20 years? For 60 years?"

"Not unless something drastic is done about our own racial problem in the United States, and take our rightful place in international affairs," said Bos'n's Mate First Class Edward Denger, 29, of Clarion, Iowa.

"There are influences inciting violence by appealing to prejudices and fostering a persecution complex among classes and colors. It's a big problem, but I believe one of the first remedies is to give better educational opportunity to the Negroes. They are entitled to the same opportunities as any other citizen."

Denger, tall, wiry and leathery-complexioned from several years of exposure to the elements aboard ship, had some definite thoughts and expressed them well.

"Another thing we've got to do," he volunteered. "We've got to get racketeers out of labor unions. Why it got so bad in many cities that you had to buy a job from labor leaders—in the United States of America!

"It cost me $63 for a union card before I could go to work at Coffeeville, Kansas. I wouldn't have minded a smaller fee. And then after I got the card, I was informed it was only a 'B' card, and I'd probably have to wait some time for a job. But-for $15 more I would be issued an 'A' card. So it cost me $15 more to get an 'A' card and a job."

"Labor unions have done a lot of good. They must remain. We don't want sweat shops. But the racketeers must go."

Make no mistake that servicemen are doing a lot of thinking, and that veterans will play an important role in politics after the war. I mean in national and international affairs—not just in legislation for veterans.

"I'm going to belong to the Veterans of Foreign Wars," Denger added. We've still got a lot of fighting to do for the right to live at home and make a living."

Shamrock Coyne thought we will have at least 20 years of peace after this war, but probably not 50 or 60 years.

"There are too many people in this world who don't know what love is," he said. "They just care for themselves."

"But we can't just dream our way to peace. We can't play ostrich. We must look realistically at the world in which we live. The United States must take a strong place in international affairs. They all know we're the strongest nation. And they all know we're not interested in building a world-wide empire. So let's let them know we'll use our moral strength to help bring right and justice and freedom in the world."

Yes, Shamrock knew what he was fighting for—with all of his 200 Irish pounds.

"When anyone says we don't know what we're fighting for it makes me so mad I can't talk," he said. "When you're stabbed in the back, by God you should have enough red blood to fight back. To hell with letters of apology. We've got to beat the Japs down to their knees. They've got a rotten philosophy. We're fighting for freedom— the right to do and say what we please, to choose our own jobs and our own wives."

Prevailing sentiment of the men favored active U.S. participation in international affairs as a means of helping preserve peace. They know that airplanes and rockets have made our world small indeed—as the late Wendell Willkie said, "One World."

The last few days aboard ship we were busy getting briefing lectures on the topography and defense of Okinawa...learning bout the natives...stocking up with ammunition...packing "D" and "K" rations in our knapsacks.

We learned that the rugged terrain, the caves, the bombs, stone walls and coral-reefed shoreline all stacked up in favor of the defense. We know what the Japs threw at the Marines at Iwo Jima. Our turn was next.

"It's surprising the high morale of our whole outfit," commented Master Technical Sergeant Warren Hemmer the morning before D-Day. An efficient, clean appearing 21-year-old, his home was Belleville, Ill. He had been married six months previously.

"When I was out last time no one smiled for a week before we went into Guadalcanal," he said. "This looks like it may be a lot rougher than those other campaigns, and now everyone's joking. That's the way it should be."

It turned out that our campaign was pretty rough...mighty rough for Hemmer and a lot of other fine boys.

"What are your emotions? Are you a bit scared?" I asked dozens of Marines, Soldiers and Sailors.

"Right now, I'm not afraid," said Dick Koch-Church. I believed him, for he had snapped completely out of the nervousness he displayed a few weeks earlier when he began learning the extent of Jap defenses on Okinawa.

"But I probably will be scared when we hit the beach," he continued. Those certainly were prophetic words in his case.

And what was Dick fighting for?

"Jim, did you see the picture the other night, 'Thousands Cheer?'" asked romantic Dick. "Did you see all those beautiful American dolls on the screen? That's what we're fighting for.

"Freedom to go where we want... do what you want...not to kow tow to Hitler or any other dictator...to achieve success... to love pretty girls!"

Bill Carver wondered how tough our campaign would be...how many men would be lost. He gave me the name of a buddy of his to write to, just in case.

"I've lived a lot. I'm ready to take my chances," he said.

Shamrock Coyne had been through campaigns before.

"We've got some misery ahead of us," he said. "I wonder how soon I'll be able to take my clothes off...take a shower...shave...sleep in a cot instead of a fox hole...use a toilet instead of a slit trench. I'll dive in my fox hole during alerts and keep my head out of danger. But I'm concerned about typhus and other diseases on the island.

"But you and I are damned well coming back, Jim. I'll be the silliest slap-happiest guy on the ship when we head for home. And I'll get down and kiss the dirt when we get back to the United States—just like this."

He dropped to his knees, leaned far forward and kissed the deck, while we panicked with laughter.

On the eve of D-Day, the elements were a bit turbulent, and so were our thoughts. We were within easy range of Jap bombers, suicide boats, submarines and possibly even shore batteries, 'ere long.

D-Day was Easter morning, so both Protestant services and Catholic Mass were held right after midnight, when Easter morning was just born.

Having been temporarily assigned as a Marine combat photographer, I attended both the services and took photographs. Never before have I seen such impressive services—impressive not for the ceremonies nor the surroundings—the mess hall—but for the humbleness, reverence and devotion which permeated the room and the very souls of the congregations like an electric charge. Brave men were thankful for an opportunity to worship...to renew and strengthen their faith...to lean more completely than ever before on the Almighty.

"May the beauty of the Lord be upon us all throughout this coming day," said Ship's Chaplain Ogden in the prayer opening the Protestant services.

Then Marines, Soldiers, Sailors and Seabees intoned hymns with fervent voices.

"Every brave endeavor, every devotion to freedom, every righteous deed, all go forward under the same banner on Easter morning," Lieutenant Ogden said in his brief sermon.

"All things virtuous arose when Christ arose...after the darkest night the world had over known...

"May everyone in this room say a silent prayer before leaving."

Father S.G. Horvath of Newark, N.J. the Catholic chaplain who was assigned to the Second Marine Air Wing and going ashore with us, also took cognizance of the forthcoming ordeal which induced humbleness the like of which I never before had witnessed.

"Knowing what we are about to face, let us, like Christ, be strong," he said. "We are looking for victory...we know it will come... the price may be hard.

"Pray hard, pray frequently. When everything seems dark, remember...Christ is by your side."

In a simple baptism ceremony, with an all-male congregation, three men entered the fold. They were Private First Class Kenneth W. Norris of Pekin, Ill., Private First Class Voyd Lacy of Fennville, Mich., and Sergeant Kenneth B. Moreton of Melrose, Mass. Norris and Lacy were Soldiers—Moreton a Marine.

There were no emotional outbreaks—no hallelujahs and amens which used to spring spontaneously from congregations at revival services I attended when young.

Instead I encountered and witnessed and felt in the men the presence of deep, silent devotion.

At mass I saw Joe Vance, pale and proudly erect, singing in sweet tones, with youthful fervor, Big John Thomaselli and husky Shamrock Coyne were there...kneeling...counting beads...receiving communion, so were Ship's Captain Twomey and Major Lombardo. And at protestant services was bog Moose Matthews standing in the front row and singing hymns reverently. There were troubled souls...then solaced souls...pallid faces radiant with holiness... a spirit of faith, hope and abiding peace. It was good for us to be there.

When the services ended at 1:30 A.M., I strolled aft to the fantail before turning in. The wind was subsiding. Now flashes from big Naval guns pummeling Okinawa illuminated the sky...told us we were nearing our objective. Outlined in bright moonlight against cumulous white clouds were the huge hulks of our fast convoy...riding the waves defiantly... invading shores of an island the Japs considered part of their homeland. We had emerged from the stifling tropics and a cool, crisp breeze whipped across the deck. It was invigorating.

We had come all the way...8000 miles...through minefields, sub-infested waters... darkness and storm. We were hurling a mighty invasion Army and Navy into the snarling teeth of the Jap warlords. The ship's bows cut white troughs of foam. I thrilled at the sight. My pulse quickened. I felt eager for the chase and the kill...a tingle with adventure...avid for retributive justice.

As I hit the sack for a few hours of sleep I was tired, curious and apprehensive of the morrow, but not really scared. No, I can truthfully say I was not afraid. It wasn't until some days later that I came to know what fear really is.

Chapter 8

Invasion

Dark, ominous clouds lurked on the eastern horizon at daybreak. Suddenly a blood-red sun arose to glare insolently on the forming battle scene. Its scarlet rays danced on the China sea and fell like a mantle of blood on the crests of nearby hills—the sanguinary hills of southern Okinawa.

It was Easter Morning, but it was L-day***landing day***"Love Day" in the military voice letter alphabet, but a loveless day on Okinawa.

I was up at 5:30 a.m., after a few fitful hours of sleep interrupted by the startling clang of the general quarters gong sounding alerts five different times as bogies flew near, or approaching submarines menaced us. On all the alerts the troops were required to lay below to their compartments... wondering... while ship's crew members manned their battle stations. There were submarine, suicide crash boat and suicide plane attacks, but none against the Allendale.

Shamrock Coyne, Bill Carver and I joked and laughed boisterously at morning show, but Bill's nonchalance seemed slightly forced. Our joviality drew surprised or disdainful glances from more than one pair of somber, wondering eyes.

Returning topside, we saw surprisingly calm seas—a lucky beak for our landing forces—and bright sunlight.

Now the roar of big naval guns—14 and 16-inch cannon—reverberated from battleships clearly visible offshore. Destroyers, light cruisers and heavy cruisers joined the battleships in the cannonading which had blasted and rocked the southern half of Okinawa incessantly for eight days prior to L-day, sending 4500 tons of projectiles crashing into shore defenses and other targets.

Thick-winged, hump-backed Avengers from unseen aircraft carriers droned overhead in small but frequent formations to dive-bomb key Jap coastal defenses, smaller single-seater Hellcat fighters, loaded with bombs and rockets, also joined the aerial procession pummeling the enemy.

Destroyers raced to and fro feverishly, dropping depth charges which kept Jap submarines from scoring a single hit. Then the anti-sub activity subsided.

Apparently the enemy was running out of pig boats. Our planes and ships had bombarded Jap submarine pens at Uten Ko on the northeastern coast of Okinawa for several days.

On L-minus two-day and L-minus one-day our fighter and bomber planes from aircraft carriers had shot down 17 enemy aircraft, damaged 19 in the air and on the ground, sunk 14 motor torpedo boats, cargo ships and other small craft and destroyed mills, barracks, bridges, radio stations, pillboxes, buildings, docks, gun positions and other installations.

The bombardment thundered with increasing crescendo as we waited tensely for Love—A-hour—8:30 a.m. We waited, and wondered about the Marines and soldiers who soon would hit the beaches. Being an aviation squadron, our job was to come later. We would wait several days before going ashore to start aerial operations on airfields to be wrested from the enemy.

However, most of our ship's landing boats had been lowered to help take ashore assault troops from other ships. Through field glasses we could see them, laden with heavily-armed assault troops, approaching the shoreline. We watched...intently...and wondered.

Then synchronized watches showed 8:30 a.m.; a subdued silence fell on the ship. The Jap creed is "Death to anyone who sets hostile foot on our shores." We waited. Then, from the ship's speaker came the dramatic announcement:

"Attention all hands. The first wave has hit the beach. Some of the LCPs (Landing Craft, Personnel) are returning."

Some are returning: What about the others? Or was it too soon?

At 8:52—just 22 minutes after the first wave hit the beach—came the announcement that six assault waves had landed along eight miles of beach. We relaxed somewhat, knowing that the battle for the beaches must be going well. Soon we heard that assault troops were walking ashore upright and meeting virtually no resistance.

For a change, the Marines had an easy landing. It was the casual start of one of the bloodiest and most violent campaigns of the bitter Pacific war.

We had surprised the Japs by landing much farther north than they anticipated. Our land batteries on captured Kerama Retto had pulled the Japs off balance by shelling the southern beaches and Naha airfield, but the Doughboys and Marines hit 15 to 20 miles farther north—the central beaches opposite Yontan and Kadena airfields.

The bewildered Jap forces of Okinawa were amazed at the overpowering size of our invasion convoy. They looked with unbelieving eyes on a fleet of 1400 ships, from which poured thousands of landing craft with troops and supplies. Instead of contesting the landings on the eight mile beach front, they elected to withdraw their forces southward for a bitter, delaying defensive battle in rugged, cave and pillbox-studded terrain where Okinawa narrows to an isthmus less than three miles across. So instead of setting up an eight-mile defensive line, the Japs threw their full strength—and it proved to be considerable—into a three-mile defensive line. There the 85,000 defending troops who had been caught off balance by our initial assault would have time to reorganize nearer their principal supply and defensive points of Shuri and Naha and exact the heaviest possible toll as well as delay our conquest to the utmost.

With the Japs falling back rapidly, L-day was tame.

"This is just like a Douglas Mac Arthur landing," cracked one Marine.

"There were only a few Jap machine guns firing on the beach when our amtrack (amphibious tractor) landed," said Marine Private First Class Ted Kolovich, who came ashore on the first wave. "On our left flank a couple of Japs sneaked in and were shot by Sixth Division Marines."

But the next day five Japs opened rifle fire on Company G, Seventh Regiment, First Marine Division, and Kolovich, a 22 year-old Leatherneck from Shamokin, Pa., and a veteran of the Peleliu campaign, went to a field hospital with a wounded foot. Two others also were wounded by the Japs, who then fled northward to the wilds of the Motobu peninsula.

Corporal Robert Dunda of Pueblo, Colo., a tank gunner with B Company, Sixth Tank Battalion, complained that the tanks couldn't keep pace with the fast-moving infantry sweeping across fields and through villages.

"All that first day we just walked and chased chickens," he said.

Even the artillery brought ashore had comparatively little to do. Occasionally pilots in spotter planes called targets. The 155 millimeter "Long Toms" would cut loose with their long-rage projectiles. However, the fleet guns kept up an incessant barrage.

Our Marine Aviation groups lolled on the Allendale for several days, watching as much of the "show" as we could see from the ship and undergoing numerous general quarters alarms as suicide planes attacked our fleet. But more about that later.

On the eve of L-day the USS Clay arrived offshore at Okinawa, brimful of Leathernecks of the Sixth Marine Division. The Clay was part of a large convoy of APA's and other ships which brought troops and supplies from Guadalcanal for the invasion of the morrow.

"Well, Jim, it looks like they finally got us into combat," said Corporal Bob Pates, ex-star fullback at St. Thomas College in Minnesota. "Yep, but it's taken a long time," responded Corporal Jim Brown. "Ever since I've been in the Marine Corps it's been march, march, march...train, train, train...simulate, simulate, simulate. I'll be glad to get at those little Jap bastards who've caused me all this damned work."

A small cluster of Marines from "I" Company, Third Battalion, 29th Regiment, was on the Clay's fantail talking casually about the unknown path which lay ahead over Okinawa's white beaches, verdant, tomb-dotted hills and brusque, cave-riddled ridges.

"You'll have plenty of chance to get even with the Japs, Jim," chuckled Gunnery Sergeant Harold E. Taylor, a former "China Marine."

Prior to enlisting in April, 1942, "Gunny", whose home was Escondido, Calif., had served a four-year hitch in the Marines Corps starting in August, 1934, and was with a detachment of the famous Fourth Marines on embassy guard duty at Peking.

"Gunny, you've been pretty quiet tonight," Jim shot back at him, "What are you thinking about?"

"I'm thinking about my wife," said the stocky, 32-year-old Taylor meditatively. "In fact, I think about Mary just about all the time." He paused, then added "This may be a rough campaign."

Then he laughed—a deep, chuckling laugh. His row of even, white teeth flashed in the bright moonlight. Gunny, the old salt, never would be one to spread alarm—no matter what the danger.

"It may be rough, but it couldn't be any worse than Iwo Jima," spoke up "Frenchy" Francoeur, a tall, dark-complexioned youth from Westbrook, Maine. "If the Marines could take what they did on Iwo Jima, I guess we at least can take what's ahead of us. But gosh! It's such a pretty night. It's a shame to be fighting."

However, Corporal Raymond C. Francoeur had a bellicose as well as an artistic side. A former baseball and hockey player as well as a skier, he was wiry, rough and ready.

"Those Japs aren't going to like us," mused Corporal Brown. "Nope they aren't gonna like old Jim Brown."

The fuedin' blood was beginning to simmer in his six-feet frame. For Jim Brown was a descendent of the notorious McCoy's who feuded with the Hatfield's in the hills of West Virginia for 90 years—from 1863 to 1923. He was a son of the former Bessie Mae McCoy and a great grandnephew of "Lark' McCoy. Soon, over the Okinawa hills and valleys not unlike those of West Virginia, Jim Brown was going fuedin'... not for Hatfield's, but for Japs. And with his modern weapon he was going to help put Japs away on the sub-tropical island of Okinawa, a lot faster than any of his ancestral rifleman ever cleared the atmosphere of Hatfield's.

Born at Logan, West Virginia, Jim was a football and boxing star in high school, and was middleweight boxing champion at Marshall College, which he attended three years. He loved a fight and feared no one.

"Well, guess we'd better turn in boys. Got a big day coming up tomorrow," said Gunny Taylor.

They hit the sack about 11 o'clock and slept soundly except when a general quarters alarm clanged at 1:30 a.m. They fell right back to sleep, and not until the next morning did they learn that a suicide plane had nearly hit their ship, zipping right over the fantail in a hail of ack ack and disappearing in the thick smoke screen laid by the ships.

Brown, Pates and Frenchy were up early and put finishing touches on their packs, rechecked their ammunition supply, and then crapped out. They knew their 29th Regiment was not on the first assault wave, but would go in shortly afterward. Gunny Taylor was remaining behind for two days to keep supplies rolling from the ship. He was on detached duty with the quartermaster department of the Third Battalion, 29th Regiment.

The Leathernecks waited restlessly—keyed up and spoiling for a fight. Then in mid-morning came the skipper's voice over the ship's speakers:

"Now hear this. "I" Company go below and prepare to debark."

Soon they were at their debarkation stations, with rifles and extra bandoliers of ammunition slung over their shoulders, hand grenades swinging from their belts, bowie knives and bayonets at their sides.

"Look out, Japs, here we come," said Pates as he swung over the side and moved rapidly down the debarkation net to a bobbing landing boat.

"Gung ho!" shouted Brown as he followed.

"Keep your heads down and your rifles well oiled," Gunny Sergeant Taylor called after them.

Some called it Love-day and some said L-day. But to Gunny Taylor it was Love-day—his wedding anniversary.

By the time their flat-bottomed landing boat bounced away from the USS Clay, the shoreline of Okinawa was busy as Michigan Boulevard in Chicago. Landing boats of all sizes, amtracks, ducks, alligators, weasels and other amphibious craft jammed the water and jostled for landing space on shore.

The Doughboys and Marines were quick to exploit the advantage of light resistance on the beaches. Already trucks were roaring up and down Okinawa's western coast coral roadway, and so were amtracks, ducks (amphibious trucks) jeeps, tanks and road graders. Troops swarmed ashore in hordes, and vast quantities of ammunition and supplies followed.

The landing boat carrying Corporal Brown and his buddies collided with another, but none was hurt. When they neared the shore the amtrack scheduled to transfer them to the beach was stranded on a coral reef. So Jim and his buddies waded ashore.

All knew by then that it was virtually an uncontested landing, but they expected at least token resistance.

"Where are the Japs, Bob?' Jim asked.

"Dunno," replied the 205-pound Pates. "This really has me snowed."

"Did we hit the wrong beach?" asked PFC Carlton K. Smith of Bridgeport, Main.

"I don't know, but this is a hell of a lot easier than our training maneuvers," replied Frenchy Francoeur.

Their outfit stood around on the beach, drying their clothes and waiting for further orders. That is, all but Jim Brown. No sooner was he ashore than he spied an elderly Okinawa man, two women and a boy, walking rapidly across a field. He took after them on the double. The Okinawans stepped up their gait, but Brown quickly overtook them. With jargon and gestures the native man indicated vehemently that he must continue.

Corporal Brown brandished his Garrand M-1 semi-automatic rifle, and with one gesture convinced them they would go with him. Down the road he marched them, and up to battalion headquarters for screening and transfer to a civilian camp. As he passed his platoon, Jim was bombarded with cat calls.

"I see you're getting on the ball there eager beaver," jibbed his buddy, Bob Pates.

"Hmmm! Not bad," shouted another.

Military government personnel were busy from the first interviewing and segregating civilians, screening out any disguised Jap soldiers and putting them in prison camps. Bona fide civilians were grouped in re-location camps, and fed with rations brought from the United States expressly for that purpose, and with food stuffs captured from retreating Jap soldiers.

The Third Battalion, being in reserves, crapped out that day near the beach. Jim and Bob immediately took off on a sight-seeing and foraging tour, and wandered inland more than a mile. They returned, both astride a native pony, carrying chickens they had caught.

"Boy, this invasion has me snowed," exclaimed Pates as the two Leathernecks, looking awkward as Don Quixote with their rifles slung over their shoulders, jogged along atop the captured steeds. "They haven't got us into battle yet, Jim. We haven't fired a shot."

"Maybe the Marines taught them a lesson at Iwo Jima," speculated Brown. "Or maybe they have some traps set to ambush us."

Meanwhile assault troops rolled roughly and rapidly inland across a patchwork of half-acre cultivated plots of rice, sugar cane, sweet potatoes and cabbage, over wooded hillocks and through shell and bomb-blasted villages. Tanks, machine guns, rocket-firing trucks, flame-throwers and riflemen surged forward. The attackers took no chance on possible ambuscades. They unleashed stunning barrages of steel and fire, leveling and burning native villages, making a clean sweep. Troops swept past hundreds of well-placed but deserted caves and pillboxes, blasting or sealing the few from which resistance came. Jap soldiers in the scattered pockets of resistance were quickly dispatched. One of the native tombs near the beach was used as a pillbox, but was blown up and its small Jap garrison sealed inside with bones of dead Okinawans.

By 11 a.m., the Marines had overrun and captured a grand prize, the large Yontan airfield, about a mile and a half inland from the beach, and soldiers had taken Kadena airfield, about the same distance inland some two miles farther south. A gullible Jap pilot who believed the Tokyo radio propaganda saying the Okinawa invasion was repulsed with heavy American losses, landed on Yontan airfield in the afternoon. Marine riflemen eager for a live target, waited until the flier stepped from his plane. When halted, he foolishly reached for his pistol but was never quite able to get it out.

Heavy guns brought ashore shelled installations on the islands. Big Naval guns boomed all day long. Smoke and dust rose like funeral pyre columns over the Okinawan landscape.

By nightfall the assault troops had expanded their beachheads to a three mile depth at several points, and controlled seven miles of the north-south coastal highway, as well as east-west roads leading to Yontan and Kadena airfields.

Grasshopper spotter planes began operating off Yontan on L-plus one day, observing enemy targets and giving radio direction for shelling and bomb attacks.

During the first-day operations, four Jap suicide planes attacked feet units offshore, and were shot down by ships' anti-aircraft fire. The Japs lobbed a few mortars and shells onto out shore parties unloading supplies on the beaches. But on L-day and for several days thereafter resistance was weak...casualties light.

Then slightly stiffening Jap resistance presaged the forthcoming hideous, bloody battle. Sixty-two miles long, malaria-ridden, typhus-infected leprosy-scourged Okinawa was a rich prize, for it would give our planes land bases less than 400 miles from Kyushu in southern Japan, and within fighter plane range of Tokyo and most of the Jap homeland. And it would open to us the crucial shipping lanes to the China coast.

Some 435,000 inhabitants of Okinawa posed a perplexing problem for Lieutenant General Simon Bolivar Buckner Jr., commanding general of the invading Tenth Army, which was composed of four Army divisions and two Marine divisions, with another Marine division (about 15,000 Leathernecks) held in reserve.

The natives far outnumbered the invading forces, and would be in the way of operations frequently. Furthermore, Jap soldiers would disguise themselves as civilians, hoping to remain at large as spies or to incite the natives to violence and guerrilla warfare.

Propaganda leaflets by the thousands were dropped on native villages before and after L-day, admonishing the natives to surrender and promising them food and fair treatment. They were warned not to travel at night, lest they be mistaken for troops passing through our lines and be killed.

Soon the Jap anti-American propaganda, which had so frightened the Okinawans in advance, boomeranged and reacted in our favor, making the civilian handling job easier. For the word quickly spread that we were treating the civilians well, and above all were feeding them and giving them medical care. Instead of setting up a false-front, puppet government for Okinawa, we set up a military government under which Okinawan affairs would be administered until the country's future political fate would be settled at a peace conference.

The Okinawans must have thought us a race of giants—so small are they. There were wrinkled old men wearing dark kimonos, squatty, bare-footed women with babies trussed papoose-fashion on their backs, and round-cheeked youngsters who quickly learned to besiege troops with cries of, "Candy! Candy!" All were rounded up, screened and then moved in motley procession to civilian, receiving stations, bewilderment and doubt reflected on their faces, in their eyes and in their nervous, walking-running strides.

Young children balanced amazingly heavy loads of hastily gathered household effects on their heads. An old woman led two live chickens on a cord...eggs would be scarce.

Japanese-speaking officers and enlisted men of the military government section quickly won the confidence of many of the leaders, and civilian handling progressed with minimum trouble. Some of the elderly Okinawans, particularly the better educated ones, welcomed the Yanks and saw in the invasion an opportunity to cast off the yoke of servitude imposed by Japan.

Predators of every ilk had preyed on the Okinawans for centuries, making their political plight miserable. In ancient days Jap pirates, who in fearsome junks, looted ships on the China Sea and specialized in every known form of Oriental torturer and brutality, made their headquarters in coves at Okinawa or the nearby islands.

Shorter and darker than the Japanese, the Okinawans have the same basic characteristics. However they are a mixed racial group. Anthropologists believe the first inhabitants of Okinawa were a bunch of the hairy Ainu and Kumaso peoples who inhabited Ryukyu and other islands of Japan. Later the Jap freebooters brought captured women from northern China, injecting the Mongolian strain. Immigration and invasion added Malayan blood, and inter-marriage eventually fused Okinawans into a slightly distinctive strain.

The Okinawans maintained their own succession of kings for approximately 700 years as part of the Ryukyu Retto. As early as 600 A.D., periodic Chinese invasions and raids began. For years the Chinese influence was strong. Then in the seventeenth century the Japs conquered the islands. The shaky Ryukyu kingdom maintained its precarious rule only by acknowledging the suzerainty of both China and Japan, the poverty-stricken citizens paying tribute taxes to both nations.

In 1879 the "king" was reduced to a non-imperial prince of Japan, and the island was incorporated into the Jap Empire Okinawa as prefecture. Finally, in 1894, China recognized Nip rule of Okinawa, but some of the enlightened citizens dreamed of future freedom and independence.

On the evening of L-day Corporal Jim Brown and Corporal Bob Pates began preparing their foraged chicken dinner while other Marines of "I" Company were breaking out their package of K rations. When their chicken was only half-done, a red alert sounded as Jap aircraft approached. They had to extinguish their fires, lest they reveal their positions to enemy planes. But quickly they improvised a shield with shelter halves, re-lighted their fire and broiled their chicken.

"This really has me snowed, Jim," exploded Bob, wolfing a drumstick ravenously and watching a Jap plane go down in flames, victim of a terrific ack ack barrage. "You know, Okinawa doesn't seem like such a bad place." "I'm sold, but how about those pretty Geisha girls?" asked Jim. "I like blooming-breasted babes. But those sad sacks."— He gestured toward the civilian camp. "Those remind me of cocker spaniels' ears."

A bit barrel-chested, Jim was a man's man, but he was also a lady's man. Handsome, personable, self-assured and full of blarney, he was virtually mobbed by palpitating pulchritude at the station when he entrained for boot camp late in 1943. Five dewy-eyed damsels were there to bid him good-bye, and almost started a spite war of jealous indignation among themselves.

"This overwhelmed me," said quick-thinking Jim. "Line up, darlings and I'll kiss you all goodbye."

With that he grabbed each bundle of charm in turn and kissed her fervently, while the others giggled good-naturedly.

During training days at Guadalcanal prior to the push off for Okinawa, Corporal Brown and three of his tent mates formed an undefeated quiz team, winning nine Straight contests against all comers. As prizes they were taken on picnics... with Red Cross girls for dates. As a crowning prize Jim sat next to Actress Martha O'Driscoll when she was on the Canal entertaining troops.

"Ah, Martha O'Driscoll," he reminisced. "She was really wonderful—super-duper."

But for a number of lonely months there was to be a feminine famine for him and his buddies...in fact, for all of us in the Okinawa campaign.

Lieutenant Colonel Erma A. Wright, 33-year-old commanding officer of the 3rd Battalion, 29th Regiment, set up a perimeter defense and bivouacked his troops about 500 yards from the beach the first night. Only one Jap, armed with grenades, tried to infiltrate their lines during the night. He failed.

Still in reserve, the 3rd Battalion moved across already captured Yontan Airfield the next afternoon and bivouacked half a mile east of it—in position to repulse any sudden Jap counter-attack. With his men dug into excellent defensive positions, Lieutenant Colonel Wright awaited further orders.

※

Chapter 9

Baptism of Blood

The tenth Army continued its lightning advances on L plus One-day, with Major General John R. Hodge's 24th Army Corps Doughboys slashing all the way across Okinawa to split the Jap defending forces in two.

While the Army forces were completing this five-mile gain in two days, the Leathernecks of Major General Roy S. Deiger's Third Amphibious Corps advanced rapidly northward in hot pursuit of the retreating Japs.

Supplies rolled ashore rapidly, and the campaign was so far ahead of schedule that ground units of the Second Marine Aircraft Wing went ashore April 3, L plus Two-day, and began digging in and setting up service and repair facilities to keep the Marine Corsair and Hellcat fighter planes flying when they alighted at Okinawa April 7 from aircraft carriers. But preceding them were two members of Marine Observation Squadron One, also of the Second Marine Air Wing, who went ashore on L-day.

At Yontan and Kadena airfield troops found a number of Japan's new Baka, a piloted rocket bomb launched from Jap twin-engine bombers to make one-way suicide rocket flights at ships or ground targets.

The First and Sixth Marine Divisions, paced by tanks and supported by artillery batteries, gained from two to four miles on April 3, reaching Okinawa's east coast and cutting off the Katchin peninsula. Army's Seventh and 96th Division troops pressed southward. By the night of April 5 the Marines had advanced more than 20 miles northward, still meeting only nasty little pockets of resistance, while the doughboys began encountering stiff Jap resistance.

To the south, the Japs set up a stubborn defensive line half a mile long near Ginouan town in the path of the advancing 96th Army Division. At noon the Japs lashed out with their first sizeable counterattack of the Okinawa campaign, with three tanks in the lead and with machine guns, rifles, mortars and artillery blazing away at the Doughboys. But the 96th, veterans of the Leyte campaign, knocked out one of the tanks, two machine guns and five pillboxes and killed 174 Japs, hurling them back to their original line.

Farther westward, near the coast town of Uchitomari, the 96th met another line of stiff enemy resistance. Pushing the Japs back, the Doughboys killed 53, exploded three pillboxes and knocked out an anti-tank gun. But the Nips knocked out two of our tanks in the torrid encounter.

Army advances ranged from one to two miles that day, with resistance strong in places; light in others. But that was the last easily won ground in Southern Okinawa. Subsequent advances were measured not by miles, but by yards...and by killed and wounded Americans. The Army had advanced some seven miles in five days. But it was going to take 11 weeks to push the remaining 14 miles to Okinawa's southern tip.

It was on April 5 that Japan's tottering Kosio Cabinet fell, unable to keep face in view of the fall of Iwo Jima, B-29 raids on the homeland, the growing success of the Philippine Islands campaign and now the spectacular gains by Unites States forces on Okinawa—Japan's doorstep. The Kosio regime began July 22, 1944, when our conquest of Saipan forced Hideki Tojo's administration to step aside.

In ousting Kosio, the Japanese Emperor chose 77-year-old Admiral Baron Kantaro Susuki, president of the Privy Council, to form a new cabinet. Admiral Susuki expressed "deepest humiliation and regret at the development of the situation which has allowed the enemy to take possession of an integral portion of the Empire." Warning that "developments do not warrant optimism" in the "present momentous crisis," he endeavored to sound a rallying call by saying "there is no excuse for us, as subjects of His Majesty the Emperor, to Permit the enemy to soil any part of our country."

Yes, the thinking Japs who were the least bit well-informed knew then that Japan was doomed to lose the war. The big question, though, was how long would they hold out and try to save face? One thing we knew for certain. As long as the war continued, their resistance would be fierce and fanatical.

There was a bit of good-natured banter when Gunnery Sergeant Taylor went ashore the afternoon of April 3 and rejoined this buddies of "I" Company, bivouacked on Okinawa.

"How many Japs you killed, eager beaver?" Gunny asked Corporal Jim Brown.

"Hell, we haven't seen anything yet but women, children and old men," Jim replied. "It would have been safe for even you to leave the ship and join us sooner, beer-belly."

"Say, I'm glad to be on land," Taylor retorted. "This is a lot safer than sitting on board ship with suicide planes diving at you."

Then Taylor saw Gunnery Sergeant Donald D. Doerr, an old-timer from Lake Alfred, Fla. kindling a fire to heat his K rations, and hailed him:

"Hey, machine gunner, What's the good word?"

"Our vacation's over," Doerr replied. "We're jumping off pretty soon."

Early April 5 the Third Battalion, 29th Marine Regiment, was on the march. That night it bivouacked 16 miles farther northward. And the next day the outfit marched nearly as far, moving up the western coast of Okinawa toward the Motobu peninsula, a body of land aimed northwestward into the China sea like an Indian arrowhead. Scouting parties stemmed from the main column to round up Jap soldiers lurking in caves of the rugged, scenic hills covered with evergreen trees similar to our pines.

At the end of the second day's march the first "casualty" occurred—a peevish Okinawa pony kicked Corporal Jim Brown in the left knee and knocked off his demolition pack, which fortunately didn't explode. But Brown did! Captain Walter E. Jorgenson of San Pedro, Calif., "Y" Company commanding officer, sent Gunny Taylor back with the word:

"If animals give you any trouble, shoot them,"

"Aw, let the ornery critter live," growled Jim. "Maybe he'll kick someone else. Besides, I don't want to dirty my rifle. I'm too tired to clean it."

"Say, that horse knew just who's fanny to kick" Bob Pates razzed. "Passed up all the others and let Brown have it. You may fool the Nips and these 'Okies,' Jim, but not the horse."

"Aw, blow it out your ear," snapped Brown. "Why Pates, you're not man enough ever to have a son. You're going to have nothing but girls, sure as shooting."

"I'll bet it is a boy," countered Bob, scheduled to become a father soon. "Why, I just can't miss."

"Bet you a case of beer it's a girl," retorted Brown.

"It's a deal."

And it was a boy, Garly L. Pates the proud father learned later.

On April 7 the Third Battalion encountered huge holes which natives had dug in the Motobu peninsula coast road to block the advance. The tanks which had been leading the advance waited for construction battalions to move up, but the Marine infantrymen marched onward. Tanks and supplies could come later. After an eight-mile advance, Lieutenant Colonel Wright drew the Third Battalion back two miles for safe bivouac. He knew he was nearing the Japs' northern forces. Now the advance would be slower, with more scouting parties used.

The Third Battalion had been moving rapidly, and Gunny Taylor was walking and sweating away his protruding paunch, developed with the aid of many-a pleasant beer. But he made never a hint of complaint. In training camps, and in standby bivouac areas, Marines bitch constantly. Waiting—eternal waiting—and inactivity get on their nerves. But in combat they don't bitch. I never have heard a Marine complain about a thing—lack of food or water, or about any other hardship—when in combat.

One 13 man scouting party, led by Sergeant Frank Lilly of Eric, Pa., flushed some Jap soldiers from a small village, burning the houses with fire grenades and then checking the ever-present caves nearby. Suddenly they found themselves under rifle fire from Japs concealed in undergrowth on high ground nearby. Sergeant Lilly dispersed the Marines in a wide skirmish line. Then they swept forward on a broad front, concentrating their fire on the enemy.

Private Grover C. Shankle, a North Carolina lad, killed three Nips, Lilly mowed down two more with his Tommy gun and Private First Class Dan Slade of Brooklyn, N.Y., accounted for another. None of the Marines was hit.

Two days later a hairy, withered old woman—one of the ugliest and meanest looking humans imaginable—walked spryly into the bivouac area of the advancing Third Battalion. Her scrutinous, black eyes observed everything in view.

"Look at that horrible bitch," said Brown. "I think I'll shoot her."

"Aw, let her live," suggested Sergeant Frank "Smoky" Fodero of Buffalo, N.Y. "She's just a harmless civilian."

Later Jim wished he had followed his hunch and killed her, or at least imprisoned her. For she disappeared into the hills and immediately set fire to a native hut which sent up a huge column of smoke, like a signal. Soon a heavy barrage of 72 millimeter mortar shells rained from distant hills beyond the burned shack. They fell all night, wounding and killing 16 Marines. Now there was no doubt; the witch-like bag was a spy.

"I" Company's first casualty occurred that day when Bugler Anthony Peralta of East Rochester, N.Y., who had abandoned his bugle at Guadalcanal and become a runner—a hazardous assignment—sustained a bad leg wound from shell fragments.

At an early hour the angry Leathernecks pushed forward, with Corporal Pates leading the point of the advance with a fire team of riflemen and Browning automatic riflemen, and with Corporal Brown and Corporal Ralph Shinn of Elba, Neb., following to ferret out land mines and booby traps, which they exploded with small TNT packs. But this was leaving the road in such bad condition that an engineering unit moved up and took over the job, disconnecting the wires and removing the mines—ticklish, dangerous duty.

"Brown, our planes have spotted Jap gun emplacements on this hill to our right, about 500 yards from here," said First Lieutenant Lawrence P. Sullivan, ex-Notre Dame football tackle who was leader of the third platoon. "Take a fire team up there and blow them. They should be right here." He penciled an x-mark on a map.

Corporal Brown led a party of four rifle and BAR-men (Browning Automatic Riflemen) and a map reader up a wooded trail.

"Keep intervals of 10 to 15 yards and watch out for snipers," he cautioned.

Cautiously the patrol advanced.

"There the guns are," said Brown, as they reached the summit. "They look deserted, but we'll take no chances. Spread out and keep me covered while I investigate."

The Japs had retreated, leaving two well-concealed 47 millimeter guns mounted on rubber wheels. With demolition packs the Leathernecks blew up the guns, and an ammunition dump. They also burned a food dump.

The returning demolition team was just overtaking "I" Company, which meanwhile had advanced some three mile up to Motobu peninsula road, when Jap 77 millimeter cannon fire from a distant ridge began falling amidst the troops. Jim dived into the nearest ditch. It was a sewer!

Up front at the "point" of the advancing company, Corporal Pates riflemen saw ahead and sent back a query:

"Are those Japs, or Marines on patrol?"

His answer came quickly. The Japs opened fire.

"That did it," said Bob, firing back savagely and deploying his men. "Our war's really started now."

During the hot rifle and machine gun fire fight which ensued, Private First Class Dorrall R. Smith of Cincinnati, O., dashed across an opening seeking a better position for firing upon the Japs. Nambu machine gun fire cut him down. Unhesitatingly his buddy, Corporal Jim Joiner of Jacksonville, Fla., dashed out and dragged Smith to protective defilade where he would be shielded from Jap fire. Joiner evacuated Smith, but in so doing left himself exposed too long. Cross-fire from three Nambus killed him instantly. Others carried Smith to an aid station on a poncho, but he died shortly afterward.

It was a cold, dismal day and rain was falling almost incessantly. The Marines were ankle and sometimes knee-deep in mud, but they didn't mind. Jap mortar shells fell in their camp area all afternoon but did no damage. The ground was so soft that the mortar shells dug in deeply, and merely threw mud instead of showering fragments of metal in all directions.

The skirmish, which took place near the Manna river, was the first sizeable contact "I" Company made with the enemy. A number of Japs were killed and wounded, while the Marines suffered two fatalities...Smith and Joiner...the first from "I" Company to die on Okinawa.

When the Japs withdrew late in the afternoon, "I" Company dug in and set up a perimeter defense for the night. Every man dug a foxhole for protection against fragments from enemy mortar and artillery shells which exploded sporadically in the bivouac area all that rainy, miserable night. Rubberized shelter halves protected them from rain for awhile, but soon their fox holes filled with water. Wet, and shivering from the cold April nights encountered on Okinawa, the Marines had to crouch low in their water-filled fox holes for protection against the shelling.

The first platoon advanced the next morning as a scouting party to locate the Japs' big guns, and "H" Company withdrew until a larger force could be mustered.

First Lieutenant John P. Stone, tall, ruddish-complexioned veteran from Montville, O., who enlisted in the Marine Corps in November, 1939 and rose through the ranks, was leader of the first platoon. Returning with his scouting party, he reported to Lieutenant Colonel Wright that the Japs' big guns were emplaced in a high ridge, later to become known as Green hill. Observing their fire, Lieutenant Stone pinpointed their position with compass and map.

Lieutenant Colonel Wright requested an air strike, and naval fighter-bombers blasted Green hill with bombs, rockets and machine gun strafing the following morning. Then "I" Company moved out on a combat reconnaissance mission with orders to feel out the enemy and return that evening.

The pilots were accurate with bombs on their strike, but the wily Japs, with mobile defensive strength, had sheltered themselves and most of their weapons in caves during the attack, emerging immediately afterward to set up their positions again.

Over rugged, wooded land between which tiny farm plots and rice paddies were sandwiched in narrow, flat valleys, the two companies advanced. Climbing upward, they formed a skirmish line as they neared Green hill, and moved up and over a broad knoll which lay in the center of a horseshoe-shaped amphitheater of high ridges, densely covered with undergrowth and evergreen trees.

All knew they were nearing the enemy, but there was no sight nor sound of Japs. Forward moved the skirmish line. Lieutenant Sullivan led the third platoon over the top of the knoll, while the first platoon, under Lieutenant John L. Porpst of Sheldon, Ia., proceeded on the right flank.

Then Frenchy Francoeur in the first platoon heard noises...the subdued voices of nearby Japs. Now he heard the clicking of enemy rife bolts as the Japs cocked and loaded their weapons. That was enough for Frenchy. He opened fire, and so did other members of the first platoon, shooting as they advanced. But they were shooting at unseen targets. The Japs held their fire a bit longer, letting the Marines get closer.

Then at point blank range the Japs unleashed a terrific curtain of machine gun and rifle fire. The Marines dropped their packs and advanced, now carrying only weapons and ammunition, and firing at the unseen enemy. Suddenly a tremendous barrage of artillery and mortar fire opened, and missiles began exploding on all sides. Sergeant Carl J. Clayton of Norristown, Pa., and Corporal Chester Gencay of Worcester, Mass., both on the point of the advance, were killed. So was Private Charles H. McKown, a rifleman. Five in Lieutenant Stone's first platoon were injured.

The Leathernecks found themselves pocketed in the core of the enemy's crescent defensive line approximately half a mile long. It was a perfect defensive position which the Japs had chosen for their biggest stand on the northern half of Okinawa. They outnumbered "I" Company more than three to one and had the advantage of well camouflage defensive positions.

Ninety millimeter (3 ½-inch) mortars dropped in the third platoon section, wounding three men. Many of the Marines dived for sheltered into nearby hand-dug trenches, but they proved to be "booby trenches"—a diabolical Jap invention. No sooner were the men in the trenches than mortar fire began landing squarely in them. The Japs already were sighted in to drop mortars in the trenches, where they anticipated the Marines would take shelter.

Quickly the Leathernecks bounced out of the trenches and sought battle positions elsewhere. First Lieutenant Sullivan, a husky six-foot-two hulk of a man with a broad face and brusque jaw, was shouting orders and exposing himself to fire from the cleverly concealed Japs. He began placing his men in a defensive line behind whatever shelter could be found.

Instinctively, Jim Brown darted behind a stone wall three feet high on the forward slope of the knoll.

"Get up here, Sullivan," Brown shouted. "They can't hit you here."

The big ex-gridster took the suggestion, and moved a full squad of men, one by one, behind the protective wall, placing them at five to 10-yard intervals, thus giving each a broad field of fire and keeping them spread for maximum protection against artillery and mortar shells.

Private First Class William R. Wiggins, radioman for the company, tuned in to Third Battalion headquarters and began broadcasting the position of the ambushed Marines. Unmindful of seeking shelter for himself, his first thought was to get word back of his company's plight. Nambu machine gun fire found him and he died, his radio transmitter still on and carrying sounds of battle back to headquarters.

On the company's left flank Platoon Sergeant John D. Heim of the first platoon exposed himself to Jap fire while dashing back and forth along his platoon's fire-swept line to reform the left portion of it and get a heavy hail of fire going to keep the Japs low in their caves and pillboxes while casualties were evacuated. Heim hadn't taken time to drop his pack, and it was quickly riddled by Nambu machine gun fire.

"Keep as many men as possible on the line and keep them firing, Frenchy," shouted Heim, who still remained exposed to direct his men.

In battle most of the firing is not done at live targets, but at defensive positions to keep the enemy pinned down. You know approximately where the enemy is, but get only occasional glimpses of him.

Marines of "I" Company put up a heavy barrage of fire, but mostly at an unseen enemy.

After machine gun fire hit and killed Sergeant Clayton, squad leader on the left flank, Heim put Corporal Frenchy Francoeur in charge of that section. Frenchy kept three BAR-men and four riflemen firing and spaced at proper intervals, while pouring clip after clip of caliber .30 bullets at the Japs from his own chattering BAR—a shoulder machine gun type of rifle.

Lieutenant Stone ordered a withdrawal of his platoon to a more protected defensive position, as soon as the causalities could be removed. Sergeant Heim darted back and forth to direct the orderly withdrawal. Now a sniper's bullet ripped his shirt. Still he stood erect and fired. A Jap bullet smashed his rifle and knocked it from his hands. But Heim, a 24-year-old veteran Devil Dog from Black-water, Mo., loved a brawl of any kind. The fate of his platoon—his buddies—hung in the balance. He grabbed a wounded man's BAR and sprayed Jap positions until he ran out of ammunition. Then he grabbed still another weapon, an M-1, and continued firing—an inspiration to his men, most of whom were in their first major battle.

As soon as the Japs started firing, Heim's closest buddy, Gunnery Sergeant Doerr, in charge of the company's automatic weapons platoon, quickly set up his machine gunners in the best spots available to bring heavy fire on the Japs and keep them low while the Marines withdrew. Lacking a good position for himself, he set up right in the open to rain hot lead at the Japs. Like Heim, Doerr was shouting for the men to pull back, one at a time, and set up a defensive line in better positions. Heim seemed to have a charmed life that day, but not Doerr. A Jap bullet crashed into Doerr's shoulder. Still he fired. Short, but powerfully built, with bulging muscles like a wrestler, it would take a lot to stop Doerr.

The entire company always respected Doerr, and feared him a bit. He didn't talk much, but his word was law. A rougher Marine sergeant never came down the pike. He had fought with the famed First Marine Division at Bougainville and Vella La Vella. Operating a machine gun is grim business, and he was an expert at it... could make a machine gun talk. Wounded, he never ceased firing... just kept pouring lead at the enemy... hundreds of rounds.

With the left flank moving back to better positions, Platoon Sergeant Heim, now armed with a carbine, dashed over the top of the knoll to check the position of the rest of the company and keep his platoon's lines properly tied in. He jumped in beside Jim Brown, whose section still was pinned down by frontal and flanking machine gun fire.

"Where the hell are the Japs?" asked Brown.

"You can't see 'em unless you get your head up and look for them, Jim," Heim replied. "There's a Jap Nambu sitting in the corner of that rock wall. You'd better use your BAR to make sure we get him. It's a little far for my carbine."

It was the Jap Nambu which had killed Radioman Wiggins.

A high scoring expert rifleman at boot camp, Brown put his BAR to shoulder and rested the barrel on the stone wall. Then he emptied a full clip—20 rounds—into the Jap. It was kill number one for Brown, who was destined to scourge the Japs incessantly throughout the entire Okinawa campaign. With grim satisfaction he watched the Jap's riddled form. But Heim wasn't so please.

"Damn it Jim, you shouldn't have used the entire clip," he said. "It not only wastes ammunition, but gives your position away. You're apt to draw mortar fire."

As he spoke a single rifle shot rang out and a Jap sniper fell from a tree above the dead Nambu gunner. It was the result of some fancy shooting by Corporal Marcel Wicka, a 33-year-old Virginian who was another veteran "China Marine."

A former professional boxer whose home was Arlington, Va., Wicka held the middleweight, light-heavyweight and heavyweight boxing championship of Marine forces in China although he weighed only 155 pounds. His previous hitch in the Corps was from 1929 to 1933.

Silencing the Nambu and the sniper freed First Lieutenant Harvey F. Brooks of Nattapan, Mass., the company executive officer, who had been pinned down by incessant fire. Now he joined Lieutenant Sullivan and ordered the third platoon to fall back to the next hill and set up a defensive line tying in with the first platoon, which already had moved back and set up. Then he contacted Lieutenant Stone and Lieutenant Propst, giving them orders to being a withdrawal.

The withdrawal started, but Brown grabbed a carbine with a grenade launcher and all the rifle grenades he could find, and remained at the front, firing one grenade after another into the Jap positions.

"Get out of there, Brown, you'll get killed," ordered Lieutenant Sullivan after all the others had moved back.

"Wait a minute," said Brown. He continued firing, his inherent McCoy feuding blood now boiling. A few minutes later Lieutenant Sullivan commanded:

"Brown! Get back here on this stretcher and help carry this wounded man out."

Brown returned and saw Private First Class Donald J. Mollica, a BAR-man from Brooklyn, N.Y., lying a short distance back from the wall and bleeding from half a dozen wounds.

"Let me put him on my back and carry him out, Chick," said Brown. "The fire's too heavy for all of us to try to get out of here with him."

"No, Jim, he's wounded too badly," said Medical Corpsman Robert L. "Chick" Demuth of Sharon, Pa. "He's hit in the stomach."

"Well, come on then, Chick," said Jim. "I'll make way for you. Let's get him out of here."

There were plenty of men for stretcher bearers, so Jim dashed a short ways around the knoll to give protective fire against any attack.

"Come over this way," he called. "There's no fire over here."

But the procession didn't come, and then a Nambu sprayed bullets at Jim from the right. Back he dashed, and found the stretcher bearers had gone over the top of the knoll and taken temporary cover in a hollow, where Chick was bandaging another of Mollica's wounds.

"You've got to get him right out of here," said Lieutenant Brooks.

"I've got to finish putting this bandage on first," replied the corpsman calmly.

Back up the knoll dashed Brown with his Browning Automatic Rifle to cover the rear. Everyone else had withdrawn—that is, all but one. Brown saw a Marine pinned down by hot rifle fire and crawling on his stomach back toward the reformed Marine lines. Two Nip riflemen were firing on him from a ledge above.

Five staccato slugs from Jim's automatic rifle killed the first Jap, and a like burst dispatched the second one.

"It's old Wick, Jim," said the crawling Marine. "Please don't shoot."

"Come on up, Wick," said Jim, who now recognized Corporal Wicka. "I wasn't shooting at you. I killed those two Nips over the top of your head. They're the ones who were shooting at you."

Wicka sprinted up beside Brown and exclaimed:

"God! I thank you, my wife thanks you and my children thank you for saving my life."

Lieutenant Brooks then called to Brown:

"We don't have any communication with battalion headquarters, so we're pulling out of here. Is there anyone left out in front of you?"

"Everyone's out except Wicka, and he's up here with me," Brown replied.

"All right, come on down then. Let's get going."

In a hail of fire Brown and Wicka stood up and ran top speed down the knoll, rejoining Lieutenant Brooks and several others deployed in a rear protective line. The other Marines had gone ahead to carry out Mollica. Jap machine gun fire then concentrated on the remaining Marines, so they dashed down a saddle and over another knoll to the reverse slope, where they set up a skirmish line and again opened fire on the Japs.

Wicka saw a Marine shot in the leg, and summoned Pharmacist's Mate Second Class Johnny Pauk of St. Louis, Mo., a fast-working Naval corpsman who had been exposing himself to enemy fire all afternoon while bandaging wounded and administering plasma. Pauk bandaged the Marine, whose wound was not bad, and then started him back toward Battalion headquarters under his own power.

Meanwhile on the left flank the withdrawal to the new skirmish line farther back had been completed, all the time under heavy fire. One at a time the Marines dashed back while the others poured fire to keep the Japs low and their return fire down as much as possible. Each Marine on the new line then resumed fire to give protection for the others.

Only after all the others were back did the wounded Gunnery Sergeant Doerr grab up his machine gun and run back to a new position. His heavy fire, and his coolness in helping direct the withdrawal, had kept casualties down and helped prevent a rout.

Reaching the rear position, Sergeant Doerr set up the machine gun in a fox hole and again began firing like mad, assisted by Private First Class Harry L. Burr Jr., whose parents lived in Chile where his father worked for an exploration company.

The Japs trained a mortar barrage on Doerr. Closer and closer came the shells as the Japs sought the range. Still he fired. One shell landed only a few feet away, and showered dirt and rocks on Doerr and Burr.

"Rat-ta, tat, tat, tat, tat, tat..," answered Doerr's machine gun.

Then another mortar shrieked down and exploded in the fox hole between Doerr and Burr, killing the latter instantly. Doerr's left leg and left arm were dangling—almost blown off. Frenchy heard a moaning and saw Doerr trying to crawl from his fox hole.

"Come get me out of here," said Doerr. "They've got me pretty bad this time." He forced a grim smile.

Quickly Frenchy dived to Doerr's side, grabbed his jacket collar and dragged him to a safe defiladed position nearby. There he rolled Doerr onto a poncho and got three other men to help carry him behind the lines to a doctor.

"Cut off my arm, Frenchy," Doerr requested in low, steady tons. "The damned thing's no good now."

The doctor began administrating blood plasma at once.

Then Doerr looked up and saw his old buddy, Wicka. "Isn't this a hell of a way to go back?" asked Doerr.

"You really gave 'em hell, Doerr," replied Wicka. "A lot of us owe our lives to you."

Strong arms started the wounded Marine back to camp on a poncho.

"Those Jap bastards..," muttered Wicka as he looked after the procession. Then he dashed back to the line and spoke his fury with more rifle bullets.

Doerr was cheerful on the way back.

"Think I can get a drink when I get back to sick bay, Doc?" asked the old gunny sergeant.

"You surely can," replied the doctor.

But Doerr grew more quiet as the trek continued. Before they reached the battalion aid station he lost consciousness, never again to awaken.

The "I" Company mortar section was hard hit by the first barrage of Japs shells, and suffered more than 50 per cent casualties. Sergeant Orua Johnson of Hickory, N.C., in charge of "I" Company's mortar section, was killed instantly. So were Corporal William F. O'Malley of Buffalo, N.Y., and Private First Class Francois H. La Cobee of Shreveport, La., also of the mortar section, while Corporal Abner Baker of Bulan, Ky., was wounded. But the remaining mortar men moved in to close range and continued firing at the Jap positions.

Soon the Japs, moving under protection of rifle trenches which ran the length of the curving battle line, moved in on the left flank and began pouring Nambu machine gun fire until all their ammunition was expended.

One Jap machine gun nest was raking the field with withering fire. Armed only with a pistol and two hand grenades, Private First Class Stephen J. Spano of Jersey City, N.J., charged it and knocked it out. He, too, paid with his life, but he saved a lot of his buddies.

While some kept up heavy rear fire, others helped evacuate the wounded. Meanwhile, the Japs were advancing stealthily in their trenches and setting up more flank positions with their Nambu machine guns, which are light and portable, with a convenient carrying handle on the top of the barrel, and which spit lead at terrific speed.

Returning to the front, Jim Brown spied PFC Bob Sampson, a runner who had been wounded while helping carry Mollica's stretcher. Quickly Jim applied a bandage to a badly bleeding wound above Sampson's heart, then helped him to a sheltered position behind the new line. Just after they moved over a hill a big 77 millimeter Jap shell exploded on top of it. They hit the deck. In the Marine Corps, as in the Navy, everyone calls the ground the "deck." Snafu!

Scouting for the best evacuation route, Jim ran across a rice paddy and crouched behind a raised, dirt walk, invariably found in Okinawa rice paddies. This gave him shelter from a Nambu on his right.

"Come on, what's keeping you," he shouted to Sampson.

As Brown raised up, another Nambu from the left kicked up dirt around his feet. He left that hot pocket in nothing flat, running to another knoll and across it. Sampson was following, so Brown struck out across another rice paddy. He made the shelter of another hill, but Sampson fell in the paddy. Jap Nambu fire sought Sampson from several directions. He got up and made a staggering dash for the hill and fell down beside Brown. Sampson now was bleeding from another wound.

"Did they hit you again, Sam?" Brown asked.

"No. But my arm's paralyzed," answered Sampson. "See what's wrong with my shoulder."

There was a big wound in the back of the shoulder where the bullet which hit over his heart had come out. With no more bandages available, Brown took the bandages from the chest and put it on Sampson's back to stop the flow of blood. The first wound had clotted pretty well, although it still trickled a small crimson stream. Sampson had lost a lot of blood, and was beginning to have a yellow appearance...like a dying person.

Suddenly Private First Class Walter T. "Rocket" Ryan dashed over the knoll and jumped down besides Sampson and Brown.

"They got me too, Jim, but it isn't bad," said the Rocket.

He had a clean wound in the arm, and it wasn't bleeding badly. Under a continuing hail of Nambu and rifle fire, the three made their way back to the battalion sick bay, Ryan and Brown half-carrying Sampson. They had made it in time, and with quick medical attention. Sampson began making a rapid recovery. Brown asked and received permission to return and help evacuate more wounded. With him went Heim, who had helped another wounded man back, and Gunny Taylor, Corporal Carl Cook Jr., and Private First Class William M. Kemp of Corinth, Miss. On the way up they met many of the battle casualties...walking wounded and stretcher cases...bandaged and bleeding. They were told where to find Corporal Baker, the mortar man who had a hole blown in his back near the shoulder. They placed him face downward on a poncho and brought him out.

Big Bob Pates was wounded in the stomach while helping carry out a comrade, Corporal Moss Miller Jr., of Ashville, N.C.

"Boy, ain't we having ourselves a time here, Bob," said Miller.

His remark became the battle quip which helped relieve tension and bring a laugh to "I" Company in many future tight situations.

"Yes," replied Bob. "Now we're really snafu (situation normal-all fouled up).

Meanwhile Captain Jorgenson, who had remained at battalion headquarters that day with a swollen infected foot received word from a runner that his company had been ambushed and was having a rough time.

Quickly he made his way to the battlefield and setup a rear defensive line to hold the Japs while wounded were being evacuated and the withdrawal completed.

The Marines evacuating the badly wounded PFC Mollica were under a terrific hail of Jap fire. First Sampson, whom Corporal Brown had helped evacuate, was wounded while helping carry Mollica. Then Nambu fire hit another of the Leathernecks carrying the makeshift stretcher. Grimly the tragic trek continued. Nambu struck another.

"Let me down to rest a minute," Mollica requested.

They complied, and the former Brooklynite painfully edged away a few feet, drew his automatic pistol and tersely command:

"Beat it, or I'll shoot,"

The Leathernecks protested.

"We can't do that, Mollica," said one.

"You've got to." He gestured with pistol. "There isn't a chance for us to get out through here, and I don't want to be responsible for any of you to get bumped off. Now scram!"

They knew he was right—that it would be suicide to continue exposing themselves under cross-fire of those fast-spitting Nambu machine guns. Reluctantly they crawled back after concealing Mollica in a protected position.

First Sergeant Richard L. Berry, a big Marine from Pensacola, Fla., helped evacuate Corporal Archie E. Unstead of Van, Pa., who was wounded in the foot by a bullet. Then after helping Captain Jorgenson setup the skirmish line to protect the withdrawal, Sergeant Berry began checking the muster roll and getting reports on the wounded and missing.

It was a dark day for "I" Company. Ten were killed, two were missing and 33 wounded two of them fatally. Private First Class Frank M. Greska of Hudson, Mass., and Private First Class Duff T. Stackhouse of Chandlers Ville, O., died later from their wounds.

The missing men were Private First Class Mollica and Sergeant "Smoky" Fodero, a platoon guide, who was hit in the head with shrapnel.

Others wounded included Platoon Sergeant Charles P. McQuilliam, Sergeant Claude W. Killiam, Corporal George A. Buck Jr., Corporal Allen A. Furbush of Manchester, N.H., Corporal Floyd S. Miederer of Titusville, N.J., Corporal Walter A. Schneider of Manchester, N.H., Corporal Hervey C. Sharp of Adrian, Mich., Private First Class John J. Christopher of Charlott, N.C., Private First Class Donald C. Corrica of New Bedford, Mass., Private First Class Joseph S. Kelly, Private First Class Pasquale J. Patruno of New York City, Private First Class George J. Pope of Fort Washington, N.Y. Private First Class James A. Saylor, who was shell shocked, Private First Class Nicholas A. Scarmozzino of Waterberry, Conn., Private First Class James C. Scism. Private First Class Wendell M. Sullivan, Private First Class Eugene L. White of Grovestone, Va., Private Charles W. Estes, Private Edward H. Hoahn of Saluda, N.C., Private Leo F. Homan, Private William H. McKinney, Private Harry D. Simmons and Private First Class James P. Menefee.

When all the forces had returned to Third Battalion headquarters, Corporal Brown heard that Mollica was left behind. By then it was getting dark.

"I wish permission to go get Mollica," Brown said to Captain Jorgenson. He's up there wounded."

"Do you know how to give blood plasma?" the captain asked.

"Yes sir. I used to be a chemist," replied Brown.

He never had given plasma, but planned to get full instructions from a corpsman and do the task. Captain Jorgenson consulted the corpsman who had treated Mollica, and then called for Brown.

The corpsman tells me he doesn't see how Mollica could still be alive," said the officer. "I don't want to risk losing anyone else on such a long chance."

"Please let me go," pleaded Brown. "My God, the man's wounded and needs attention."

"I'm sorry Brown. I can't give you permission," said Captain Jorgenson, with a catch in his voice.

Jim walked away, hot tears coursing down his cheeks.

Crafty Captain Jorgenson snapped him out of it shortly by inviting Brown to accompany him and Lieutenant Colonel Wright to a nearby hill to observe and spot Jap artillery.

Back on the now-deserted battlefield, Private First Class Mollica waited grimly, and wondered, as evening approached and dark descended. He lay there alone—wounded—with loneliness gnawing at his heart.

After a few fitful hours of sleep he awakened in the morning with a tremendous thirst. He looked about and saw a corpsman's kit which had been abandoned. Slowly he dragged himself to it, and bandaged his own wounds.

But the exertion made his thirst grow stronger...his brow feverish. Glancing around almost desperately, he spied a canteen 75 yards away. With great effort he painfully dragged himself along foot buy foot, yard by yard—finally reaching the canteen. It had been punctured by a bullet, and was empty...

His head throbbing until it seemed like it would burst, Mollica pulled himself to the shade of a nearby tree.

There he slumped down... exhausted... feverish... thirsty... living, but living the agonies of war.

Chapter 10

Victory on Motobu

Lieutenant Colonel Wright called for heavy shelling of the Jap positions on Green Hill by the Sixth Marine Division's 155 millimeter (5 inch) Long Tom guns. With this bombardment in progress, he held his forces back two days, waiting for other elements to move up for a coordinated attack.

He knew the Japs well, and planned a bold, powerful assault to blast them from the rugged bastion of strength to which they had cunningly retreated for their large-scale ambuscade and last ditch stand.

A veteran Marine officer, Lieutenant Colonel Wright was ordered to the Pacific when trouble with Japan first appeared imminent. He was at Pearl Harbor when the Japs stuck there on December 7, 1941, and later fought them at Guadalcanal.

After 42 months in the Pacific, he returned stateside. Eight months later he brought a Marine artillery unit back to the Pacific combat zones, but soon was assigned to the Sixth Division which was training for the Okinawa campaign.

As commanding officer of the Third Battalion, 29th Regiment, Lieutenant Colonel Wright sent his men through rigorous battle maneuvers at Guadalcanal, which had become a training and staging area by late 1944 and early 1945.

Originally from Langdale, Ala., he was graduated from Auburn College with an Army commission following four years of R.O.T.C., military training. But he chose the Marine Corps, and advanced rapidly in it. Now the 33-year-old Lieutenant Colonel was ready to hurl his battalion at the stubbornly resisting Japs who held the advantage which goes to a well-entrenched defensive force.

But this time it was the Japs who were due for a surprise.

Instead of one company, he was hurling all three of his companies at the Japs, but that wasn't all. His forces were coordinated for the attack with the Fourth Marine regiment. The Fourth Marines had steamrollered up the east coast of Okinawa, making a clean sweep as they went. Now they were called over to the Motobu peninsula for a surprise flank thrust at the insolent Japs. The battle plans were drawn... the first phase of the well-calculated attack set for April 14, 1945.

Then back to the bloody battlefield of Green Hill Lieutenant Colonel Wright sent the Third Battalion.

Up a high ridge the Third Battalion assaulted. Now the Marines knew they were fighting for more than freedom, right and home. They also were fighting for their own necks, and to avenge their wounded and killed buddies. It had been a rough mental jolt for "I" Company members to see their ranks hit so hard. Now they were ready to strike back, and in full measure.

As the attack developed they soon ran into heavy barrages of machine gun and rifle fire. Marine tanks had caught up with the fast-moving infantry by now, thanks to some fast road repair work by construction battalions. The tanks threw their hard-hitting, mobile fire power at the Japs, who also were pounded by Marine artillery, mortars and two more air strikes by Corsair-flying Leatherneck pilots.

Moving ahead and driving Jap machine gunners backward, the Marines reached their first day's objective on high ground, set up a perimeter defense and bivouacked for the night. Lieutenant Colonel Wright was covering the ground carefully and completely.

With the battalion entrenched in a strong position for the night, a scouting party skirted the Japs to reconnoiter the outskirts of the previous battlefield.

Under a tree they saw a motionless form—Private First Class Mollica—lying near the parched canteen. Sadly they walked up to the place where he lay.

"Gee, I'm sure glad to see you guys," said Mollica, raising his head. "Gimme a drink of water."

His overjoyed buddies showered him with water from their canteens, and then formed a makeshift stretcher and evacuated him. The doctor who treated him upon his arrival at the aid station was amazed at this vitality and at finding him still rational after being wounded in half a dozen places and going without food or water for two days.

"That's great news about finding Mollica," said Corporal Brown as the word spread.

"Yes, and they also found Smoky Federo," replied Gunnery Sergeant Taylor. "He was stunned and blinded when hit in the head by shrapnel, but recovered and was picked up by the Fourth Marines after wandering blindly for two days."

Lieutenant Colonel Wright pushed his forces forward the following day against increasingly heavy machine gun and mortar fire. But the heavy fire power of the Marines, who were pitching plenty of mortars of their own, pushed the Japs backward toward their original position on Green Hill. The "I" Company, which was being held in reserve on the first phases of the assault, had no more casualties on the first two days of the advance. But torrid action was in store on the morrow.

At 8 a.m., on April 16 "G" Company of the Third Battalion assaulted up the steep west flank of Green Hill in the face of intense Jap machine gun and mortar fire. Leading the assault was First Lieutenant Jim Green, former Purdue football player who had come up through the ranks. He was leader of the second platoon, "G" Company.

Pistol in hand, Lieutenant Green led the fast-charging Leathernecks. A hidden Jap tossed a grenade. It struck the officer's shoulder, exploding as it hit. Jagged fragments served his jugular vein.

First Lieutenant Sherman B. Ruth ran to assist the fallen officer, but he was beyond assistance. Lieutenant Green died almost instantly on the hill which now bears his name.

Quickly Lieutenant Ruth reformed the lines of the hard-hit second platoon, tying them in with his own first platoon. Then furiously the Leathernecks charged, advancing up the hill above most of the Jap positions and then sweeping forward and downward, throwing grenades into Jap trenches from the rear. Then they followed in with bayonets to finish the remaining enemy with cold steel. Demolition men with their powerful, square packages of TNT sealed cave after cave and forever silenced big Jap Naval guns found on Green Hill.

Hot on the heels of "G" Company came "H" Company, slashing across the ridge at a lower point, cleaning out Jap pillboxes and trenches and sealing caves as they advanced. By 12:30 the Marines held the west forward slope of Green Hill.

After this bold flank attack took the Nips by surprise, "I" Company charged forward, tying in on "H" Company's left flank. Lieutenant Sullivan led the third platoon around the right side of the knoll which had been under such heavy fire during the ambush on April 12, while the second platoon, led by Second Lieutenant Propst, skirted the knoll to the left.

Another heavy barrage of mortar fire from the reverse slope of Green Hill descended on the advancing Marines, but this time they passed up the "booby trenches" which had proved so costly before.

"Forward," shouted Lieutenant Sullivan. The two platoons charged, skirting the knoll and joining forces in front, at the base. Then they swept forward into a draw to join their lines with "H"

Company's left flank. Riflemen and BAR-men advanced without opposition down the draw. Then came the machine gunners.

Suddenly there was a roar of Nambu machine gun fire at point blank range from a concealed Jap machine gun nest which covered an opening in the draw. Lieutenant John. L. Propst was killed instantly, and so were Private First Class William M. Kemp of Corinth, Miss., Private First Class Richard E. Walter Jr., of Williamstown, N.J., and Private Bernard A. Kaeame of Waltham, Mass., all machine gunners. Another machine gunner, Private First Class James H. Knight Jr., of Ferndale, Md., was wounded. The Japs had waited for the machine gunners, then opened fire.

Rapidly "I" Company cleaned out the Jap nest, sealed more Japs in caves and then continued a hot fire fight with the enemy until dark. During the bitter battle, Private First Class Russell E. Hamilton of Harve de Grace, Md., also was wounded, and Corporal Nicholas A. Cipriano was wounded slightly but returned to duty a few days later.

While suffering some heart breaking casualties, the Third Battalion killed 157 Japs and sealed many more in caves.

While Lieutenant Colonel Wright's forces were assaulting and winning the forward slope of the west end of Green hill, Colonel Alan Shapley's Fourth Marines completed a long, rapid advance which took the defending Nips by surprise. With the Third Battalion's assault at its height, over the hills from the east swarmed the Fourth Marines—most of them veterans of the famed Marine Raider battalions. Flushing small pockets of Japs whom they killed or drove before them, the Fourth Marines advanced up the northeast side of Green hill and tied their lines in with the Third Battalion.

Black night fell over the battlefield, bringing a lull broken only by the muffled roar and tremor of grenades as Japs committed hari-kari in the caves where they had been sealed by Marine demolition charges.

About 10 p.m., the Nips began a stealthy infiltration movement toward the positions where "I" Company had dug in for the night. Marines could hear the approaching Japs, but waited, holding their fire as long as possible lest they betray their own positions. Nearer came the muffled sounds of footsteps, of snapping twigs, of rustling leaves.

Then a sharp explosion shattered the silence as a hand grenade exploded in a fox hole, wounding three Marines. A rifle shot rang out and a Nip fell, a bullet between his eyes. A small group of fanatical Japs charged upright toward the Marine line. Withering bursts from a Browning Automatic Rifle operated by Corporal Carl J. Cook, one of

Brown's long-time buddies from Logan, W.Va., mowed them down. He killed four of the Nips.

Sporadic fire and hand grenade blasts continued all night as the Marines remained in their fox holes and repulsed Jap infiltration attempts. Numerous Nips, armed with bayonets, hari-kari razors and hand grenades, ended their nocturnal assaults in death. Three Marines were hit by grenade fragments, but remained silently in their fox holes throughout the harrowing night. They were Private First Class Robert W. Luddecke of Hartford, Conn., Private First Class Eugene B. Sims and Private Myron I. McMahon.

At daybreak Private First Class L.D. Sparks of Roxburrough, N.C., crawled to the foxhole where Lieutenant Sullivan and Corporal Brown were crouched, and said:

"We've got three men wounded. They need a corpsman."

"Give them a hand, Brown," said Lieutenant Sullivan.

Brown awakened Pharmacist's Mate Second Class John Pauk of St. Louis, Mo., who immediately started to the aid of the wounded men. Then he awakened Pharmacist's Mate Second Class "Chick" Derauth. The startled corpsman jumped straight up. Brown lunged at him, slamming him back into his fox hole, but not in time. He saw a Jap 10 yards away toss a grenade. It exploded in the fox hole, wounding Brown and grazing the corpsman. A piece of shrapnel struck Jim in the forehead, two more dug into his shoulder and one ploughed into his side.

With blood streaming down his face and saturating his jacket, Brown accompanied the shaken corpsman to Lieutenant Sullivan's fox hole. Then he went after the Jap. Now Jim's feudin' blood was coursing through his veins like molten lava. His pulse beat fast. Possessed with an all-consuming rage, he wanted only revenge. He felt like nothing could stop him—not even a hundred bullets.

Grabbing a Browning Automatic Rifle, the wounded descendent of the McCoy's stalked the Jap who had narrowly missed killing him. The Jap took one look as the wrathful Leatherneck approached. Then he turned and fled.

Madly Brown pursued. He didn't shoot. He just wanted to seize the Jap in his powerful hands... pound him... crush him... choke him to death!

Rapidly he closed on his quarry. The Jap stopped, dropped to his knees, and, facing his captor, bowed low in an Oriental gesture of servitude and surrender. Jim was only five yards away. Two more paces and the quarry would be in his clutches. But some instinct must have warned him. He stopped short and his BAR broke into an angry roar. He rode trigger on a full clip of 20 bullets which blasted away the top of the Jap's head.

With grim satisfaction he took the dead Nip's bayonet for a souvenir. Then he saw how close he himself had been to death. For as the Jap bowed forward, his finger found the pin of a fragmentation grenade carried on his belt. In another instant he would have pulled the pin, straightened up and blown both himself and Brown to oblivion.

The fully awakened "I" Company now looked about and took inventory. Four from the third platoon were wounded, but the Japs had paid with 11 dead.

Then another sniper shot rang out and wounded Corporal Gaylor F. "Pop" Leach in the left buttock while he was sitting down eating his morning rations.

"Corpsman," bellowed Leach, double-timing it to his fox hole on hands and knees, and then holding his fanny.

"Where you gonna wear your purple, you old fossil?" asked Brown, who had received first aid and was awaiting evacuation.

"Right here," said Leach in his polite, nasal voice, while pointing to his wound and laughing through his heavy black beard of three weeks' growth. "More people have looked at my fanny than ever looked at my face."

Pop, a wiry, wizened Marine from Malone, N.Y., was 39, but spry as a colt and just as tireless. Four missing teeth kept him out of the Navy when he was young, and he had a long argument before being accepted by a Marine recruiting sergeant for duty in World War II. But that sergeant can well be glad he let Pop Leach in, for he did a terrific job on Okinawa.

And Pop's 18-year-old son, with a full set of incisors, bicuspids and molars, was heartily welcomed by the Navy.

Jim Brown, Pop Leach, and the other wounded were taken to the beach and transported by landing craft to the Marine evacuation hospital on the Okinawa beaches near the place where the first landings were made on L-day.

The Japs had thrown everything they had the day before, but still the hard-shooting Leathernecks advanced, gaining strategic positions for the final push. It came on the morning of April 17.

The "Gung Ho" Devil Dogs of the Fourth Marines, many wearing khaki overseas caps instead of steel helmets, unleashed a terrific barrage with rifles, sub-machine guns, hand grenades, bazookas, flame throwers and demolition charges, driving the Japs westward right past the Third Battalion, whose lines were set up at the top of Green Hill.

All hands had a field day mowing down the disorganized and routed Japs. One Jap took a look at the assaulting Devil-may-care Marines and fled over a hill screaming:

"Banzai! Banzai!"

His back riddled with bullets, he died in the fastest reverse bonsai charge on record.

"Maybe he meant that the Marines were putting on a bonsai charge of their own," suggested Gunny Taylor.

That day the Marines sealed eight ammunition caves, destroyed two eight-inch naval guns and killed more than 300 Japs, wiping out the strongest point of resistance on the northern half of Okinawa. The Marines pushed forward the next day, sweeping westward to the China sea and wiping out remnants of the Jap army.

At the evacuation hospital where Jim Brown and Pop Leach were taken, a corpsman put tags on them the first evening.

"What does this mean?" asked Brown.

"It means you'll be evacuated to the Marianas tomorrow," replied the corpsman.

Leach looked at Jim.

"Are you thinking the same thing I am, Jim?" he asked.

"Shall we take a powder now?" asked Brown.

"No. Let's get a good night's sleep," counseled Pop. "We'll take off right after morning chow."

After eating a hearty breakfast they gave away their souvenirs; then departed through a restricted area set aside for Okinawan civilians. Hitch hiking back to the Motobu peninsula on military vehicles, they got caught in a torrential rain storm between rides, were fired upon by a sniper and had no weapons with which to return fire, and finally arrived on the Manna river to find that the Third Battalion had moved by truck the day before to the other side of the island.

Their wounds needed fresh dressings, so they went to a sick bay.

"Will you bandage us without asking any questions?" asked Brown.

"Okay," replied the doctor, who thought they were fresh battle causalities. But soon he discovered the true story.

"We just got damned tired of that hospital," said Pop Leach. "It's all fouled up There are 90 corpsman. 85 Seabee construction men and only 32 patients."

"Damn it. You two are over the hill from the hospital," replied the officer. "But I'm glad to have you back, and I'll call the Colonel and explain it."

While brown and Leach were in the hospital the Sixth Marine Division had enjoyed good hunting—both for the Japs and for souvenirs.

With time on their hands, Private First Class John O'Leary of Brockton, Mass., and Corporal Brown hitch-hiked to the Third Marine Amphibious Corps headquarters and "borrowed" a jeep, which they took back to the native village where their outfit was bivouacked.

But it proved to be pretty hot property—the property of a captain.

O'Leary was caught red-handed, so Jim admitted his part. Word quickly reached their platoon leader, Lieutenant Sullivan.

Brown and O'Leary saw the giant Sullivan striding toward them. Quickly they darted into their shelter halves and emerged in native kimonos, saying:

"Me civilian. No Okinawan."

This antic brought only a deeper scoul to Sullivan's set, Irish jaw. They knew by now the big ex-football tackle was furious enough to dispense with reading them off, and wade into them with his large hands. Wanting no part of that, they fled, shouting:

"Bonsai."

Soon word came to them through Gunnery Sergeant Taylor that each would do 10 hours of extra police (cleanup) duty.

While the Fourth and Twenty-Ninth Regiments were securing the Motobu peninsula, the Twenty-Second Regiment, also of the Sixth Division, had slashed through dense, semi-tropical jungles of the rugged northern portion of Okinawa.

By April 19—two days after conclusion of the battle for Green Hill—there were no more enemy front lines, and the Japs were capable only of scattered guerilla warfare. The 29th Regiment killed 27 more Japs on the 19th and a patrol from the Seventh Marine Artillery Battalion killed five. "I" Company had another casualty that day when shrapnel wounded Private First Class Orman H. Duck of Liverpool, N.Y.

Major General Geiger announced the following day that organized enemy resistance of Motobu peninsula and in northern Okinawa had ended, and the Marine's portion of Okinawa was secured. Only mop-up and patrol activity remained.

The First Marine Division had participated in the beach landing on L-day, then gone into reserve and patrol activity. But it was to see plenty of action later in southern Okinawa.

During the 20-day campaign the Marines of the Third Amphibious Corps had killed 2741 Japs and taken 44 prisoners while their own casualties totaled 273 killed and 1169 wounded in action.

Lieutenant Colonel Wright's Third Battalion had been in the middle of the hottest fighting of the campaign and had a casualty list of 148—30 killed and 118 wounded, in addition to six accidentally injured in action and 21 non-battle casualties. And what did the Third Battalion do to the Japs? It killed 602 of the sons of heaven.

Before arriving at Okinawa we were warned about poisonous snakes, malaria, plague, leprosy and other pestilences. But most of us never saw a live Habu, or any of the other poisonous snakes, and little sickness developed, aside from fungus (athlete's foot), principally among infantrymen who were so busy battling day after day that they had no time to change or wash socks, and seldom had enough water anyway. However, some of the Sixth Marine Division men were bitten by Habu, but no fatalities from this venom were reported.

As for leprosy, the percentage of lepers is higher among Okinawans than any other people. I saw some natives who looked like they were afflicted, and the Sixth Division discovered a colony of 800 lepers on Yagachi Shima, a tiny island on Unten Ko (bay) on northern Okinawa.

And on Unten Ko another pestilence existed—Jap submarine pens—until the Marines arrived and took over.

With their first major assignment of the Okinawa campaign completed, Major General Geiger's Third Amphibious Corps Marines stood by awaiting further orders. That is, all but the Marine artillery battalions. After the first week of the Okinawa campaign the Third Phibs Corps' Long Toms and 105 millimeter guns were attached to Army units and began blasting Jap positions on southern Okinawa.

On the narrow isthmus of southern Okinawa a few miles north of Naha, the capital city of the island, the main Jap forces elected to make their big defensive stand. They were entrenched on rugged ridges and in concrete and dirt pillboxes and caves supported by the heaviest batteries of guns and mortars encountered by our forces anywhere in the Pacific. The Army's 7th and 96th Divisions First contacted the Jap defenses in this sector April 7.

Directly ahead of the advancing 96th Division lay Kakasu ridge, a sheer bluff extending from almost the western edge of the island to well past the middle. The great Wall of China was 16 feet high, and an effective barrier in its day. Kakasu ridge is 300 feet high, slashed in places by gullies and flanked by other smaller ridges. Each ridge or knoll was completely encircled with caves and pillboxes, with particularly strong, well-concealed machine gun, anti-tank gun and mortar positions on reverse slopes. Ahead of 7th Division near the east coast rose a higher crest—Hill 178—not as long as Kakasu ridge, but surrounded by similar lesser ridges and knolls honeycombed with caves, old tombs and concrete and log pillboxes.

On April 8 both divisions pushed forward from 200 to 800 yards in the face of angry machine gun, mortar and artillery fire, with the Japs unleashing the heaviest barrage of artillery yet encountered in the entire Pacific war. By April 8 the two divisions had killed 573 Japs and taken only a handful of prisoners since landing on Okinawa. The Doughboys' casualties still were comparatively light-34 killed and 163 wounded in action.

On April 9 the 7th Division made slight gains, while the 96th, accompanied tanks and supported by terrific barrages of artillery, mortar and machine gun fire, assaulted up the slope of Kakasu ridge. The attack started at 6:20 a.m., against comparatively light resistance at first. But once the Doughboys reached the steep slope of Kakasu ridge the Japs unleashed an almost solid sheet of rifle, machine gun and mortar fire from the reverse slopes of flanking hills and from the top of Kakasu ridge, from which vantage point they also showered hand grenades on the Doughboys. The Japs' strategy was to let our troops advance up a slope, then open fire with guns already sighted in on it and kill as many Americans as possible.

In hand to hand combat on Kakasu ridge the Doughboys tossed and received hand grenades. While the Japs were on commanding heights and well dug in, the Doughboys had to find whatever slim shelter the steep, barren slopes would afford.

It was difficult tank terrain. The usual impression of tank warfare is to have the steel-shelled Goliaths charging in big numbers across open fields, overrunning bushes, knocking down small trees in their path and taking ditches and bumps in stride, all the time belching armor-piercing projectiles to shatter enemy pillboxes or other targets. That's essentially the way tank warfare works under favorable conditions. But on the Okinawa battleground there were no open fields to be found. Most of the terrain was too rugged for tanks to negotiate once they got off the few available roads. And the roads were heavily mined, and thoroughly covered by camouflaged anti-tank guns. The tanks had to advance slowly, with bomb disposal men going ahead to spot land mines. Then the tanks would reach a point of vantage and stop, firing into caves and pillboxes as they were spotted, but seldom being able to strike at the reverse slopes of the many interlocking ridges and knolls. And while they were in position firing, they were sitting ducks for Jap anti-tank guns and mortars, with which the Japs were very proficient.

Despite the handicaps, the tanks did an effective job on Okinawa and helped mightily in blasting Japs from hills and crags. But tank causalities were high, and the scenes of Okinawa battles now are littered with rusting, twisted carcasses of blasted and broken tanks. The tank toll was heavy on that first Kakasu ridge assault.

For six bloody hours the battle for the ridge continued, with some of our elements cut off from the rear. The soldiers killed scores of Japs, but even more appeared to replace the fallen Nips. Their bodies soon were stacked up like cordwood, but the slope of Kakasu ridge also was littered with our wounded.

Under smoke screen and heavy protective fire, the doughboys evacuated some of their wounded into a gully protected from rifle and machine gun fire. But no sooner were they in the gully than the Japs started arching mortar shells in their midst. Casualties mounted rapidly, and some of the once-wounded were hit again. Finally at 3:30 p.m., with their ammunition virtually all gone, the troops withdrew from Kakasu ridge.

That night more than 1500 rounds of mortar and artillery fire fell in the 7th Division's sector, and the 96th was hit almost as hard. With some elements assaulting Tombstone Ridge, from which the Japs were sending withering flanking fire, the 96th moved forward again the next day and captured the western nose of Kakasu ridge.

A week later the 96th still was clinging to the forward slope of Kakasu ridge in positions which had changed hands several times. The Japs counter-attacked time after time, always holding the advantage of defensive positions on commanding heights overlooking our positions. The Japs also had defense in depth, raining heavy spigot mortars 13 inches in diameter and five and eight-inch artillery shells from the reverse slopes of still higher ridges extending back to Shuri castle in the center of the isthmus and three miles to the rear.

The soldiers called the Japs' 13-inch spigot mortars "Ash cans" because they looked big as a G.I. rubbish cans coming through the air, and they blasted craters as wide as 40 feet in loose dirt. On hard rock, they did even more damage because more fragments flew in all directions.

Meanwhile the 27th Army Division had moved in to drive a wedge on the west flank of the 96th and take over part of the terrific battling for Kakasu ridge. The Doughboys encountered catacombs of interconnected caves several stories high, and with numerous small firing ports. They threw smoke grenades into one entrance, only to see it pour out as many as 15 others.

On the east side of the island the 7th Division captured ground leading up to Hill 178 several times, each time being driven back by flanking fire and Jap counter attacks.

And each night the Japs made the battlefront a roaring, screaming hell with their heavy shelling. One night they fired 4500 rounds of shells into our positions. For the first time in the Pacific campaign the Japs used batteries of guns, instead of single guns.

Small bands of Japs, loaded with hand grenades and satchel demolition charges, attempted to infiltrate the lines every night to blow up tanks and other heavy equipment, or to slice the throats of weary Doughboys sleeping in their fox holes. There were a few, small bonsai charges.

Meanwhile numerous ships lying off shore stepped up the tempo of their incessant shelling, raining projectile after projectile into the rear slopes of Kakasu ridge and Hill 178. Army and Marine artillery joined in the pre-attack bombardment, and Marine and Navy pilots from carriers, and Marine pilots from Yontan and Kadena airfields on Okinawa, flew 648 sorties on one day, dropping 300 tons of bombs. It was by far the heaviest bombing and shelling preparation for any attack in the Pacific war.

The big assault started April 19, with the 7th Division, paced by flamethrower tanks, again moving forward but being stopped short of Hill 178. In the center of the line the 96th Division finally cracked the defenses and stormed to the top of Kakasu ridge on a broad front, after heavy exchanges of rifle, machine gun and mortar fire, and a terrific hand grenade pitching dual. Opposition again was light at first, but terrifically heavy after the troops reached points where they came under the Japs' fierce flanking fire.

On the west flank the 27th Division drove southward along the shore, capturing Machinato village and reaching the edge of Machinato airfield. Other elements of the 27th gained the top of a rugged escarpment and by-passed Kakasu town on the west, but failed in an effort to by-pass that strong point on the east and encircle it. On the five-mile front across the island the advances ranged from 500 to 1500 yards in the all-out offensive by three divisions.

Following up on its gains of the previous day, the 7th Division captured the crest of Hill 178 on April 20, but lost it again. In one cave pillbox the 7th killed 36 gunners in one position. But each time the persistent Japs brought up another replacement from the tunnels and caverns below and continued their stream of fire into our ranks. It wasn't until April 24 that the 7th finally captured and held Hill 178.

Meanwhile the 27th had been driven back from its portion of Kakasu ridge, and the 96th was battling for life to hold its position atop Kakasu ridge in the middle of the island. On April 24, the 7th finally entrenched itself firmly on Hill 178 overlooking the east coast highway and Yonabaru airfield, and the 27th Division retook and held all of its section of Kakasu ridge.

For 17 days the battle had raged along the Japs' natural man-made barrier, and the average gain for the three divisions for that entire period was about a mile. During that time they killed more than 14,000 Japs, while their own losses were 1132 killed, 317 missing and 5966 wounded in action, plus 3075 non-battle casualties—a total of 10,490.

During the next few days all elements advanced slowly against bitter resistance, and on April 28 and 29 the 27th Division captured another big prize, the Machinate airfield.

On April 30 the Marines were called in to help on the bloody campaign for Okinawa. The First Marine Division began replacing the 96th Division, while the 27th Division was replaced by 77th Division which had captured Le Shima, killing 2,062 Japs between the landing date of April 16 and the time the island was secured on April 21.

Le Shima is a small island lying off the point of Motobu peninsula, and containing Jap air bases from which hundreds of our fighter planes were to begin flying in a few weeks.

The 27th Division was sent to the northern portion of Okinawa for patrol and mop-up duty against scattered remnants of Jap soldiers who were organizing guerilla bands of soldiers and natives to ambush vehicles and make surprise raids on small outposts.

The 96th Division was withdrawn to an area behind the lines for rest and for replacements to decimated ranks. Casualties in many of its companies ranged from 30 to 50 percent.

On April 30 I talked with one of the 96th Division officers and asked how the Okinawa campaign compared with Leyte in the Philippine Islands, where the 96th Division distinguished itself in its first campaign. He replied:

"Leyte was a picnic."

As the battle-weary doughboys came off the front lines of Kakasu ridge, tragedy was on their stubbled faces, drawn cheeks, dragging feet and staring eyes. It's a sight you'll never forget, once you see it. One

soldier bespoke the thoughts of many when he said to Private First Class Gil Feinstein, a combat correspondent from Los Angeles, Calif:
"Thank God, we're still alive."

Chapter 11

Eagles and Vultures

As our enormous invasion fleet lay off the western shores of Okinawa on L-Day pouring troops and supplies ashore, weird, fantastic ceremonies were in progress in Japan.

Japanese aviators of the new Kamikaze corps of suicide pilots were wined, dined and festooned in the gay but grim orgies fraught with Oriental fatalism and fanaticism...funeral feasts and services for the living who were about to die. Music of joyous life and violent death mingled in the flower-strewn Nipponese banquet halls.

Now out to their waiting planes, which were loaded with bombs and TNT, strode the doomed pilots of Japan's "Special Attack Air Corps"... strange sky battalion of a once-insolent but now losing, frenzied nation, whose inferiority complex and cheap appraisal of human life, resulted in the most drastic battle strategies ever employed. Some of the Nip airmen still clung to the flowers which had been showered upon them. A few even wore black robes. But most of the "divine wind" attackers dressed no differently then other Jap pilots.

Then into the sky reared this flock of hateful, emotionally wrought vultures to hurtle themselves and their planes in body-crashing attacks against our ships.

The setting sun flamed the western horizon with a vivid, burnt orange glow, followed by purple twilight and ashen gray. Then a big, round moon swung picturesquely like an oriental lantern over the haze-shrouded China sea. Clang..clang..clang.. sounded the general quarters alarm on the USS Allendale, warning us of approaching bogies.

Suddenly our ship's guns barked angrily, joining in tremendous barrage of anti-aircraft fire which rose from our mighty fleet. The sky was a latticework of red hot tracers. The Kamikaze boys were arriving.

Now one was diving at a nearby ship. Tracers found their mark. The Jap suicide plane exploded. Like a flaming chariot of death...like a fast-burning comet...it arched across the sky and plummeted to a sizzling death in the black waters, missing its intended target. The pilot was intent on death and destruction. He achieved no destruction...only death...with the aid of perhaps the largest curtain of anti-aircraft fire ever to lighten the Pacific skies.

A wild, exultant cheer arose from the ship's crew, and my voice joined it. Because I was an acting Marine press photographer, I was permitted to remain topside with my camera and watch this unforgettable start of the most bitter air sea battle the world ever had seen.

In 11 separate waves the suicide planes winged in from bases in southern Japan—only two or three hours away by plane. Night fighters from aircraft carriers intercepted some. Others got through. Crack gunners of our fleet knocked eight of the planes down as they made their death dives. Time after time the sky was nearly crimson with tracers.

Early in the evening the Allendale began circling and making runs away from the island. Other elements of our fleet were with us, circling and running through a night made dark by heavy smoke screen where all of us were laying. There were tight turns...sudden stops...much sounding of fog horns and whistles...a number of near collisions.

Shortly after midnight death struck close to our ship. A dark, batlike object reared out of the night in a suicidal dive at our convoy. So suddenly did it appear that not a shot was fired. With terrific impact a Sonia bomber crashed into the USS Achernar, a freighter transport only 200 yards behind our ship. Down through Higgins boats swinging in their davits crashed the place, bursting into flames on the deck. A 500-pound bomb it carried crashed through the ship's side and exploded in the mess hall, where ship's crew members were sleeping.

The Achernar was loaded with supplies and carrying members of the Marine Nighthawks Night fighter Squadron, VMF (N)-543. Quickly Marine pilots and officers of the squadron manned fire extinguishers and hoses and battled the roaring blaze. After the fire was quenched, five dead and 80 wounded were counted in the mangled mass of humanity. Three more died later. Most of the troops were in forward holds, and all but four of the Marines were unharmed. While the ship was afire they stood by to abandon ship if necessary. But quick action by the fire fighters saved the ship.

The Achernar put in at Kerama Retto the next day for repairs, and for the burial of the dead.

With many of the crew members missing, the Marines aboard turned seamen, manning anti-aircraft guns, swabbing decks and even stringing new rigging on damaged cranes. The marine squadron's medical officer, Lieutenant Commander Richard E. Kelley of Houston

Tex., was in surgery constantly for eight hours and performed approximately 30 operations the night of the attack.

The next day our carrier fighter and bomber planes lashed back at the Japs in the air and on their airfields on islands north of Okinawa, shooting down 45 Jap planes before they could reach our fleet units. Still more kamikaze pilots came. That night seven groups approached within an hour—some penetrating our outer defense of night fighters and hurtling themselves at our fleet. Eleven were shot down in flames. Several others missed their intended targets and crashed into the China sea. Day and night the attacks continued. A few of the planes found their mark at times and caused casualties and damage. Some light warships were sunk, and larger ones damaged. But the Japs paid a tremendous price, and sank no large ships.

Restlessly we awaited our turn to unload men and supplies on Okinawa. It took many days to pour all the men and material of our convoy onto the beaches. We began unloading on L-plus three-day, and it was a happy bunch of Marines who contemplated getting their feet on shore again. I had to remain aboard ship several more days with a work detail to unload our supplies. Technical Sergeants Shamrock Coyne and Pancho Carver went ashore in the same landing boat, and near the beach transferred to an amphibious tractor. No longer was the China sea calm. A strong breeze whipped up angry whitecaps, and large swells hit landing boats broadside as they headed shoreward.

As the amtrack reached shallow water, the driver shifted from propeller power to land power. The broad tractor tracks dug in and moved the huge, steel shell up a coral reef. Then a big swell hit it broadside and nearly tipped it over.

"It was a helpless feeling," Carver told me later. "We were packed so tightly we couldn't move. I thought sure we would turn over and I just sat there crossing myself."

On its fourth attempt at the coral reef the amtrack tipped dangerously again, but got across and proceeded up the beach without further trouble. Even the effervescent Shamrock was quiet, but all laughed once they reached the beach. The shore party worked day and night handling supplies which we sent ashore, while others went inland a couple of miles to set up our new camp area and quartermaster dump near one of the airfields.

By mid-afternoon that day the sea grew so rough that we had to discontinue unloading of supplies. The surf was so churlish that our landing boats could not approach the Allendale and be taken back on board, for fear of disaster. Our sailors had been working around the clock, but kept plodding on mechanically.

On the morning of April 5, Seaman First Class Paul E. Mestayer of Loreauville, La., who had been working every day and was out every night on a smoke-making boat since L-Day, collapsed from exposure and exhaustion and was brought aboard on a stretcher. Several others had like experiences later, and had to go to the ship's hospital for rest. One sailor was so busy and had so few hours of sleep that he didn't take off his clothes for a week.

The Japs, who had made no appreciable dent with their suicide plane attacks, redoubled their efforts on April 6 and 7 in hopes of breaking up and scattering our convoy, and then following up with a task force strike led by the 45,000-ton battleship, Yamato.

We had three general quarters alarms in one hour aboard the Allendale, and I began to feel like a high school track man, running full speed from unloading hatches where I was toiling to get a point of vantage for taking pictures in case some of the attackers came close. At 5:15 a.m., on April 6 our ship's guns broke into a roar. A Jap suicide bomber, a Val, had made a strafing run across the narrow island of Okinawa at low altitude, and now was coming right at us in a long 20 degree glide. Seemingly thousands of guns from nearby ships fired at the approaching vulture. There was the flash of a direct hit. A wheel fell off. But the plane didn't flame. On it came. I wondered; will it hit us? How does the pilot feel? I snapped a picture, then prepared to take another.

The plane, which had been diving straight at our ship, veered slightly to the left upon being hit, and went just off our fan-tail. Our guns were barking incessantly, and now the Allendale's five-inch cannon roared, probably scoring a direct hit. Scores of small tracers also were finding their mark. Now the Jap plane was heading directly toward an LST. Suddenly it went out of control, did a wingover to the left and plunged head-first into the sea, missing the LST by only a few yards, and coming close to a nearby hospital ship, painted white. There was a great roar of triumph from men aboard every ship in the area.

Now we saw other single-engine and some twin-engine Jap planes attacking other ships and being shot down.

At about the same time Bill Carver, Tech Sergeant Don Houseman and others of our shore party were on a pontoon pier, unloading supplies from landing crafts. A Jap Zero, carrying a bomb, swooped low over the beach and made a strafing run at the pontoon. Carver and Houseman saw a pattern of bullets coming straight at them. They took refuge at first behind a generator, then turned and fled toward the gaping mouth of an LST moored at the pier. Both were knocked down after only a few steps.

Carver was wounded and calling for help. Houseman dragged him back to the generator and removed his shoe; then discovered that he also was bleeding. First Lieutenant John J. Logan, a tall, husky ex G-man and attorney from San Angelo, Texas, picked Carver up in his arms and carried him aboard the LST. I was still on the Allendale when Carver and Houseman were brought aboard for hospitalization. An operation was necessary to remove a big chunk of flak which lodged against the bone in Bill Carver's foot. He also had some flak in his other leg. Houseman had flak removed from his right arm and one piece from his right instep, while other pieces of flak were deeply imbedded and still remain in his instep and in his right thigh, near the groin. They were the first battle casualties from Marine Aircraft Group Forty-Three, Second Marine Aircraft Wing.

"Somehow, someway, I want to kill just one of those Jap bastards," Bill told me.

The same plane which strafed the pontoon continued in a circle over the water where Dick Koch-Church was going ashore in a landing boat with a load of our sea bags.

"Tracers from hundreds of anti-aircraft guns were following the plane, and it was coming right toward us," said Dick. "A 20 millimeter shell hit the boat. I manned a caliber .30 machine gun and fired at the plane. But I don't know if I hit it or not. I never have been so scared in my life. The plane was hit, but made a suicide dive on an LST. The LST caught afire, but didn't sink."

A few minutes earlier the plane which narrowly missed the LST near the Allendale, crossed directly above the small landing boat, and Dick and the crew crouched low as ack-ack bullets rained nearby.

After this flurry of excitement we saw other single and twin-engine Jap planes making suicide runs and crashing into the water—some in flames. It was happy hunting for the fleet.

"This is just like a fox hunt," said Sergeant Frank Treuting, one of the many Marines who volunteered to pass ammunition to the ship's guns.

I saw nine of the Kamikaze planes go down, and the score for the day in our area was 53 kills and more then 50 suicide planes were shot down the next day as the Japs continued their attacks.

We unloaded supplies feverishly as we heard the Jap Task force definitely was headed our way. All day, all night and the next morning we worked and sweated in the stuffy holds, then swarmed down the landing nets and started ashore at 7:30 a.m., on April 8. But we cruised and drifted off shore until mid-afternoon before our turn came to land. Meanwhile, we heard good news about the Jap task force.

Lieutenant Richard L. Simms of Atlanta, Ga., and Lieutenant James R. Young of Central City, Ky., sighted the task force on April 7 when they flew their twin-engine navy patrol bombers close to the Jap homeland. They radioed the position of the battleship Yamato, two cruisers and eight destroyers. Soon the sky was full of planes from Vice Admiral Marc A. Mitscher's fast carrier task forces.

Hellcat fighter-bombers screeched down in near-vertical dives to drop bombs, launch rockets and strafe the ships. Big Grumman Avenger torpedo bombers dropped bombs or sent their torpedoes into the side of Japan's biggest battleship.

The Yamato made frenzied turns. Her guns—from small machine guns to 16-inch cannon—blasted away incessantly at the attackers. Still they came. Eight aerial torpedoes and eight 1000-pound armor-piercing bombs, as well as some 500-pounders, crashed through her thick hide and heavy decks. In a roaring explosion she went down, and with her the two cruisers and three destroyers. The other destroyers were badly damaged and left smoking or flaming.

Of her once-haughty navy, Japan now had left only five battleships, all slower than the Yamato, probably six carriers and as many cruisers and about 20 destroyers.

Right on schedule the Jap airmen renewed their attacks on our shipping the following day, and Admiral Nimits announced that "the attacking enemy aircraft pressed their attacks with desperation and succeeded in sinking three of our destroyers and smaller craft."

But in two days the Japs lost 361 planes—245 shot down by our carrier pilots. The others were shot out of Okinawa skies by ships' gunners.

Into this bitter death struggle of the skies Marine Corsair pilots were catapulted on April 7. The first kill for the flying Leathernecks came even before their wheels touched Yontan and Kadena airfields on Okinawa.

No sooner was Marine Captain Ralph G. McCormick of Detroit, Mich., catapulted from an aircraft carrier in his gull-winged Corsair than he saw a twin-engine Jap bomber approaching. Quickly Captain McCormick, a veteran pilot with one Zero to his credit from the Guadalcanal campaign, gained altitude. The bomber was racing full speed at the aircraft carrier. Seconds counted. Captain McCormick bore down swiftly on the enemy plane from above and the rear. His six machine guns broke into a roar. Hot tracers and armor-piercing bullets ripped into the bomber's fuselage and flamed the left engine.

The crippled bomber, only 50 feet above the water, began losing altitude, but continued its swift suicide run on the carrier. Now it was only a few hundred yards away. Another Corsair piloted by First Lieutenant Joseph Doherty made a diving pass. His aim also was true. The bomber's right engine burst into flames. The attacking plane crashed head first into the water and exploded...only 100 feet from the carrier.

That was the Japs' introduction to the Hells Belles Marine Fighter Squadron, VMF-311. With the skies now clear of bogies, the Marine pilots swung their planes shoreward and landed at Yontan airfield late that afternoon. The Hells Belles and other Second Marine Air Wing fighter squadrons which arrived at Okinawa April 7 flew combat air patrols until dark to protect our ground forces and shipping from Jap planes. Every day thereafter the Corsair pilots flew combat patrols to intercept the enemy, and soon Marine night fighter pilots began patrolling the skies at night in single-seater Hellcats to shoot down the Japs' nocturnal intruders.

Three speedy Jap fighter planes identified as Oscars bore down on our shipping the following evening just before dusk. Corsairs of Fighting Wildcat Squadron, VMF-224, got on their tails and made short shrift of them. First Lieutenant A.C. Satterwhite of Crockett, Texas and Second Lieutenant R.M. Tousley of Lesuer, Minn., quickly get on the tail of the first Oscar. The Jap pilot made diving turns, climbing turns and in desperation even looped his plane. But the corsair out climbed and quickly splashed him into the sea some 10 miles northwest of Okinawa.

Now Second Lieutenant R.E. Torgeraon of Minneapolis, Minn., and James B. Bender of Denver, Pa., bore down on the second Oscar, which made a climbing turn to the left at the top speed. Rapidly they out climbed him and closed. Their machine guns spoke. The Oscar spun in and splashed.

It took only a few short bursts for Captain F. Hick of Milford, Del., and Second Lieutenant R.C. Bray of Fargo, N.D., to down the third Oscar.

The aggressive Leatherneck pilots on Okinawa never hesitated to trade bullets with the enemy, no matter what the odds. They battled the Kamikaze pilots as fiercely as Marine infantrymen battled the entrenched Nips on the ground.

Four pilots of the Day's Knights Fighter Squadron, VMF-312, sighted 24 of Japan's best planes—20 Zero fighters and four Jill torpedo bombers—approaching Okinawa on April 12. The Jills have a top speed of approximately 320 miles an hour, and the Zeros 360 miles an hour.

Outnumbered six to one, the Corsair pilots unhesitatingly tackled the formidable formation. Smart fighter tactics would dictate that our pilots fly in team sections of two, with one pilot attacking and the other flying wing to give him protection and watch for enemy planes which might get on their tail. But here was a large enemy flight ready to close its attack on our ships and airfields. The Leathernecks threw caution to the wind and hurled themselves individually at the enemy in order to shoot down more planes faster.

Diving out of the sun, they hit the surprised Japs hard on the initial assault, breaking up their formations. Captain D.H. Johnson of Neoshc, Mo., and Second Lieutenant John C. Webb of Bethel, Kas., each made kills from the rear. Their hot tracers whizzing past the other planes warned the Jap pilots of an attack.

Quickly two Nip airmen turned and made head-on attacks at Second Lieutenant R. Revnes of Beverly Hills, Calif., and First Lieutenant J.E. Holden of Mt. Vernon, N.Y. They answered the challenge, hurtling their rugged plane headlong at the oncoming targets. Now their six caliber .50 machine guns burst into roars. The Zeros flamed and went down with the Marine pilots pulling up and crossing over them just in time to avoid mid-air collisions. The first four Jap planes hit the water in rapid succession.

Then followed a mad scramble of dog fights. The Corsairs out climbed the Zeros, out sped them and outmaneuvered them, the latter mostly because of superior airmanship. The Jap pilots, turned, banked and dived, but ever the Corsairs closed on them.

Captain Johnson scored three kills, smoked another for a probable and damaged a fifth Zeke. Lieutenant Revnes destroyed two and damaged a third, all with head-on attacks which he pressed to the last instant before pulling up. Two more planes were destroyed and one damaged by Lieutenant Webb. And Lieutenant Holden destroyed one, scored a probable and damaged another.

Only after running out of ammunition did the Corsair pilots break off their attack and return to their base on Okinawa. By this time the enemy planes were in full retreat toward Japan. Fourteen of their 24 aircraft had been hit—eight destroyed, two probably destroyed and four damaged. Not a bullet struck the four Corsairs.

That same day Second Lieutenant H. H. Kyle of Sweetwater, Texas, also of the Day's Knights Squadron, shot down a big Betty bomber which was bombing and strafing a destroyer. And three more Zeros, a Tony fighter and a Betty bomber were downed by pilots of the Death Rattlers Squadron, VMF, 323.

First Lieutenant A.P. Wells, a pilot from Garden City, N.Y., who later became one of the many Okinawa Marine aces, opened the day's scoring before sunrise. Kadena airfield was undergoing a bombing and strafing attack, and a Tony fighter dropped a 250-pound bomb on the edge of the runway as Lieutenant Wells was taking off. The Corsair pilot banked westward and pursued the speedy Tony, which by then was a mile away at 1500 feet elevation. Under full throttle the Corsair closed rapidly, and Lieutenant Wells opened fire at 200 feet. The surprised Tony pilot made a steep diving turn to the left, but the Corsair matched his maneuver and sprayed the fleeing plane incessantly with six streams of caliber .50 machine gun bullets. The Tony flamed and crashed into the sea.

Another Zero went down before the guns of Second Lieutenant J.W. Ruhsam, also of the Death Rattlers Squadron. It was the first of seven kills in the Okinawa campaign for Lieutenant Ruhsam, a short, dark-haired and sparkling eyed youth of 22 from Albert Lea, Minn. Second Lieutenant W. W. Bestwick of Missoula, Mont. scored a Zero kill, and so did Captain Joe McPhail of Grand Saline, Texas, also of the Death Rattlers.

Three more pilots of the same squadron ganged up on a Betty bomber and sent it spinning into the water with both engines flaming. It exploded when it struck. They were First Lieutenants Charles S. Spangler of Philadelphia, Pa., D. L. Davis of Hollister, Calif., and Second Lieutenant D. F. Durnford of Columbus, Ohio. The latter downed six more Jap planes during his Okinawa combat tour.

Now the score stood: Marine pilots, 17 kills; Jap pilots 0.

But the Japs continued their attacks, unabated.

The small handful of Corsair fighter squadrons not only handled air defense for Okinawa and the fleet surrounding its shores, but on Friday, April 13, flew their first fighter-bomber strike missions in support of ground troops battling the Japs only a few miles south of the airfields.

Loaded with two 500-pound bombs and eight rockets each, 36 Corsairs pummeled more than a dozen Jap gun positions, mostly in caves. Several direct hits were scored by the aggressive leatherneck pilots who defied enemy anti-aircraft fire and dived down and down in their speedy flying arsenals, pulling out of their bombing, rocketing and strafing attacks at only 500 feet above the ground. None of the marine planes were hit—this time.

Thereafter they flew strike missions almost every day, their total sorties running into the thousands during the campaign. Later their fighter-bomber strikes were extended to surrounding Jap-held islands, and then against the Jap homeland itself on June 18. Dive Bombing is much less spectacular than shooting enemy aircraft from the skies, but it proved much the rougher assignment in the Okinawa campaign on strikes against many enemy positions which were heavily protected by anti-aircraft guns.

Commanding General of the Tactical Air Force, consisting of Marine fighter and bomber squadrons, and later of Army Air Forces squadrons, was keen-minded Major General Francis P. Mulcahy, the commanding general of the Second Marine Air Wing. A veteran of the Guadalcanal and Solomon Islands air battles, General Mulcahy was flying aircraft long before most of his youthful "hot pilots" were born. In World War I he was a marine bomber pilot. With all of his Irish tenacity he directed the fast-moving air battle of Okinawa, seldom taking time out to sleep.

By day he would pop up anyplace, anytime in his jeep, which he usually drove himself, checking on the most minute details of the operations and setting a terrific pace for his staff officers and the entire Second Marine Air Wing. At night three radio sets blared constantly in his tent, bringing him minute by minute news of approaching bogies; conversations between pilots and aviation ground officers, and pass by pass reports of dog fights. At any hour of the day or night he would demand and get special reports of every combat action, missing pilots or unusual incidents. His stamina was a marvel to all, and his aerial show moved at feverish pace.

Chief of staff of the Tactical Air Forces was Colonel Bernard A. Bridget, sage Army Air Corps pilot from Chandler, Ariz., who was a private in the Army during World War I, and who returned to the services in 1924 as a pilot.

Colonel Bridget's good humor, friendly personality and excellent judgment made him particularly well suited for the liaison duties he performed between the various branches of service and various commands of the large Okinawa operation. He had been in the thick of aerial warfare in the Pacific ever since the start of the war, serving successively at Pearl Harbor, Santos, Guadalcanal, Peleliu and then Okinawa. He was popular with officers and enlisted men alike.

A veteran of more than a quarter of a century of flying was Colonel Hayne D. Boyden, General Mulcahy's chief of staff for the Second Marines Air Wing. Serving outside the United States for 13 of his 26 years in the Marine Corps, Colonel Boyden made aerial maps in Santo Domingo, Panama and Cuba; flew in the first land plane flight to Fort Au Prince, Haiti, in a Flying Jenny on May 21, 1920; flew mail and strafed bandits in Nicaragua, and led an evacuation flight from Nicaragua to Washington, D.C., via Mexico on January 1, 1933. His pre-war foreign duty also included a whirl in the Virgin Islands and an assignment as naval attaché for air to Cuba from April 1940 until September, 1943. During that period he also served at Fort Au Prince as naval attaché to the American Legation, which later became the American Embassy.

Arriving in the Pacific theater of operations in July, 1944, he helped plan part of the aerial operations for Pelelieu, then turned his attention to assembling and organizing marine personnel for the Okinawa campaign. Sprightly, fast-talking Colonel Boyden, 48, of Statesville, N.C., still flies every time he has opportunity to tear himself from administrative duties.

For commanding general of the Fighter Command, Major General Mulcahy chose efficient, affable and tireless Brigadier General William J. Wallace, whose Marine Corps service also dated back to World War I. As a youth of 17 he enlisted in 1917 as a Leatherneck infantryman. Serving with the 10th Regiment, he rose to the rank of first lieutenant.

He didn't get a crack at Foreign Service in the First World War, but he has seen action aplenty in World War II. In the interim he flew in Santo Domingo, China and the Philippines after winning his wings at Pensacola, Fla., in December 1921.

General Wallace was eating breakfast the morning of December 7, 1941 when Jap planes bombed the strafed Pearl Harbor and the Marine Corps Air Station at Ewa, Oahu, T.H. As he raced to the Ewa field in his own car, Jap planes were strafing vehicles on the roads. The field was under heavy attack when he arrived.

On January 6, 1942, he arrived at Midway and organized Marine Air Group 22 consisting of two fighter and two dive-bomber squadrons which played a mighty part in turning back Japan's determined assault in the battle of Midway. Meanwhile General Wallace had returned to Ewa to organize Marine Aircraft Group 23 which was the first air group to operate at Guadalcanal.

The first squadrons landed at Henderson Field on August 20, 1942 and courageously battled the Japs whose planes outnumbered ours 10 to one. While Marine dive-bombers pounded Jap warships, troop transports and freighters furiously, other flying Leathernecks in Wildcat fighters whittled away intrepidly at Jap zeros which were superior in speed, climbing ability and maneuverability—superior in every way except for their ability to take punishment.

General Wallace gives major credit for development of our superior fighter tactics to five marine pilots whose bag of enemy shoot downs totaled 74½. The Pilots, and their scores by the end of their Guadalcanal combat tours, were; Lieutenant Colonel John Smith, 19; Major Marion Carl, 16½; Major Joe Foss, 15 (he later ran his score to 26); Lieutenant Colonel Bob Galer, 13, and Lieutenant Colonel Joe Bower, 11.

In Guadalcanal's cauldron of roaring dog fights the Marine Corps, which originated and pioneered dive bombing years ago in Latin America, made a major contribution toward developing our present fighter tactics employing the four-plane division which comprised two double-plane sections operation near each other. These tactics have been largely adopted by the Army and Navy and by most of our allies as well.

General Wallace's pilot ranks were so decimated that his group had to be replaced. In November, 1942 he became chief of staff for Marine Fleet Air West Coast on North Island, San Diego, and soon became its commanding general. He conducted a vast program of organizing new squadrons and air groups, and training them at the Marine Corps air stations along the Pacific coast. During this period Marine Aviation underwent phenomenal growth and development.

In June 1944 General Wallace returned to Ewa, Oahu as Chief of staff for General Mulcahy, and helped plan the Marine Corps' biggest aerial operation to date—the Okinawa campaign.

Responsibility for assigning fighter planes to combat missions, supervising maintenance and guiding and directing fighter tactics at Okinawa rested on the broad shoulders of Colonel Boeker C. Batterton, 41, operations officer for the Fighter Command. In that capacity, and previously as operations officer of Air, Fleet Marine Force, Pacific, at Oahu, Colonel Batterton did much of the planning staff organization work for the Okinawa aerial operation.

A Naval Academy man who was graduated from Annapolis in 1928, he served six years as a Marine line (infantry) officer. Three of those years were in Haiti, where his regiment quelled an uprising.

Soloing in 1933 he became a marine fighter pilot, and during a year and a half of his air career called the aircraft carrier Saratoga his

Home. From March, 1941 until November, 1943 he flew in Peru with the Naval Aviation Mission which assisted the Peruvian government in training pilots. Later he flew offshore patrol and search missions for any Jap submarine or surface craft which might attempt to establish a toehold in South America.

Then, as a full colonel, he became commanding officer of an air group at El Toro, Marine Corps Air Station at Santa Anna, Calif., where he supervised the training of more Leatherneck pilots than any other officer in the Marine Corps. His group had more planes, officers and pilots than a wing. And scores of the pilots he trained saw their first combat action in the Okinawa campaign. He trained fighter pilots, dive-bomber pilots and torpedo bomber pilots, all of whom learned to operate both from land or from aircraft carriers, fly by day or by night, fly on instruments, and bomb, rocket and strafe targets to perfection. If they couldn't keep up with the face pace, they were weeded out. On his staff were ace pilots who had come out on top in aerial combat with Jap pilots in the South Pacific.

The Corsair pilots who fought in the Okinawa campaign averaged more than 1000 hours of training. They were superior pilots, both individually and in team tactics. Savagely they hurtled their fast, rugged Corsairs at the fanatical Jap, and with perhaps unprecedented skill, courage, determination and daring.

Their box score was nothing short of phenomenal.

Chapter 12

Purple Hearts and White Crosses

Bombing attacks against our shipping and airfields were almost daily and nightly occurrences. Frequently there were many attacks in one day. During the first 40 days of the campaign we had more than 100 red alerts.

Between Yontan and Kadena airfields, which were some two miles apart, lay our camp area. So we usually caught part of the bombing and strafing hell hurled at each field. One night we counted 70 nearly bomb hits, but none did any damage on that occasion. Sometimes we weren't so fortunate. A few of our planes were destroyed and a number damaged by bombing and shelling, the latter from the nearby front lines.

We dug in for dear life from the moment we came ashore. Wearing leggings and carrying rifles and packs, we looked and lived like infantrymen. The first few nights we bivouacked in fox holes covered with our camouflaged, water-repellent shelter halves. But that didn't keep water from seeping or streaming into our fox holes. On Okinawa it often rains from four inches to as much as sixteen inches in a day. Tropical heat and dust storms came later.

Those were busy days. Tents for living quarters and offices popped up like mushrooms after a rain. Everyone worked. We toiled like stevedores; built cabinets and shelves in office tents for maps and supplies, typed reports, unpacked boxes, and foraged for lumber in the ruins of nearby villages and captured barracks. Shamrock Coyne and others of our large communications section strung mile after mile of telephone and teletype wires through sniper-infested territory and erected and manned telephone switchboards.

Officers as well as enlisted men dug fox holes, prepared their own meals from canned rations and sprouted beards on their faces. Most of us were much too busy to shave the first week. After working 14 to 18 hours, we would hit the sack for a few hours of sleep which invariable was interrupted by air raids. Most of us slept with our clothes on. Joe Vance and I lived for a few days in a deserted Jap cave. One cold, rainy night I slept on a wet floor, wearing a raincoat, rubber boots and my helmet, the latter in lieu of a pillow.

"That isn't a lovely way to spend an evening," Dick Koch-Church consoled me.

Few had time to take baths during those first days of mud, sweat and no beers. Our baths were sponge baths, with our steel helmets serving as basins. That system seemed unsatisfactory to Private First Class John Woods of Whitesbore, Tex., so he took a bar of soap, hiked across country and found a clear stream. After enjoying a 20-minute bath and washing his hair, he dried, dressed, and then, feeling like a new man, looked around. Not 20 yards upstream he saw the ripe cadaver of a Jap soldier. Woods hastened back to camp... for a sponge bath in the helmet.

Hot coffee, baths, and clean clothes were the most coveted items. Many had lost their sea bags when a landing boat capsized. Warrant Officer Harris, our mess officer, had hot coffee for us every meal to wash down our packaged rations. Staff Sergeant Cole made us the envy of everyone on the island when he came ashore the first day and brought steaks for all from the Allendale.

There were no snakes, but the place was infested with fleas and mosquitoes. And such mosquitoes! I've seen bigger ones many places, but never such fast ones. Just try to slap one. They were elusive as a P-38, and they packed a wicked stinger. Lieutenant Commander T.T. Flaherty of Long Beach, Calif., medical officers of the Second Marine Air Wing, soon had a big twin-engine Douglas transport plane spraying DDT insecticide over our area. We saw the big plane winging overhead, skimming tree tops, to do an effective job. Then we heard a crash. Dr. Flaherty and seven of the eight occupants of the plane were killed or fatally injured. It was an army plane, and the only other passenger from Tactical Air Force was Captain Geoffry Willoughby of Minneapolis, our competent and well-liked public relations officer. He too was killed. It was one of the many tragic by-products of war.

Snipers were killed occasionally in our immediate area, but there were so few that we never thought of them... except at night. One night there was a report of a Jap infiltration movement. Quickly sentries were posted. It proved to be a false alarm, but one sentry heard a noise and began firing—probably at a native pig or goat. Soon tracers were flying everywhere, and we hugged our fox holes.

Vance, one of the sentries, saw a light flare in a pup tent. He opened fire. One of our Negro mess men had crawled into the tent to light a cigarette. He left in a hurry, and was not to be found until the next morning. It was a sheepish bunch of "trigger happy" sentries the next day, and they got a big horse laugh from the others who held their fire. Fortunately—yes, miraculously—none were hit.

About a month later another trigger happy orgy occurred the first night after the second echelon arrived to supplement the invasion crew of Squadron Two, which was headquarters squadron of the Second Marine Air Wing. Apparently some of the newcomers believed all the snow jobs that the salty old timers dished out about Jap night attacks. During the night scores of volleys were fired, and in the morning the rifleman had something to show for it—two dead goats. I couldn't refrain from typing and posting the following notice:

DAILY BLEAT
OKINAWA-USA

FLASH!   FLASH!
MARINE   MARKSMAN
MASSACRE MEDLERS

Intrepid, fearless, unyielding Leathernecks of the Second Marine Air Wing, posted as sentries to safeguard lives and material of their camp area, unleashed a lethal barrage of rifle and machine gun fire last night to halt infiltration of menacing, nocturnal intruders who took advantage of darkness to move stealthily forward.

Yes, those Marines were not "kidding." They killed two innocent, fleecy, white kids, who attacked, bleating: "Baa, Baa, Baansai!"

Now doesn't that get your goat?

It never happened again.

Curiosity kept some of us out of our fox holes to watch ack ack and searchlights duel with enemy bombers during alerts. So intense was the anti-aircraft fire that falling flak frequently was a greater menace to exposed individuals than bombing or strafing. But after our camp area was strafed a few times we had nothing but fox hole scrambles during alerts.

One of the sure winners in fox hole races was Mess Steward Perfect S. Allen, a tall, amiable Negro from Washington, D.C., whom Shamrock nicknamed "Senator." Senator Allen had a cigar in his mouth constantly, but merely to chew. Cigars were almost as scarce as blondes on Okinawa.

" 'Cept when Ah see where mah supply is coming from, Ah never smokes a cigar," said Allen. "Ah has to make a cigar last a week."

Only when eating would he take the cigar from his mouth. Then he would put it tenderly in his pocket, and again be chewing it when the meal was finished.

Cigar-smoking Major Alfred N. Bisgard, former state patrolman from El Centro, Calif. handed Senator Allen a cigar one day.

"Here, throw that old one away," said the officer.

"Thank yo, suh! Thank yo ever so much! Ah certainly 'preciate that," said Allen, his rows of even white teeth flashing like ivory piano keys.

Then he put the new cigar in his pocket and the soggy inch and a half butt back in his mouth.

"How come you didn't throw the old one away?" demanded Major Bisgard.

"The new one lasts longer the mo I keeps usin' dis one," explained Allen seriously.

Major Bisgard walked away, shaking his head.

"Senator, do you have a rabbit's foot?" Coyne asked.

"No," replied the witty Allen, "else Ah wouldn't be heah."

Allen and his dusky companion mess stewards put on some of the best fox hole races of the invasion. Awakened at night, they would streak down a hill toward their fox hole and frequently trip over Coyne's tent ropes and stakes.

"Take it easy during those air raids," admonished Shamrock. "You'll get yourself all fouled up."

Replied the Senator: "Man, when Ah starts for mah fox hole, Ah's got mah movin' shoes on! Dat's de only way to get back to de States."

"You mean when you hear that air raid siren you're gone?" asked Coyne

"Dat's me!"

One Lieutenant Colonel West said to Allen:

"Where's your cigar?"

Mournfully the Senator replied: "It's done gone to pieces on me, Colonel West."

"I have one over at my office which you may have," said the colonel.

"Ah certainly 'preciate dat, suh," beamed Allen. " 'Cept when Ah has a cigar, Ah feels sick in the haid."

There were all sorts of scratches, bruises, twists and sprains in those mad fox hole scrambles. Lieutenant Colonel Eugene H. Hawkins of Montgomery, Ala., slipped while dashing for his fox hole, broke his arm and was evacuated. So was Corporal Harold W. Jackson, as assistant cook from Albuquerque, N. Mex., whose leg was broken.

First Lieutenant John A. Smith, with a slow southern drawl, but fast-moving feet, never lost a fox hole race during the campaign, but sometimes wished he had when others who arrived a bit later would jump or walk on him. And Lieutenant Smith, a slim, personable ex-G-man and attorney from Fayette, Ala., isn't exactly built for such punishment as he got when his cohort, Lieutenant Logan, clamored all over him and then sat on his chest with his massive feet in Lieutenant Smith's face. But such things are forgiven, and they're friends again.

On April 14 one of the Jap's speedy photo reconnaissance planes came in at extremely high altitude and made a diving pass over our airfields to take photos. It was clocked at more than 300 miles an hour in its diving sweep, and outran our fighters. The next afternoon we had one of our heaviest air raids.

After the sirens sounded the alert, we remained at our work in the intelligence section where Dick and I were assigned. Short stocky Captain Norman W. Noble, a newspaper reporter from Salina, Kansas, was at one typewriter, and I at another. We had our helmets on, but were remaining outside our covered fox hole until ack ack started. Suddenly Sergeant Coleman ran into our tent and shouted two dramatic words:

"STRAFING RAID!"

Dick, who has jackrabbit ears during a raid, was the first in the fox hole. He dived in head first, Captain Jere T. Tipton, our canny intelligence officer, made it next. I was third—I thought. But when only halfway in I was mashed against the side of the tiny entrance by First Lieutenant Alfred S. Forayth, a six-foot-three intelligence officer who formerly was a New York attorney. Like an all-American fullback he smacked that hole and gained the necessary five yards to make his goal. He swarmed all over the prone Koch-Church, and with a wild kick struck Captain Noble in the mouth.

Coleman, who had a running start, was only a poor fifth, followed by portly PFC Stevens and MT/Sergeant Plumb, who got in as best they could. Staff Sergeant John V. Walsh of Rye, N.Y., who had been overseas before, wouldn't risk getting injured in that mad scramble. Closest to the fox hole, he stood aside and was the last in.

The strafing was all too close for comfort. A string of bullets missed our tent by only 20 yards. PFC Mike Dolan was one who habitually lay on his sack during raids instead of diving for shelter. But he got cured, a 20 millimeter shell fell between his spread legs near the groin and buried itself in the ground. After that Dolan procured an old steel engine boiler for a fox hole, sinking it underground and calling it his "iron lung."

An estimated 20 planes bombed and strafed us during that night, and jitters flourished. The terrifying siren sounded at 3 a.m., just as we had fallen soundly asleep following the previous raid. Dick awakened with a start.

"Where am I, Jim?" he gasped.

Our folding cots were side by side, and he started to roll out over me. Quickly I slipped into my pants and shoes, which I had placed so I could find them easily, and went outside. But Dick got fouled up trying to find his clothes in the dark.

"Wait for me, Jim," he shouted.

I did, and suddenly he whizzed past me like a P-38, stumbled and fell full length. I couldn't help laughing.

We stood outside and waited for 15 uneventful minutes. Exhausted from long working hours and little sleep, we returned to our sacks before the all-clear sounded and flopped down with our clothes on. I fell asleep, but awakened when I heard a plane in a power dive.

"Jap plane," I shouted.

We really scrambled, while the Jap sent hot tracers uncomfortably close to our area. Then it was back to sleep again. But suddenly Dick ejaculated:

"Jim, there are more Jap planes."

"Relax son," I said. "Those are our night fighters."

"Take it easy," I said assuringly. "I know my planes, and I'm getting some sleep."

Soon he heard more of our night fighter Hellcats, which he had not yet learned to identify by sound. He exploded:

"Nuts, those must be Jap planes."

"No, don't you hear those wings whine?" I replied sweepingly. "Those are Hellcats."

Later there were so many whining wings overhead that Staff Sergeant Van Ochten dressed and spent the rest of the night in a fox hole.

As days passed we were acquiring more luxuries and comforts. We still carried water to our tents in flat five-gallon cans. But our construction crew (bull gang) built two-holer, three-holer and even four-holer privies. No longer did we take shovels and seek an open field for relief. And it was a great day when we moved into our new mess hall, which the industrious Seabees helped us build, and could sit down for hot meals.

Master Technical Sergeant Philip L. Ryan, of Milwaukee, Wis., our mess sergeant, did a swell job of feeding us. With his assistance he borrowed, begged and pilfered every choice morsel of food he could find. He and his cohorts became known as Ryan's Raiders. If their allowance from stockpile called for two cases of food, they usually hauled away four. And Gunner Harris, the mess officer, gathered souvenirs which he traded aboard ships for meat, butter and eggs.

Corporal Joe Gmur, thick-legged, under slung barber for us, from Monticello, Wis., erected a barber pole which he painted with the traditional red and white stripes, the first barber pole ever seen on Okinawa.

Second Marine Air Wing public information section nailed up a sign bearing native characters, but took it down when a linguist interpreted it. It read:

"Latrine."

An even greater pestilence to Second Marine Air Wing personnel at Kadena airfield than air attack was pistol Pete, a 150 millimeter (five inch) Jap cannon near Naha, some 12 miles away. Time and again the Japs would roll their long range gun out of a cave on tracks and fire a fusillade of high explosive projectiles; then roll it back to shield it from our bombing and shelling attacks.

PFC James L. McLeod of Dallas, Texas who was transferred from our group to another air group of the Second Wing at Pearl Harbor, described Pistol Pete's periodic poundings at Kadena, where Mac was stationed.

"One night Pistol Pete put about 30 shells in our bivouac area," he related. "But I was only really scared one other night. Five of us were in a dugout, with sand bags on top. Shells screeched over us, and we held our breaths each time until they landed. Several struck within 30 feet of our fox hole, knocking out a number of tents and showering our sand bags with rocks and shrapnel."

"Did you have the shakes?" I asked.

"You just ain't kidding," replied Mac. "I was shaking like a hula dancer, and so were the rest of us."

When you get the shakes during a raid, it's hard to stop, as just about everyone who has been under intense bombing or shelling attacks knows. I learned about the shakes the tragic night of April 20.

"Boy, look at that bomber's moon," commented MT/Sergeant Morris Fry that evening. "We'll hear plenty from the Japs tonight."

Condition red was at 7:22 p.m. Several of us in the camp area watched a Jap fighter strafing nearby Kadena air field. Many were in our big community shelter, but a few of us sat outside watching the show.

The Japanese fighter swung back and headed directly toward us. I dived for the small entrance to the shelter, but two others collided and jammed the opening so the rest of us couldn't get inside. We flattened ourselves to the ground.

At the last instant the Jap planes swung and made a strafing run on Yontan air field and we breathed easier. He was a plenty hot pilot, flying up valleys and keeping so low that our machine guns had difficulty following him. We saw him vividly in bright light from the half moon above. For a while longer a few of us remained outside the shelter to watch any excitement.

"Well, I guess the show is about over," said young Major Feasley, our squadron commanding officer who had been outside the shelter all the time.

"Good night, men."

Lucky for him, he departed for his tent, and so did Sergeant John H. Carter, short jovial mustachioed marine from Redding, Calif., I too shoved off; then decided to look at another fox hole nearer my tent in case I needed shelter in a hurry some time, an alternate landing field, as it were.

Tech Sergeant Joe West of Washington, D.C. and Staff Sergeant Ken Pine of San Francisco, Calif., said I could share their fox hole. I crawled into the low-roofed shelter with them. Then we stepped out.

A twin-engine plane roared loudly overhead. We heard a murderous swishing whine, like the rushing wind.

"Bomb!" shouted Joe.

I dived for the fox hole. West already was in. As I dived I saw a blinding flash 200 yards away... then another 50 paces away. Almost simultaneously I hears explosion... Ka-whoomp! Ka-whoomp! I saw more flashes. The enemy plane had missed the airfield a long ways and laid a string of five bombs through ours and two adjoining camp areas. Pine was seated at the fox hole rear entrance and concussion knocked him in. A piece of shrapnel missed him by a foot and ripped full length through a sand bag.

I darted out. Black smoke marked explosion points. Men were running. Voices called excitedly. I dashed toward the scene of action.

Cole came running down the road.

"What happened?" I asked.

"Show me to a fox hole, Jim," he said, half hysterically. "They've killed all our cooks and mess men!"

"Right down the path," I said and started onward.

He grabbed my arm.

"Don't leave me Jim. Take me to a fox hole."

Quickly I took him to the fox hole and left him with Pine and West. Then I grabbed a small shovel and ran top speed to a big shelter I had left only three minutes before. A 150 pound "daisy cutter" bomb which exploded on contact had made a direct hit on our big shelter, and showered jagged steel fragments in all directions. I saw dead and dying lying outside the shelter or half buried by dirt and twisted debris. Cole and a number of others had emerged from the shelter dazed and shocked, but unhurt.

"Take it easy now, and help get this man out," said our medical officer, Lieutenant Commander Dawson A. Mills of Pittsburg, Pa., a veteran of the Solomon Islands campaigns where he was attached to the First Marine Air Wing.

Quickly he worked with his staff of medical corpsmen, giving morphine injections to ease the pain, then removing the injured and sending them to the nearby aid station for blood plasma transfusions.

Carefully but rapidly we dug dirt and wrestled with shattered timbers and steel rails which supported sand bags covering the main shelter and another adjacent fox hole. Staff Sergeant William R. Smith, 25-year-old chief cook from Carlisle, Ark., was badly wounded by shrapnel as he lay in his bed in the small fox hole.

Valiantly Smitty worked to help extricate his partner Tech Sergeant Alvin R. Raburn Jr. 25, of Long Island, N.Y., our group baker. We lifted Raburn carefully onto a stretcher and carried him to the sick bay. Then Smitty collapsed.

I dashed back to help carry another stretcher, then got several Marines and raided nearby tents for more cots. Many hands were calmly and efficiently helping. The medical corpsmen worked rapidly and expertly.

PFC George D. La Duke, a smooth-faced youth from Detroit, Mich., was in the shelter. Unhit, but shocked, he dug dirt from the face of a buddy and watched him die. Then La Duke grabbed a shovel and helped cover gasoline spewing from a truck parked nearby and riddled with shrapnel, causing a dangerous fire hazard.

"Don't light any matches or cigarettes around this gasoline," ordered Dr. Mills.

Heavy fumes of gasoline and gun powder permeated the air. As long as I live, the odor of gasoline will cause that ghastly scene to flash again in front of my eyes.

As an ex-police reporter, I had seen numerous persons who were injured or killed in automobile and other accidents. But never had I seen a sight like this. I felt pretty humble and small as I realized how close I had come to death. But since the calamity occurred, I was glad to be there to do what little I could to help the wounded.

Telephone lines were down, so I dashed to the Intelligence tent to call for more ambulances. I broke news of the tragedy to Lieutenant Forsyth, Morris Fry, Dick Koch-Church, Marion Stevens and Ralph Plumb. At first they were incredulous. We hadn't yet felt the full crush of war.

Bill Carver and Don Housemen had been our only previous wounded. Our casualties had been much lighter than expected, and we had come to believe it would continue that way. We were unprepared for a shock like this.

Our telephone line was intact, but our power line had been severed by fragments from the explosions. We huddled in darkness in the small, cold shelter, and the full significance began to sink in on the others.

Then another bomb went Ka-whoomp...then another...a whole string of bombs. Actually the string of bombs was going away from us, but as we sat there tensely it seemed each one came closer this time. I believe all of us got at least a slight case of the shakes, and not just from the cold, although that contributed. I wished to return and see if I could be of further assistance. But Lieutenant Forsyth ordered us to remain in our fox hole until the all-clear sounded at 11:10 p.m. Back at the sick bay the tragic toll was tabulated. There were five dead, and six badly wounded.

Four were killed outright, and MT Sergeant Warren H. Hemmer, 21, of Belleville, Ill., died within a few hours without regaining consciousness. It was he who had told me on L-minus one-day that this campaign might be rougher than his previous one at Guadalcanal. It was for him.

Tech Sergeant Melvin Reed Jr., 20, of Milford, Ind., died without seeing and holding his baby daughter who was born January 24—the day we sailed from San Diego.

With him went one of his closest buddies, Staff Sergeant William P. Curd, 20, a tall athletic youth from Plattsburg, Mo., who with Reed worked in the Sergeant Major's office.

Tall, silent and amiable Sergeant Joe H. Butler, 26-year-old field cook from Acme, Tex., was another killed outright. His wife and small daughter, Jo Ann, reside at Midland, Calif.

The other Marine who paid with his life was another field cook, Sergeant Alan, B. Cook, 21, of Fort Arthur, Tex.

Our headquarters squadron was small, and most of us knew all the men well. Two of the wounded occupied the tent with Dick and me.

One was Staff Sergeant LaVerne Ochten, 21, of Essexville, Mich., who worked in the Sergeant Major's office. The other was Private First Class William L. Rehkemmar, a 19-year-old farm lad from Oelwin, Ia., who was a carpenter and always busy building something new for our tent. They were wonderful tent buddies, alert, agreeable and each possessed with a fine sense of humor. Both had proudly showed us pictures of their pretty sweethearts back home. Both planned to go to college after war. Both were wounded seriously.

Our Sergeant Major, Master technical Sergeant Robert B. Wray, 28, of Sioux City, Ia., was severely injured. He was an efficient Sergeant Major, and always took time to listen to the problems of any members of the outfit.

Tech Sergeant Rabun was critically injured. He lost his right leg and left eye. Rabun was one of the best bakers I ever knew. The bread and pastries he baked and served to us made our meals a pleasure. Aboard ship he and Sergeant Joe butler brought a couple of loaves of hot bread from the kitchen to our hold almost every night so some of us could enjoy a late snack.

Severely wounded was Corporal Howard W. Stovell, 23, an assistant cook from Yankee Hill, Calif. Quiet but friendly, he had a fine singing voice. He really knew how to prepare chow.

Smitty, an outstanding cook, was severely wounded by shrapnel. After being evacuated to Guam for hospitalization, Smitty insisted on rejoining our outfit. He did a fine job for us for two months after his return, but finally had to give up because of headaches and nervousness. We loved him for his spunk and eternal cheerfulness, which he managed even when he didn't feel well.

It was really hitting below the belt for the Japs to kill and wound so many of our cooks.

Others who were huddled in the rear of the shelter when the bomb struck were shaken and shocked. Private First Class Thomas E. Oliphant, 21, of Kernes, Tex., another hard-working cook, suffered concussion, Our mess officer, Warrant Officer Harris La Duke, MT Sergeant Ryan, Cole and Private First Class Frank J. Kristunas of Hartford, Conn., all from the commissary section, were in that hell hole. They were not injured, but showed the effects of shock and grief for days.

PFC William K. Gibson of Cleveland, O., Corporal Francis D. Dorsey of Keyser, W. Va., and Technical Sergeant John F. Keese, aerial navigator from Milwaukee, Wis., also underwent the full shock of the blast in the hole.

Concussion was so strong that it knocked down Sergeant Frank Treuting who was standing in front of his fox hole 100 yards away.

With the wounded treated and evacuated, we still had our hands full quieting and consoling the shocked occupants of the blasted shelter. Arm in arm, La Duke and Ryan sat in Dr. Mills' office sipping medicinal brandy. Ryan was badly shaken, and grief stricken for his many assistants who were killed or wounded. La Duke was consoling Ryan, and held up admirably until Ryan was taken to the tent of Staff Sergeant Sam Winfree and Shamrock Coyne to spend the night. Then La Duke broke down. Cole and Oliphant were jittery but holding up well.

"Stay right with me and don't leave, Jim," La Duke said to me.

I sat beside him and he clutched me tightly, telling over and over again in lurid detail just what had happened—how he uncovered the face of a buddy and watched him die. Others were there, and we kept turning the conversation to cooking and baking; of how he helped forage for food under the army's nose. But he always returned to the bombing.

"Don't leave me Jim," he repeated, clutching me still tighter and crying on my shoulder.

A jeep engine started outside.

"Air raid," he yelled, and jumped up.

We sat him down and consoled him; assured him the planes overhead were friendly. But he doubted it. Then shortly after midnight the air raid wailed a loud warning of more approaching bogies. La Duke let out a wild shriek and leaped for the door, then dashed back and grabbed frantically for his helmet. Others took him to an already crowded fox hole, and I looked about for Cole, who I had promised to take to a fox hole near my tent where I crouched with Dick Koch-Church and Keese.

Soon more strings of bombs landed nearby, and then Pistol Pete the Jap canon, began sending its screaming projectiles overhead. They were exploding about 400 to 800 yards from us. We sipped a tiny bottle of medicinal brandy I obtained at sick bay. It braced us, but still Dick and I felt nervous. Keese, shaken from his ordeal in the shelter where the bomb hit, had the shakes, badly.

After the raid, which lasted an hour, I found Cole and Oliphant and took them to the tent of PFC Albert B. Washington Jr., of Willis Tex., a slender young Marine who was holding up like a veteran. I got PFC John Donovan to move into the tent with them. One of the older men in our squadron, Donovan was calm and had a good line of Irish blarney. Then I returned to La Duke, and didn't get away from him until morning.

He sacked down on a cot in sick bay, and I pulled another alongside it. With one hand he held on to me incessantly, sleeping fitfully, starting at each sound and asking repeatedly if I were still there. I had no blanket and between the cold, his jitters and Pistol Pete's screeching barrage exploding nearby, I too developed a case of the shakes, which wracked me violently. I reasoned with myself and mustered all my will power, but could not entirely overcome the shakes. I know, now, how it feels to be afraid. Fear seems to be something which originates in your tissues, your nervous system, and over which your mind at times has no control. It stems from the strong instinct of self-preservation. Mentally, I didn't feel afraid; but physically I did. Finally I got up and found two thick blankets. Soon I was warm, and relaxed and went to sleep.

The next morning La Duke walked with a nervous gait and talked constantly about the previous night's ordeal, describing it in detail to all who had time to listen.

"Give him some hard work," advised Dr. Mills.

We kept busy all morning helping a new outfit dig fox holes. All were digging deeper and stronger shelters.

Soon we learned that the same string of bombs which hit our area also killed three and wounded 15 in the nearby Second Marine Air Wing Headquarters Squadron area.

The dead were: Captain David B. Thayer of Brookline, Mass., Master Technical Sergeant Raymond H. Bubb of Huntington Park, Calif., and Chief Pharmacist's Nate Leon A. Rutberg, the big medical corpsman from Los Angeles, Calif. Rutberg was one of the closest buddies of Ray Flaherty, and it was a double blow to Ray after losing his brother. Captain James G. White of Washington, D.C., commanding officer of the wing headquarters squadron, had taken cover in a cave, but left to disperse a large crowd of men and officers who were congregated near the mess hall. As he approached the bomb fell, and he too was wounded. However, he refused to be evacuated.

Bare headed, we stood the next afternoon at the First Marine Division cemetery where Father Horvath, the Second Wing chaplain, conducted funeral services for the eight Marines whose bodies were shrouded in white.

Stooped and bent with grief and shock, La Duke stood there crying. And there were plenty of others misty eyed, including mine.

I looked sadly at the eight lifeless forms. Gallantly and uncomplainingly these young men—our buddies—had gone into the combat area to fight for freedom, opportunity and happiness for many. They helped assure these things for others, but their own ambitions and futures would never be realized. For they had made the supreme sacrifice.

"Greater love hath no man than that he lay down his life for another."

Within me welled a burning resolution that their deaths must not be in vain; that we must use our nation's moral strength and physical strength, if necessary, and assume our just share of responsibility for international peace and justices.

Ever since The civil war we have enjoyed peace among our many states. We must help accomplish the same for nations. International problems are infinitely greater and more complex. But answers can be found to these problems if we approach them honestly and unselfishly. The answers must be found to these problems. This must not happen again!

The funeral services were simple and brief.

"Think of these men in the days to come, and always remember what they did," said Father Horvath.

Then he called for pall bearers. Four marines took each stretcher. La Duke stepped forward and helped one... crying, bent with grief and shambling along... a pathetic sight and yet an inspiring example of intrepid fortitude.

Then he insisted on returning and baking a big batch of bread for us, using Rabun's recipe and taking over as chief baker. Day after troublous day, night after haunting night, he fought his fear and continued to work, now harder than ever because we were short handed. For more than a month he slept with his clothes on so he could dash quickly to his fox hole when the frequent alerts were sounded. During the alerts he always was seized with the shakes... haunting fear... and memories.

But gradually he won that hardest of all battles—the battle against fear. La Duke remained with us throughout the campaign and completely overcame his jitters during raids. His was one of the hardest battles on Okinawa.

We of MAG 43 will always remember our buddies... the price they paid ... their purple hearts and white crosses.

Chapter 13

Dauntless Defenders

Furious air battles raged as dauntless Marine Corsair pilots clashed violently in mortal combat with fanatical, unswerving Jap Kamikaze fliers intent on wreaking death and destruction at any cost.

The flying Leathernecks found frequently that lack of weather reports, rapidly rising storms, and soft, narrow, pockmarked runways were even more dangerous enemies than the Japs. Our first pilot casualties were by these elements.

Corsair pilots on dusk combat air patrol flew late the evening of April 19 to give maximum protection to ships off Okinawa. A heavy storm front moved in quickly and enveloped the planes. The ceiling dropped far below minimums for safe flying. Smoke, which screened the nearby fleet, blew over the airfields, and brought zero ceiling and zero visibility.

Second Lieutenant R. M. Tousley of Le Suer, Minn., who had helped shoot down an Oscar fighter the day before in his only contact with the Japs., found the shrouded field, but crashed into a hill on his approach and was killed. First Lieutenant A. C. Satterwhite made it back to the field but crash-landed on the runway. His plane was demolished, but he escaped without serious injury and later shot down a Jap fighter plane.

"Lost in the Soup" as pilots call encompassing clouds, were Second Lieutenant R. W. Hager of Columbus, O., Captain R. L. Green of Titusville, Pa., First Lieutenant J. L. Williams of Welton, Ariz., and Second Lieutenant J. C. Hale of New York City.

"Missing in action" was written by their names.

Another marine pilot lost in the pea soup fog and clouds was Second Lieutenant Charles E. Coppedge, 26, of Halifax, N.C., a member of the Blackjack Squadrons. Because of his dark complexion, his fellow pilots called him "The Gook". For more than two hours he flew on instruments, waiting for a weather break, which never came. Finally he made radio contact with a ship and was brought in over it. At 6000 feet his motor cut out, the gasoline all gone. Nosing the plane upward, he slowed the speed so the slipstream of air would not be too violent for him to bail out.

Quickly he rolled back the cockpit, clambered out and then stepped into space. It was his first parachute jump, and on the darkest of nights. Down he plummeted in the black abyss. He pulled the ripcord. Only one of the parachute leg straps was buckled. The chute opened and there was a violent jerk, which felt like it would pull him in two. Slowly he descended. As he hit the water he slipped the parachute off, inflated his rubber life raft and climbed aboard.

For an hour Lieutenant Coppedge drifted, unable to see any landmarks and knowing only that he was on the China Sea. Then faintly he heard a ship, so quiet that it might be a submarine. He blinked his flashlight; then stopped. It might be a Jap ship. Then he decided to take a chance. It was an L.C.I., one of four landing craft supports, a small picket patrol vessel.

Rescued pilots are treated like royalty aboard ship. The ship's doctor, Lieutenant (j.g.) E. H. Vick of Selma, N.C., gave him a quick bracer of medicinal brandy. The personable skipper, Lieutenant (j.g.) George Smith, who formerly was a U.S. embassy man to Argentina, treated Lieutenant Coppedge with all the hospitality, which would be accorded a guest of state.

The dark peppery pilot who a few years before was a football halfback and baseball shortstop, immediately became a great favorite of the crew. There was no way to return immediately, so he relaxed and enjoyed himself, but only the first two days. Then came the Kamikaze pilots.

At 2 p.m. on April 12 the tiny craft found itself the prey of some 25 Jap suicide dive-bombers.

One of the dark vultures opened the attack with a power dive at the vessel. Anti-aircraft guns barked loudly. Nearer and nearer came the diving plane, strafing madly all the while. Now tracers were streaming into it. It appeared certain that the plane would crash into its target. But suddenly it spun in, a scant 200 feet away.

Quickly the gunners swung their fire at another suicide diver. This time they weren't so fortunate. The plane flew through the thick ack ack barrages, hit the conning tower and exploded near the bow. It seemed incredulous that the tiny craft could take such punishment, but it did. Several of the sailors were burned, some wounded by shrapnel and others stunned. A 20 millimeter gun was knocked out, but the gunners continued their fire until the last instant, unmindful of seeking cover or protecting themselves. Lieutenant Coppedge dragged hoses and helped extinguish the blaze.

Another plane made a suicide dive and was shot down, this time a little farther away. Then another pilot pressed his attack and crashed onto the fantail, his plane's engine burying itself in the hull. Still the sturdy support ship refused to sink, although the explosion was so violent that it blew several of the crew overboard. Now it was Lieutenant Coppedge's turn to help pull them out, their life jackets having kept them afloat. Two men were wounded by the plane's strafing, but remained at their posts and continued to load guns.

Still another suicide plane roared in on a long gliding dive. The ack ack boys scored kill number three; then kill number four. The plane hit the water and exploded 300 feet away.

Now three Navy Hellcat and four Marine Corsair fighters came to the rescue and began knocking down attacking planes. The crew was too busy to count them, for another Jap plane was approaching. Lieutenant Coppedge manned a caliber .50 machine gun after its crew was knocked out.

The anti-aircraft guns threw everything they had at the plane. Flying low, the pilot came in level, then zoomed to 1200 feet directly above the ship, did a wingover and dived almost straight down. By now most of the guns were jammed. With a spiraling dive the plane found its target and crashed on the bow, killing two gunners who remained on their weapons, firing to the last.

Water gushed in, flooding all the holds. All the pumps were working, but not fast enough. The crew began throwing everything possible overboard. The craft was trying to return to its anchorage but the steering apparatus was fouled. The valiant crew extinguished another fire which raged fiercely where the last plane had landed. Dr. Vick and one corpsman worked frantically to treat the wounded.

Now another landing craft came to the rescue, pulling alongside and adding its pumps. Slowly, but still afloat, the craft limped back to safe anchorage. As the flier bid farewell to all hands, the skipper's parting words were:

"For God's sake, when you get back up there knock down some of those Jap planes."

"I'll do my best Captain," the pilot replied. "And I'll always remember the coolness and courage of your crew."

Four days later Lieutenant Coppedge saw Jap planes for a second time, but now he was in the cockpit of his speedy Corsair. Leading a four-plane division, he saw a Val making a suicide run on a destroyer.

"The Gook" peeled off so fast that he lost the other three planes in his division. Down he thundered. His machine guns broke into a roar. The Jap plane burst into flames, then crashed near the ship.

The pilot pulled up and saw another Kamikaze plane attacking. Quickly he got on the Val's tail. Under a withering blast from the Corsair's six caliber .50 machine guns the enemy plane began flying to pieces, then flamed and crashed, not 300 feet from the destroyer.

Pulling up to look for his division, he saw a third Jap plane diving toward the ship, with a Corsair in hot pursuit. Lieutenant Coppedge made a diving turn and helped shoot down the "divine wind" attacker, who splashed near the ship.

In less than five minutes he had scored two and a half kills, sharing the last with the other pilots of his Blackjack Squadron who were engaging the enemy.

More than 30 planes had attacked the destroyer, which broadcast a distress call at 9:35 a.m. Even as member of the Blackjack Squadron approached they saw a suicide plane crash into the ship.

First Lieutenant William W. Eldridge, a 22- year-old basketball and football star from Chattanooga, Tenn., who hadn't seen his three-month-old son, was flying wing to wing with First Lieutenant Selva E. McGinty, a quiet, pint-sized Irish kid of 21 from Oklahoma City, Okla.

"Bogies at 9 o'clock, "Eldridge radioed to his division leader, 9 o'clock meaning directly to his left.

"Tally ho if you see him, Eldridge," replied the leader of the four-plane flight.

Eldridge and McGintry peeled off in power dives after five Jap planes which were in steep power dives at the destroyer. Eldridge immediately jettisoned his auxiliary belly gasoline tank and shot water injection into his engine for full war emergency speed and power. McGinty kept his tank and gave full throttle without injection. Rapidly they closed.

Eldridge got on the tail of a Val and opened fire. It flamed, exploded and spun in, a quarter of a mile from its intended target. McGinty shot down another Val flying beside the first one, and it splashed only 200 feet short of the ship. Another Val went down before McGinty's guns. It hit the water only 50 feet from the destroyer. Some of the debris rattled against the ships hull.

Now at terrific speed Eldridge closed on another Val. There was a burst of machine gun fire...an explosion..another Kamikaze pilot joined his ancestors.

Four of the five attacking vultures were dead, but the fifth now was diving 300 miles an hour and closing rapidly on its target. Eldridge's machine guns spoke again. The Val smoked, fell off slightly, but continued. It struck the frantically twisting and dodging destroyer just below deck level. But the valiant destroyer refused to sink. The pilots had temporarily saved the ship by their last instant interception, only one of the five attacking Vals hitting the destroyer.

With his Corsair now cleaving the air at 450 miles an hour, Lieutenant Eldridge leveled off and saw several Navy Hellcat fighters trying to close on a Jap Betty. With his terrific speed he shot past them and opened fire on the Betty at 300 yards, giving the big bomber a long burst. It flamed and he ceased firing. Down it dropped, but bounced off the water and continued flying. The Corsair pilot slackened his speed and unleashed another fusillade. His tracers streamed into the bomber's cockpit. Apparently the pilot was killed and fell forward on the controls, for the twin-engine aircraft dived sharply into the sea.

Dangerously close, the Corsair passed only 10 feet above the dying plane. Lieutenant Eldridge looked back over his port wing and saw the bomber hit the water...the fire go out...a red "meat ball" insigne (the rising sun) slip beneath the surf.

Now Lieutenant McGinty saw a Zero which had made a pass at the destroyer. With a side burst into the cockpit he flamed the Jap fighter and scored his third kill for the day.

With six Jap planes to their credit, the two pilots joined up and patrolled back and forth, searching for more bogies. Lieutenant Eldridge was first to see another Zero, which was making a speedy dive at the destroyer. Giving his corsair water injection again, he closed rapidly and shot the fighter down just short of the ship. Simultaneously other Blackjack pilots had been battling still more Jap attackers.

Captain Floyd C. Kirkpatrick, a short, solidly built pilot from Klamath Falls, Ore., who attended the University of Oregon, peeled off and got on the tail of a death-diving Kamikaze plane which was only a few hundred yards from the destroyer. Seconds counted. With reckless fury the Leatherneck pressed his attack, diving through anti-aircraft fire and closing within 20 feet of the Jap plane to make every bullet count. The Val flamed. Now Captain Kirkpatrick realized he was too close. He pushed forward quickly on the stick and dived under the blazing plane as it spun in, just short of the ship. Then the Corsair pilot had to pull up rapidly to get out of ship's anti-aircraft fire which still continued.

Later he described his first kill as "a hell of a big thrill," but he had little time to think of it at the time. Quickly he got on the tail of another Kamikaze pilot only 400 feet from the destroyer. Again he closed within 20 feet to pour every bit of lead possible into the enemy, whom he again had to follow through a tremendous hail of ack ack. The Val blew up almost in his face and hit the water just 75 feet short of its target.

Pulling up, he quickly tailed another Val which had dropped a bomb at the ship and was turning to make a suicide run. For the third time Captain Kirkpatrick closed within 20 feet of his quarry and sprayed bullets into it. With his plane mortally wounded, the Jap pilot swerved suddenly and pulled up, trying to crash into the Corsair. An abrupt wingover saved the marine pilot, and he saw the Jap plane splash and explode a few hundred feet from the ship.

On his first and his last kills Captain Kirkpatrick was fired upon and his plane hit by rear seat gunners in the Jap planes. And he dived through the ship's ack ack to make all three kills. Machine gun bullets ripped his Corsair's wings and rudder, and a 20 millimeter shell from the ship crashed through his cockpit and missed his head by inches.

On Captain Kirkpatrick's first interception his wingman, Second Lieutenant Larry Friess of Hudson, Mich., attacked with equal courage and abandon, pressing close to make the kill and save the ship. Either ack ack from the ship or fragments from the exploding Jap Val struck his plane. Or possibly it collided with the destroyer's superstructure. One of his wings was sheared off and he spun in, his machine guns still firing.

Second Lieutenant Marion I. Ryan of Atlanta, Ga., nicknamed Rowdy because he was so quiet, collided with another Corsair and had to hit the silk. The other plane escaped serious damage, and Ryan was picked up.

The destroyer was in bad condition, but managing to remain afloat. Like swarms of angry hornets, the Jap suicide planes continued attacking.

Tall, dark- complexion First Lieutenant Will Dysart of Kopperl, Tex., flamed a Val at 3000 feet but it continued its death dive at the ship. At the last instant, however, it fell off and struck the water, so close that it bounced into the ship's side. His wingman, Second Lieutenant Clay Whittaker of Lafayette, Ind., peeled off at the same time and flamed another Val which crashed only 100 yards from the destroyer.

Then together they downed another Val which had dropped a bomb and missed. But they had to fly through ship's ack ack to score the kill, and Lieutenant Whittaker's plane sustained a huge flak hole in the stabilizer. So fiercely was Lieutenant Desart pressing the attack that he missed crashing the flaming Val by a scant six feet.

Navy Hellcats and ship's ack ack had knocked down a number of planes before the marine pilots arrived. Then the Blackjack pilots with their faster and more powerful Corsairs roared in and took over the show, shooting down 15½ Jap planes in less than five minutes. Not one of more than 30 Jap planes was left. The ship was saved, though badly wounded. Had the Leatherneck fliers arrived even half a minute later it might have been too late. Only by attacking with the most reckless abandon, flying through ship's ack ack and pressing their attacks at such close range that the Jap planes blew up in their faces, did they complete their job in time.

A few weeks later Captain Kirkpatrick shared in another kill, then scored two more to become an ace. In all but one of his shoot downs he flew through ship's ack ack to score his kills. It's difficult for ships to identify planes diving at them. The ship's gunners held their fire when possible. But in mortal danger from suicide attacks, their policy has to be shoot when in doubt.

"Why did you risk your plane and your life so many times by flying through ship's fire?" I asked Captain Kirkpatrick. "Was it just to add another kill to your score?"

"Well, our primary mission is to protect the ships," replied the marine pilot.

He paused, then added: "I figure that risking one plane and myself may save a ship and several hundred men. How could I let those men down? But you really get a lonely feeling after you shoot down the plane and the ack ack keeps right on firing at you."

"Yes, those tracers look big as baseballs," chimed in his wingman, Second Lieutenant George E. "Peewee" Lantz, Mansfield, O. A vivacious five-foot-four kid of 23. Peewee looked more like the saxophone player he used to be than the hell for leather pilot he had become.

Captain Kirkpatrick felt a lot of justified satisfaction from his kills.

"I kind of think I had it coming," he said. "I'd been waiting a long time. My dad wondered what was wrong with me last time when I came home after 16 months in the Pacific and hadn't shot down a plane. He couldn't seem to understand that there just weren't any Jap planes to shoot down at that time in the mid-Pacific, where we were flying patrol missions. He ribbed the hell out of me. I'll really give it back to him now!"

Lieutenant McGinty, who downed three of the suicide planes, later shot down a Betty bomber and a Zero to become an ace. Lieutenant Eldridge, who scored four kills in his first furious encounter, returned from his tour of duty without again seeing a Jap plane.

But one pilot who saw all the Jap planes he wanted one day was Second Lieutenant Frederick Kelb Jr., of the Blackjack Squadron. Answering a distress call of a picket ship being attacked by 10 suicide planes, he and his wingman, Second Lieutenant Elliot F. Brown, sped to its aid but became separated in thick clouds.

Lieutenant Brown sighted a Val above him, made a zooming attack and damaged it, and then followed it down and shot it into the water. After patrolling for some time he returned to base without finding Lieutenant Kelb or any more Japs.

Meanwhile Lieutenant Kelb saw a Val, and in a high side run ripped pieces from it with his roaring machine guns. The badly damaged plane started downward, but poor visibility kept him from seeing it crash. He scored it as a probable.

Then he saw eight more Vals. Unhesitatingly he attacked the entire formation, at the same time calling for help. Back at the base his fellow fliers heard a dramatic monologue on the radio, with Lieutenant Kelb as the announcer, saying:

"I'm in a hell of a fight over here...I'm outnumbered eight to one...Send some help...Splash a Val!" Machine gun chatter punctuated the broadcast.

There was a pause, then:

"Send some damned help over here...I'm getting shot up pretty badly...Aw hell, splash another Val."

Japanese planes had gotten on his tail and mortally wounded his Corsair. He radioed his position and hit the silk. While getting shot down himself, he scored two kills, confirmed by the ship, and a probable. After his bold attack the Japs turned back without attacking the ship. It was a grateful ship's crew which rescued Lieutenant Kelb.

If the Kamikaze suicide attacks were a surprise to some people, the resolute and daring determination of Marine pilots was equally as surprising to the Japs.

One day Captain Kenneth L. Reusser of my former home city of Portland, Ore., the "City of Roses", observed vapor trails at 35,000 feet over Okinawa. His four-plane division, from the Days Knights Squadron, was patrolling at 10,000 feet. He and his division zoomed skyward. At 32,000 feet two of the Corsairs refused to climb higher, but Captain Reusser and First Lieutenant Robert R. Klingman of Binger, Okla., continued to climb.

Still above them, and in full flight homeward, was a new Jap twin-engine bomber known as a Nick. Exceptionally fast, it has a top emergency speed of 354 miles an hour, but apparently was stripped of excess weight and speeded up for photo reconnaissance missions.

Four 100 miles Captain Reusser and Lieutenant Klingman pursued the fleeing plane through the stratosphere their own wings now also leaving vapor trails. Unable to climb to its ceiling or to close, they fired half of their ammunition to lighten their planes. Then the powerful Corsairs moved in for the kill.

Captain Reusser closed to effective range and with several long bursts damaged the Nick's right wing and famed the right engine with his remaining ammunition. Lieutenant Klingman moved into range, but in the sub-zero temperature at almost 40,000 feet his guns froze. The Jap bomber continued its homeward flight handily on one engine, returning with valuable photographs of our fields and defenses. But Lieutenant Klingman had just begun to fight.

The Leatherneck pilot flew into the tail of the Jap bomber and with his propeller chewed off the tip of the rudder, then pulled away. The Nick continued in controlled flight. The horrified rear seat gunner in the Jap plane was firing frantically and scoring hits, but Klingman closed again. This time he cut the rudder completely off and damaged the right stabilizer. On a third pass he severed the stabilizer. The Nick went into a long, circling spin and crashed in to the sea. No parachutes were seen to open, so apparently the entire crew went down with the plane.

Jap machine gun bullets made many holes in the Corsair's engine and wings, and bits of the Nick's tail were stuck to the cowling and propeller. The propeller was badly bent, and the tip was sheared from one of the blades.

Losing altitude at the rate of 300 feet a minute, Lieutenant Klingman eased what little power he could from the damaged engine and stretched a long glide 150 miles back to his home field. Barely reaching the runway, he made a safe landing and saved the plane. The engine and propeller were junk.

"The best part of the show was to see the look of stark terror on the face of the Jap rear-seat gunner," said Captain Reusser.

One of the wildest melees of the campaign occurred when Captain L. H. Smith, First Lieutenant J. W. Leaper and First Lieutenant W. L.

Milne of the Bob Cats Squadron tally hoed a Jap Betty bomber at 7000 feet, with three flights of Zero, Jack and Oscar fighters flying cover for it. For identification purposes, we usually bestow masculine names on Jap fighter planes, and female names on the egg-laying bombers.

Captain Smith opened the assault on the Betty with a roaring overhead run, but his electrical system failed and his guns remained silent. He broke off the attack and Lieutenant Miloe bored in, his tracers hitting the Betty's left engine. The rear-seat gunner was firing 20 millimeter cannon shells at him during his assault. Quickly Lieutenant Leaper closed with a flat run and shot the enemy aircraft down in flames.

A few minutes later Lieutenant Miloe tally hoed another Betty bomber at 7000 feet, covered by four Zeroes 4000 feet higher. In the face of fire from the Betty's 20 millimeter cannon he tailed the plane through a series of evasive maneuvers, keeping it under constant fire. His own 10 millimeter shells blasted huge chunks from the Betty's engine nacelles. Then the right wing disintegrated. The Japs had lost another bomber.

As the Betty rolled over, Lieutenant Miloe saw attached to its underside a piloted rocket suicide bomb known as a Baka. Down went the Betty with its Baka, and struck the water with a tremendous explosion. Few of the Baka bombs were used during the Okinawa campaign, and there never was a report of one causing damage. We named the Japs' piloted rocket bomb the Back because in Japanese Baka means "foolish."

While Lieutenant Miloe was engrossed in destroying the Betty, Lieutenant Leaper was flying wing on him and calling:

"He's shooting at you, Pappy."

Then the four Zeros dived, and Lieutenant Leaper, using water injection for greater power, zoomed to meet the challenge. Three broke off, but the fourth roared straight at him. He couldn't get his Corsair's nose up fast enough to bring the Zero into his sights, but the Jap had him cold. Machine gun bullets shattered the Corsair's bullet-proof windshield. The Zero passed over Lieutenant Leaper, pulled out and maneuvered to bring Lieutenant Miloe once more under fire.

But a quick turn brought Lieutenant Leaper on the tail of the Zero, which still held an altitude advantage. The Corsair pilot, climbing at a 30 degree angle from below, opened fire. He led the enemy plane, aiming his 20 millimeter cannon shells slightly ahead of the Zero. The Jap flew head-on into the deadly stream of fire. Pieces flew from the fuselage and wings. Its tail was riddled. It turned into a diving barrel roll, trailing smoke, and spiraled into the sea.

Lieutenant Leaper fired a short burst into the Betty bomber as Lieutenant Miloe was finishing it off, then pulled up and fired a short burst at another Zero diving to attack Lieutenant Miloe.

That was the last of his ammunition, but Lieutenant Leaper, an aggressive flier from Hopkins, Minn., wasn't through. With a split S turn he quickly got on the Zero's tail and closed rapidly. From 20 feet below, the Leatherneck pilot pulled up to cut the tail off the Zero. The Corsair's shattered windshield was covered with oil from the overworked propeller, making visibility poor. Missing the tail, the Corsair's propeller struck the Zero near the cockpit, almost cutting the plane in two. But the Corsair also was a wreck. A gas tank exploded, blowing off the right wing, and the plane went into a high speed spin.

Lieutenant Leaper tried to bail out over the left side, but centrifugal force of the right spin held him in. Finally he took a chance of being hit by the plane, and bailed out over the right side. The plane cleared him by inches as he pulled the rip cord. The chute opened immediately, but because of his terrific speed it ripped from the top center to the rim of the canopy.

The sudden jerk caused the pilot to black out. He recovered to see another Zero diving at him. Quickly he pulled the shroud lines and collapsed the chute. Six Corsairs got on the tail of the fiendish Jap pilot, and took care of him. Lieutenant Leaper plummeted downward three or four thousand feet. Then his chute opened again, and he floated down to the sea.

As he landed he unbuckled his gear and the chute fell forward about 75 feet. A strong swimmer, he quickly reached the chute but could not find the seat pack containing the life raft. He looked around and saw it about 100 feet away. Quickly he swam to it, inflated it and climbed aboard. Tracers from his pistol attracted search planes, and an hour and a half later he was picked up by a destroyer.

Meanwhile Lieutenant Miloe was attacked by three Zeros, so he discreetly dived away from them. Then he saw another Zero at 2000 feet, and shot it down. His score for the day was a Betty and a Zero, while Lieutenant Leaper's was a Betty and two Zeros.

During the first month of aerial combat, the flying Leathernecks of the Fighter Command downed 209 Jap planes, while suffering only two known losses in combat with the enemy. One day the Marines shot down 60 Jap planes without a single loss. Nine of our planes disappeared that first month in what General Wallace described as "the worst flying weather I ever have seen." Possibly the Japs shot down some of them. Even adding those nine to the two known lost in contact with the enemy, the score was 209 to 11, or 19 to 1 in favor of the Marine pilots.

The Leathernecks again were making aerial history. With their daring, determined attacks—flying through ship's ack-ack and even chewing enemy planes apart with their propellers—they were constantly going above and beyond the call of duty to protect the lives of all of us on Okinawa and aboard the nearby ships.

The fanatical Japs were no match for the aggressive marine pilots.

Chapter 14

Air Victory Over Okinawa

Air victory over Okinawa rode on many wings, with hundreds of skillful pilots scoring shoot downs of enemy planes. Many became aces in the roaring sky battles, but there was not one pilot with an outstanding lead in the number of enemy kills. However, one squadron was far ahead of the pack in running up its total of sky victories. It was the Death Rattlers Squadron—VMF 323.

The Death Rattlers shot down 91 ½ planes between April 12 and May 12 for a new Marine Aviation record for that period of time, and then ran their string to 124 ½ kills for the campaign. Twelve of the Death Rattlers became aces. The squadron ran out of enemy air targets by mid-June.

Major George C. Axtell, a hard-driving 24-year-old pilot from Baden, Pa., was commanding officer of the Death Rattlers.

"It's just damned hard work over long periods of time that makes an outfit click," he told me.

Possessed with this unswerving conviction, he drove his squadron relentlessly through its training syllabus in the States. He promoted ground crew members who maintained the feverish pace, and demoted any who didn't. He grounded pilots who he felt could not keep pace, reasoning that he was doing a favor both to the government and to the individual. It isn't everyone who is physically and mentally constituted to be a fighter pilot. They fly in a fast league.

"If a job is necessary, I expect a man to finish it if it takes him all night," said the major. "These mechanics and service crews are working incredibly long hours here on Okinawa. They work as much as 20 hours a day. And it's really paying off. Ground crews who remain at their posts while the air field is under bombing and shelling attacks, are deserving of the utmost credit."

Major Axtell developed a healthy respect for Jap fighter pilots in his first brush with them. A pair of Jacks, Japan's new 400-mile-an-hour fighters, dived out of the sun and opened fire on Major Axtell and his wingman, First Lieutenant E. L. Abner of Washington, D. C.. Bullets crashed into the engine and a flap of the major's Corsair, and he gave full throttle to outrun the attackers.

Lieutenant Abner also was under fire, but popped open his flaps and made a tight, stalling turn which put him on the tail of the first Jap. Then he gave full throttle. His powerful Corsair surged forward and closed rapidly. Several bursts of machine gun fire struck the Jap plane. It turned on its back and exploded. Tracers again flew past Lieutenant Abner's cockpit, and again he popped open his flaps, made a tight stalling turn and bore down on the tail of the Jack which a few seconds before was closing to kill him. A Navy Hellcat fighter saw the action and raced to the rescue. Together the Corsair and Hellcat closed. Their 12 machine guns quickly exploded the Jack, and the two pilots shared credit for the kill.

Six days later Major Axtell repaid the Japs, and in good measure. Between 30 and 35 suicide planes flying through haze beneath overhanging layers of clouds were prowling for our outlying picket patrol destroyers. The Jap Val dive bombers had no fighter planes for protection, so seven pilots of the Death Rattlers Squadron abandoned all caution and lashed furiously at the foe.

Major Axtell led his two-plane section with Lieutenant Abner again flying wing for him, and First Lieutenant Jeremiah J. O'Keefe of Biloxi, Miss., led another section with First Lieutenant W. L. Hood of Benton Harbor, Mich., as his wingman. First in sections, and then individually they hurled their deadly corsairs at the Japs. Tracers flew like fingers of lightning. Exploding planes filled the sky and crashed violently into the sea.

Lieutenant O'Keefe, a tall, slim youth of 21 with a big smile and engaging personality, began building model planes when only a youngster. With his aunt he visited the World's Fair at Chicago and went home with a package of parts for his first model plane.

Now he was in a Corsair, one of the best and most versatile fighter planes in the world, with the sky full of targets. Diving from 20,000 feet, he had speed to burn, so slowed his plane with flaps and closed on a Val. The slow and extremely maneuverable Val made a sharp turn to the left, then wheeled back rapidly to the right. Lieutenant O'Keefe matched the turns. The Val flamed and exploded as bullets ripped into its wings and engine.

Pulling his flaps, Lieutenant O'Keefe raced after another Val a mile away. Again he dumped his flaps and waited for the Val to make its diving turns. The Jap pilot made a turn and ran into a hail of tracers. His plane flamed and exploded on the second turn.

Kill number three came harder. The cagey Jap pilot kept trying to turn inside O'Keefe to get on his tail. But with low throttle and open flaps the Corsair duplicated every maneuver of the Val. After the fourth turn the desperate Jap flew head-on at the Corsair. Tracer, armor-piercing and incendiary bullets sprayed from O'Keefe's machine guns. The Jap pilot flew straight at the Corsair, then pulled up and tried to crash it. A quick wingover saved Lieutenant O'Keefe, and he saw the Jap go down.

A few minutes later he saw six Vals in one group.

"I just sort of figured they were all mine," he said. "But it didn't quite work out that way."

All but one darted into protective clouds. Now the Leatherneck pilot began conserving ammunition to extend it for more kills. Flying low over the water, he pressed closely and scored kill number four with a short burst; then found himself flying through a geyser where the enemy plane splashed. The sturdy Corsair shook violently, but never faltered.

Radio orders came for the pilots to orbit and resume their fighter formations. Lieutenant O'Keefe joined up to fly wing on Major Axtell, who had shot down three enemy planes in the wild melee. Major Axtell held up three fingers and flashed a big smile. Lieutenant O'Keefe held up four fingers and flashed back a bigger smile. In fact, he laughed right out loud. Then another flight of Vals was sighted and there was a feverish race for kills.

When the Death Rattlers rejoined their formation a few minutes later Lieutenant O'Keefe held up five fingers, and so did Major Axtell. Major Jefferson D. Dorroh Jr., leader of another division of three planes which had been making hot junk of the Jap planes, made six kills to lead the day's scoring. Major Dorroh, Major Axtell and Lieutenant O'Keefe together shot down 16 planes and became aces in a matter of 20 minutes.

A rough and tumble Leatherneck from Hood River, Oregon, Major Dorroh competed in a rodeo at Eugene, Oregon in 1940 and won $60 as first prize for riding the hurricane decks of angry long-horned Brahma steers. A sophomore at University of Oregon, he plunked down $32 for tuition in the Civilian Pilot Training Program and began his brilliant sky career.

Major Dorroh had taken dizzy rides on the worst outlaw bucking horses and wild-eyed steers that ever entered the area, but never such a wild ride as he took in his Corsair on the day of the big turkey shoot. His plane raced madly, slowed down suddenly, pivoted, dived, sun fished, banked, rolled and pitched to keep first one enemy plane and then anther in its sights. He scored kills by using flaps and remaining doggedly on the tails of violently maneuvering and jinking Japs. Other kills came on lightning, 400-mile-an-hour dives and passes. When the sky finally was cleared his score was six kills, plus two probables which he hit hard and left wounded while he pressed for more kills.

The Death Rattlers' score that day was 24 ½ planes.

On April 28 the operations section scrambled a number of extra pilots to repulse a large enemy attack.

"They'll fly anybody who wants to go," shouted a pilot who received the word.

Lieutenant O'Keefe was lying on his cot dressed only in his underwear. Quickly he put on his shoes, grabbed a bag containing his flight gear, and dashed half-clad to his plane. He dressed while ground crews swarmed around, re-gassing the Corsair. A few minutes later he was in the air, again leading the second section of Major Axtell's four-plane division.

Major Axtell shot down one Jap plane that day, while Lieutenant O'Keefe scored two kills. As in O'Keefe's other kills, the enemy planes caught fire and became flaming incinerators. In civilian life O'Keefe was an undertaker. Then, it was O'Keefe—the embalmer. Now, it was O'Keefe—the cremator!

One member of the Death Rattlers who never got an opportunity to share in the kills was Captain Clarence N. Moore, a sandy-haired pilot from Douglas, Ariz. In a previous tour in the southwest Pacific his Wildcat fighter plane was ganged by a flock of zeroes and shot down. He spent eight and a half months in hospitals; then recovered and returned to combat flying. I talked to him just before he returned to the States from his Okinawa tour of duty, and he was pretty disgusted.

"This is getting boring," he said. "I haven't even seen a Jap plane in flight when I've been up. I'm ready to go home, see the folks, have a few parties and then come out again. Maybe my luck will change by then."

Many other capable pilots at Okinawa never got a shot at the Japs.

Captain Moore didn't shoot down any enemy planes, but be struck heavy blows at the Japs with fighter-bomber attacks. He was so superior on these close support strikes in front of our advancing infantry that he was assigned as flight coordinator. He would lead flights of Corsairs in their strikes, diving down first and marking the target with smoke rockets.

The secret of the great success the Marines have at dive bombing is the low altitude of release and pullouts.

"This is dangerous, but if we lose a few more planes we'll save a lot of marine ground troops," said Captain Moore. "To hit a Jap cave you have to fly down so low that you can hardly miss. Near misses aren't worth a damn. The caves have numerous openings, and concussion doesn't do much damage. You've go to score direct hits to do any damage."

He flew and coordinated many strike missions, attacking the enemy with bombs, rockets and by strafing. He strafed troops and vehicles on highways; blew up caves and gun positions; exploded ammunition trucks, and scorched Jap ground troops with fire bombs.

Marine Corsairs and Avenger bombers hammered the Japs incessantly on southern Okinawa throughout the entire campaign. At times their close support strikes were made within a hundred yards of our own front lines. The Japs had to move most of their supplies by night because our planes kept them off the roads by day.

The famous Marine Red Devils Squadron flew the first TBM Avenger bombers from Okinawa, hammering the Jap ground forces day after day. Like the Corsair pilots, the Red Devils were so daring in their low-level attacks that more than one plane was struck by debris from its own exploding bombs or rockets. Major General Mulcahy had to issue a strict order against low pullouts except when delayed action bombs were used. Close support bombing is dangerous work. We lost more planes to enemy anti-aircraft fire at Okinawa and throughout the Ryukyu islands than we did in dog fights.

During the campaign the Red Devils flew ground support strikes, observation flight, parapack drops of supplies to front line troops when ground transportation bogged down on mud-soaked roads, drops of propaganda leaflets, night heckler mission, strikes against airfields from Okinawa to Kyushu, Japan, and strikes against enemy shipping.

Army and marine ground troops were loud in their praise of the Red Devils, who were so accurate with their attacks that their pilots were permitted to make their strikes towards our own lines. This enabled them to hit the Japs' strong reverse slope defenses. Ground forces developed full confidence in the Red Devils' marksmanship, and called on them repeatedly.

One of the most remarkable feats by the Red Devils was the shoot down of a Jap plane at night by rockets. First Lieutenant Fred F. Folino saw the Jap plane over southern Okinawa, wheeled his big Avenger bomber around like a fighter and made a direct hit with his rockets.

One of the biggest Corsair fighter-bomber strikes was near the conclusion of the ground campaign in southern Okinawa. Sixty Corsairs made fire bomb attacks which spread a sea of flames over a half mile area obliterating a Japanese command post.

Additional marine fighter squadrons arrived as the campaign progressed and more airfields were completed. Alone, those Leatherneck pilots carried on the air battle at Okinawa against the constantly attacking Jap planes until mid-May. Then Army P-47 Thunderbolt squadrons began arriving and were attached to the Tactical Air Force.

With his Fighter Command growing in strength, Major General Mulcahy launched his forces into the second phase of the Okinawa air battle, and began carrying the fight to the Jap homeland. Every day that weather permitted, our fighter-bombers made strikes against airfields at Kyushu and on islands between Okinawa and Japan.

On these sweeps our planes encountered a much larger proportion of Japan's best planes. And the Jap fighter pilots were good airmen who flew smart team tactics.

Doggedly the Japs continued their attacks against our shipping and airfields and on the night of May 24 launched one of the most audacious attacks in the history of aerial warfare. Six Jap bombers carrying demolition and saboteur troops, attempted landing on Yontan airfield. Our anti-aircraft gunners did a magnificent job, hitting all of the attacking bombers and causing five of them to crash in flames. A sixth bomber made a successful wheels-up landing on the field and disgorged its suicide troops. Our pilots and ground crew closed in rapidly and killed or drove to cover all of the Jap raiders, but not before they had burned and destroyed seven of our planes on the ground.

One of the planes crashed only a few hundred yards from our camp area, and three enlisted men from Second Marine Air Wing headquarters shot and killed three Japs who lived through the crash and were recovering and reaching for hand grenades.

The next morning I saw dead Japs strewn about the wreckage of each of the planes. The Japs carried special belts loaded with grenades and fire bombs. They also carried land mines and booby traps. Obviously these suicide troops were given a formal sendoff, for we found wilting flowers in the planes—their petals falling like the heads of their owners.

Our night fighter planes scored seven kills that night—four of them twin-engine bombers which also might have been laden with suicide troops. The Japs destroyed seven of our planes on the ground, and one of their falling planes killed two men in their fox hole. But they lost 13 planes and at least 100 men. The queer little men came out a poor second on their unique attack. Again their suiciders achieved death, but not much destruction.

The next day the Japs followed up with one of their biggest daylight air raids, and our Corsair and Thunderbolt fighters made a record kill of 75 planes without a single loss of our own. Four days later our pilots shot down 40 Jap planes and added 35 more on June 4. The Tactical Air Force, now under command of dynamic Marine Major General L.E. Woods who succeeded Major General Mulcahy, boosted its total kills to 540 by mid-June.

The Japs were whipped in the air, and discontinued virtually all of their daylight attacks, making only a few sneak raids on cloudy days. But they continued their night attacks, causing occasional damage and making all of us lose a lot of sleep during alerts. Some of the bombings brought more deaths.

We depended on our night fighters for defense against the Nips' nocturnal attacks. Captain James Etheridge, who as a dive bomber pilot on his previous combat tour sank a large Jap freighter and a tanker, and probably sank a submarine, opened the scoring by night fighter pilots when he shot down a Jap Frank fighter.

Taking off at dusk in his single-seater Grumman Hellcat night fighter, Captain Etheridge saw the speedy Jap plane flash past, and immediately gave chase, pursuing the Frank over the nearby fleet and shooting it down.

Flying wing on Captain Etheridge was one of his school-day buddies from Oklahoma City, First Lieutenant John F. Sneed Jr. Concentrating on the kill, the two pilots from the Marine Nighthawks Squadron, VMF(N)-543, paid little attention to ships' anti-aircraft fire until the Jap plane went down. Then they realized their plight and scrambled. Several Jap planes were strafing the airfield, and Captain Etheridge drew anti-aircraft fire when he approached to land. But both he and Lieutenant Sneed managed to land safely, although both of their planes were pretty badly shot up. Captain Etheridge scored another night kill on May 27.

Night fighting still was a comparatively new and not a fully developed specialty when the Okinawa campaign began. But it was nothing new to Lieutenant Colonel Radford C. West, a brilliant young Marine pilot who was graduated from the naval Academy at Annapolis. During his varied air career he trained and flew with British night fighters in Europe to study their methods. Then he returned and helped organize a night fighter program for Marine Aviation.

Instead of twin-engine night fighter planes with three-man crews, the Navy turned to single-seater night fighters which could fly from aircraft carriers. So Marine Aviation had to follow suit, because the marine pilots had to be able to operate either from land bases or from carriers.

The British, with their Mosquito night fighter planes, proved the effectiveness of twin-engine, multiple-crew night fighters. Experts on night fighting agree that the multiple-crew night fighter is superior. But the marine pilots at Okinawa proved that single-seater night fighters also are effective, and they turned in the most outstanding performance in the history of one-man night fighters.

Jap night bomber pilots began dying young after the arrival at Okinawa of the Black Mac's Killers Squadron, VMF(N)-533. It derived its nickname from Lieutenant Colonel Marion M. Magruder, the squadron's blustery, boastful commanding officer.

"Just let the Japs try to come over at night," said Lieutenant Colonel Magruder. "We'll blast 'em out of the skies."

His squadron did just that, and the self-assured leader even flew patrol himself and shot down a Jap Betty bomber. He had studied British night fighter tactics in England and was an ardent for multiple-place night fighters. After the Okinawa campaign he was enthusiastic for the one-man job. His squadron set all sorts of new records for night fighting, and certainly was one of the most popular squadrons at Okinawa as far as we fox hole habitués were concerned.

First Lieutenant R. S. Hempstead of the Killers squadron shot down an Irving, a Betty and a Sally for three night fighter kills—an excellent score for a night fighter.

First Lieutenant R. E. Wellwood and First Lieutenant A. F. Dellamano each shot down three planes in one night. On May 18 Lieutenant Wellwood splashed three Bettys, and on May 24 Lieutenant Dellamano shot down a Jake, a Betty and another Jap bomber tentatively identified as a Sally.

But the number one pilot of the Black Mac's Killers Squadron was 23-year-old Captain Robert Baird, a former expert on the flying rings and trapeze at Compton Junior College in California. Captain Baird scored his first night fighter kill on June 9. On June 22, less than two weeks later, he became the Marine Corps' first night fighter ace. And just for good measure he ran his score to six shoot downs by blasting the tar out of a Betty bomber on July 14.

Owl-eyed Captain Baird, a whiz at spotting an enemy plane's silhouette or exhaust pattern in the dark, flew wild chases to close on the Jap planes and keep them in view after first sighted.

Our night fighters don't shoot tracers, because that warns the enemy pilot that he is under attack. Furthermore, the tracers would blind the pilot and cause him to lose sight of his quarry. So the night fighter machine guns are loaded with armor-piercing bullets and incendiary bullets. The incendiaries explode a bit as they strike; thus the pilot can keep on target.

One of Captain Baird's hardest kill was his first. He spied an exhaust pattern half a mile away, and from his long training knew it was not from a friendly plane. Rapidly he closed, but the enemy pilot soon discovered he was pursued. The Jap plane was a Jake, a slow seaplane used for suicide attacking. Captain Baird moved up slowly with flaps down to avoid overrunning his quarry. The Jake speeded up and dived. The marine pilot pulled up his flaps and gave throttle. The Jap made a split turn and Captain Baird overran him, but quickly turned, with the aid of flaps, and closed on the Jake.

"He burst into flames when I fired, and it was a beautiful sight," said Captain Baird. "They really make a pretty fire at night."

Blonde-haired Captain Baird had to extend his Hellcat to the limit to catch a Frances, one of Japan's fastest bombers, but he brought the big night vulture down. On two different nights he scored double kills.

Captain Baird is all for the single-seater night fighter, but would like a Corsair for the job. The Corsair is faster, has much greater pickup speed, and its special diving flaps slow it faster, making it superb for dog fighting and fast maneuvering.

Arriving after the campaign was well underway, Lieutenant Colonel Magruder's Killers scored their first shoot down on the night of May 16. A month later they had set a new all-time record for a Marine fighter squadron, with 19 planes on their scoreboard. And a month later they had increased that score to 34. Other night fighter squadrons at Okinawa also had done a good job, and by mid-July the Japs all but discontinued their night attacks, although they would cross us up at times and come in with night heckler raids.

The Black Mac's Killers concentrated almost entirely on interceptions, while the other night fighter squadrons divided their time between interceptions and flying night bomber and heckler missions against enemy airfields.

Some freakish sky battles occurred during the Okinawa campaign, but one of the strangest in the history of aerial combat was reported on

June 10. A large number of army P-47 Thunderbolts were on a fighter sweep over Kyushu, Japan, and Second Lieutenant R. J. Stone returned with this unusual combat narrative:

At 28,000 feet he and his wingman were closing on a Jap George fighter when 25 Zeros jumped them from above. Unable to get maximum power at high altitude because his induction system was damaged on the take-off, he dived and pulled out almost at the ground.

He found himself over the Nittagahara airfield. With two of the Zeros pressing him closely and others following Lieutenant Stone he swerved sharply to avoid a Betty bomber which was just taking off. Apparently one Zero matched his turn but the other didn't for they collided. Then both crashed in to the Betty. Without firing a shot he downed the three Jap planes.

He also shot down two other Zeros that day, becoming an ace and running his score of kills to seven.

The top ace in action with the Tactical Air Force was Marine Captain Kenneth J. Walsh of Brooklyn, N.Y., who scored 20 kills in the Solomon Islands sky battles to become the nation's number two ace at that time. A Congressional Medal of Honor holder, his Flying Deuces Squadron, VMF-222, arrived at Okinawa late in the campaign and he saw only two Jap planes in flight.

"Ten of us saw two Zeros at the same time, and it was strictly a race," he said. "They split, and I was lucky enough to win the race for the one which went to the right."

The 29-year-old Irishman, who began his aviation career as a mechanic and then went from grease monkey to flying buck private, flew numerous fighter-bomber strikes from Okinawa against Jap airfields and shipping. Since the start of the war he had flown more than 100 such unspectacular but highly dangerous and effective missions.

"I wish I could have been here from the start," he told me. "If the war continues I may get another crack at the Japs. But I'm not out here to try to set any record. I'm just out here to kill Japs."

The Okinawa aces of the Tactical Air Force, with their previous kills and Okinawa shoot downs, were:

Name	Previous Kills	Okinawa Kills	Total Kills
Captain Kenneth Walsh	20	1	21
Captain Jefferson J. DeBlanc	8	1	9
Captain Judge E. Wolf*	2	7	9
Second Lieutenant William P. Brown		7	7
First Lieutenant J.J. O'Keefe		7	7

Name	Previous Kills	Okinawa Kills	Total Kills
First Lieutenant Jack Pittman Jr.	7		7
Second Lieutenant J.W. Ruhsam		7	7
Second Lieutenant R.J. Stone*		7	7
Second Lieutenant R. Wade		7	7
First Lieutenant J.V. Dillard		6	6
Second Lieutenant D.F. Durnford		6	6
Major G.C. Axtell		6	6
Captain Robert Baird		6	6
Major J.C. Dorroh		6	6
*First Lieutenant Stanley J. Lustic	1	5	6
Major J.B. Mass	4.5	1.5	6
Major Perry L. Shuman	6		6
First Lieutenant F.A. Terrill		6	6
Captain H.J. Valentine		6	6
First Lieutenant W.L. Hood		5.5	5.5
Captain Floyd C. Kirkpatrick		5.5	5.5
Second Lieutenant S.C. Alley		5	5
First Lieutenant Richard H. Anderson*		5	5
First Lieutenant C.W. Drake		5	5
First Lieutenant W. Farrell		5	5
First Lieutenant William H. Mathis*		5	5
Second Lieutenant Selva E. McGinty		5	5
Captain W.E. Singler	4	1	5
Captain John E. Vogt*		5	5
First Lieutenant A.P. Wells		5	5

*Army Pilots

Another now-famous squadron which underwent the repeated bombings and shelling at Okinawa and lashed back mightily at the enemy was the Old Crow Squadron, VPB-118, of the Navy's fleet Air Wing One. With big four-engine Consolidated Privateers, the Navy's single-tail version of the B-24 Liberator, the Old Crow Squadron blasted out perhaps the best patrol bombing record in the history of Naval Aviation.

Arriving at Okinawa on April 24, the big Privateers were the first land-based bombers to penetrate the Japan Sea, and the first to fly strikes from Okinawa against Japan, and China.

Like pirates of old, the Privateers attacked enemy shipping, playing a major role in driving it from the China Sea and the Yellow Sea. The Privateers reported the positions of Jap destroyers and cruisers, and singly or in pairs tackled everything else in sight. They sank Jap freighters and tankers almost every day, and shot down many enemy fighter planes which attempted to intercept them.

I flew on one of these marauder missions with Lieutenant George T. King of Seattle, Wash., a former frosh crewman from University of Washington which he attended from 1936 to 1941. Pilot of the other Privateer in our division was Lieutenant Robert M. Finely of Holdenville, Okla. We took off after an early morning rain storm and winged northward between layers of cumulous clouds.

Soon we sighted two ships, and flew close enough to identify them as friendly destroyers. Hour after hour we droned northward... Lieutenant King and his co-pilot, effervescent Ensign Bernard Dunn of Reading, Pa. at the controls... crack machine gunners alert and ready in their power turrets. It was such a smooth flight that I catnapped at times—until we reached a position west of Korea.

To our left jutted a rugged island about two miles long with two tiny native villages tucked near the eastern beach at the base of a steep ridge. At the south end of the island on a jutting rock was a lighthouse and radio-weather station. We circled low past the villages and headed for the radio-weather station.

"All right, get on him," ordered Lieutenant King.

Tracers from our machine guns ripped into the compact cluster of neat buildings. Those naval aerial gunners can really shoot.

"Where's your bombsight?" I asked, standing at the cockpit entrance between the pilot and co-pilot.

"We don't have one. It's just seaman's eye," replied Lieutenant King.

Then I realized what he meant. He was going to fly so low he couldn't miss. Lower and lower we flew as we approached our target. It seemed as if he was trying to shear the tops from the buildings with the Privateer's broad wings. The plane was vibrating from the loud, heavy-hammering caliber .50 machine guns. Now we were only 100 yards away. Just as the target went out of sight Lieutenant King pressed the bomb release button. Our plane seemed to bounce up a bit and become lighter. We passed directly over the station, clearing it not more than 50 feet.

Then we looked back. He had scored a direct hit with three thousand pounds of bombs, armed with four-second delay fuses to give us time to clear the target. There was a terrific explosion which showered shrapnel, rocks and timber in all directions. Our tail gunner still was hitting the station with tracers. Fortunately for us, there was no return anti-aircraft fire. As close as we flew, they couldn't have missed us.

We circled and made another strafing run. Then Lieutenant Finley made an equally low bombing and strafing run from the opposite direction and dumped another 3000 pounds of bombs at the edge of the station. We saw the already damaged buildings tremble from the concussion.

In rapid succession we made two more strafing runs, then circled and winged homeward—leaving in our wake the shattered remnants of another Jap military installation.

"I'm sorry it wasn't a more exciting flight," Lieutenant King said half-apologetically as we stepped from the plane after our 1200-mile hop.

"Gosh," I replied. "I'm glad we all got back!"

Two crews from the Old Crow Squadron were lost, and so were several from other Navy four-engine patrol bomber squadron which operated from Okinawa during the latter part of the campaign.

On May 3 three of the squadron's Privateers, piloted by Lieutenant M.V. Montgomery, Lieutenant P.E. Pottes and Lieutenant H.J. Thompson, swept over Kanoya Naval air base in Japan at tree-top level. They strafed two planes circling for landings, beat off an attack by a third plane and dumped 60 100-pound bombs in crowded parking revetments.

During the next crowded four days Lieutenant Commander Arthur F. Ferwell Jr., and Lieutenant N.M. Keiser shot down two enemy planes over Kunsan air field in Korea. Lieutenant Finley entered the mouth of a cove harboring seven Jap destroyers and burned an anchored tanker. Lieutenant J.S. Serrill picked off a freighter in a convoy from under the noses of escorting warships. Lieutenant Montgomery brought back a length of hawser in the wing of his badly-mangled plane after a tanker exploded under him during a low-level attack.

Soft-spoken Lieutenant Commander Farwell of Chicago, who succeeded Commander C.K. Harper as squadron commanding officer, turned his big four-engine Privateer into a pursuit plane one day and engaged in one of the most unusual dog fights of the war. Off the Korean coast he sighted an enemy plane and gave full throttle. The single-engine Jap Val circled and danced around a string of small but high islands, with the big Privateer doing wingovers and tight turns in hot pursuit. Lieutenant Commander Farwell kept maneuvering to bring as many of his gun turrets as possible into action, while above him at 2000 feet flew his wingman, cheering him on, advising of the Val's position when it was out of view behind one of the islands, and laughing at the sight which he said looked like a cow chasing a rabbit.

In desperation the Jap pilot made an inside turn and apparently attempted a water landing. The big Privateer banked and the bow and starboard waist guns slashed the middle of the Jap plane. It nosed straight down and went in.

On the return Lieutenant Commander Farwell sank a 1500 ton freighter with two direct hits. Then he and his wingman tackled a 3000-ton oiler, and left it dead in the water. But Farwell's plane was riddled with 20 millimeter fire which knocked out two engines, the hydraulic system and the bomb release mechanism. The pilot made a water landing and the plane broke into three pieces, but after a feverish struggle all the crew was extricated. Three who were out and wounded were placed on the tiny raft which had been salvaged. Half an hour later they were rescued by a Dumbo-twin-engine flying boat, which landed in heavy seas to make the pickup. The other Privateer circled and flew escort for the rescue, and repulsed the attack of a Jap twin-engine Nick fighter.

The ill-fated flight was on May 13, and there were 13 men on the Privateer. A month before on Friday, April 13, Lieutenant Commander Farwell had to ditch a Privateer off Tinian, and on that day also had 13 men aboard.

"No more flights with 13 men aboard," chorused his crew.

On May 16 Lieutenant Commander Farwell and Lieutenant Finley were attacked by four Jack fighter planes. Both Privateers were hit by Jap 20 millimeter cannon fire. By deft maneuvering the two big planes each kept six caliber .50 machine guns firing at the Jap fighters all the time, and they shot down two of the attackers and badly damaged a third.

Once Lieutenant Finley flew over a Korean harbor in the face of heavy anti-aircraft fire and sank a 10,000-ton freighter. In two days he sank four ships.

Lieutenant Commander Farwell celebrated the Fourth of July by leading a six-plane flight over Japan. The Privateers destroyed seven trains, three railroad tunnels, three railroad bridges, one rail yard, two power stations and one weather-radio station. Admiral William F. Halsey sent a note of commendation saying:

"A well done to your boys for their anti-Casey Jones job."

During the Okinawa campaign the Old Crow Squadron sank 67 ships and damaged 76 more to account for nearly 200,000 tons of shipping. The score also included 12 planes destroyed and five damaged.

The Japs hated to see the Privateers approaching.

During the campaign the marine pilots of the Fighter Command shot down 504 enemy planes, and army pilots downed an additional 129.

The superb airmanship of these pilots, their bold and aggressive attacks, and the risks they took above and beyond the call of duty to save the lives of all of us at Okinawa—these things always will live in my memory.

One day the USS Hadley, one of our destroyers on picket patrol, was beset by a large flight of Jap suicide planes. Then came another flight of attackers... and another... several more flights. Marine and navy fighter planes sped to the rescue, and a terrific air battle ensued. The Hadley's gunners did a terrific job, shooting down attacking planes by the dozens. Still more waves of planes came. More than 100 of the Kamikaze planes hurled themselves at the destroyer. A marine pilot radioed to the ship's captain:

"I'm out of ammunition, but I'm sticking with you."

Then the Leatherneck flew his Corsair between the ship and an attacking Jap plane, causing the Jap to swerve and miss the ship. Another plane attacked. Again the marine pulled up and almost stalled, causing the Jap to turn away. A third time the Corsair pulled up in a stall. This time the attacking Jap plane swerved, then tried frantically to crash into the ship, which already had been hit by several suicide planes. The Jap missed the ship, but struck some of the rigging and crashed into the sea.

All this time the Hadley's anti-aircraft guns were firing furiously, but the marine pilot and his wingman continued to fly at masthead height through the flak and drive Jap planes away from the ship. Later the ship's captain said:

"I'll take my ship to the shores of Tokyo if those marine pilots go with me."

Chapter 15

Bartering Blood for Victory

In the bloody hills and ridges of southern Okinawa, Jap troops made their most bitter and effective stand of the war. They blasted our ground forces with their mightiest concentration of fire power. They employed battle strategies far superior to any they previously used. And they had the advantage of probably the best defensive terrain in the history of modern warfare.

Okinawa was part of the Japanese homeland... the doorstep to Tokyo... the portal of doom for the Japanese empire. Into the violent conflict the Japs hurled themselves with all the fanatical, fatalistic fervor of doomed men.

The Okinawa campaign was not a quick island blitz. It raged for 82 hellish days.

The Japs had more heavy artillery than ever before—not just single guns, but batteries of guns. They had more and bigger mortars; many more machine guns, and an endless supply of hand grenades and demolition charges. As many as 15,000 shells a day rained on our forces. The Japs' heavy concentrations of machine guns gave their ground troops much heavier fire power than they previously had when armed chiefly with bolt action rifles.

"We will take our time and kill them gradually," said Lieutenant General Buckner. "They'll have to be blasted out with a blowtorch and a corkscrew."

The marines secured the Motobu peninsula and northern Okinawa ahead of schedule; then hurled themselves into the stubborn Jap defense on southern Okinawa. The First Marine Division relieved the battle-weary 96th Army Division, and on May 2 and 3 blasted forward 900 yards in a drive toward Naha.

Early the next morning the Japs made a counter landing of 650 troops along the west coast beaches behind the marine lines, and another landing of 65 machines gun and demolition troops still farther north to strike at rear concentrations of tanks and command posts.

A bitter beachhead battle raged in early morning blackness, and the Leathernecks killed 200 of the Nips on the reefs opposite the Machinato airfield. By mid-morning the marines pocketed the main force of Japs at Kuwan, and wiped out all the attackers by night. Other marine units killed all but 10 of the suicide demolition troops who landed farther north. The remaining Japs hid and carried on sniper and terrorist activities until eliminated, one by one.

While the First Division was repulsing this surprise rear attack, it continued its forward push another 600 yards that day, and reached the Asa-Kawa estuary, within a mile of the capital city of Naha.

Moving down the center of the battle line came the 77th Army Division, which had relieved the 27th Army Division, while on the east coast the Seventh Army Division drove a tank-led spearhead 1400 yards into the Japs' east coast defenses. The 96th Division rested a few days and then returned to the lines, while the 27th was given patrol duty in northern Okinawa.

In the next few days the First Marine Division assaulted across the Asa-Kawa estuary, built a tank bridge across it despite heavy Jap artillery and mortar fire, and then began squeezing inland toward the formidable hills of Shuri Castle.

Into the battle for southern Okinawa Major General Roy S. Geiger, a commanding general of the Marine Third Amphibious Corps, now sent the Sixth Marine Division. The Sixth Marine Division pressed southward toward Naha, and then eastward.

This swung the Japs' defensive line into a huge crescent, and doubled the length of their line which they had hoped to keep short across the narrow isthmus of southern Okinawa. The First Marines Division pressed southward and eastward toward Shuri. The two Army divisions were employing similar tactics on the eastern half of southern Okinawa.

"Well, Gunny the European war is over, but we've still got lots of Japs here to kill, said Corporal Jim Brown as "I" Company, 29th Regiment, Sixth Marine Division, moved toward the front lines just over ridge from the outskirts of Naha.

"Yes, the war started in the Pacific and it's finishing here," replied Gunnery Sergeant Taylor meditatively.

More than 400 Jap artillery and mortar shells landed in the small area where "I" Company bivouacked that night. The next morning, Sunday, May 13, the company moved into the battle lines, and I accompanied them. I wanted to learn more about these infantrymen who fight face to face with the enemy and have the roughest and bloodiest assignment of war.

Sergeant Joe Dube, former New York United Press writer who was a marine combat correspondent, went with me. The stench of dead Japs filled the air. Artillery, machine gun and rifle sounded constantly. We were hitch-hiking in the jeep of a sight-sear, who didn't want to get too close to the front lines. He looked about nervously every time a shell exploded.

"Those are our guns, and the front lines are about five miles ahead," lied Joe.

A quarter of a mile farther we found the "I" Company boys and thanked the jeep driver for the lift. He started to drive on southward.

"I wouldn't go any farther," advised Joe. "The Japs are sweeping the road with machine gun cross-fire about 50 yards ahead."

At that instant machine guns barked savagely over the next knoll. The frenzied driver wheeled his jeep about and took off like a Corsair.

In single file we advanced eastward through a narrow valley, keeping the crests of ridges between ourselves and the enemy positions.

"Keep 10-yard intervals and look out for duds and land mines." ordered Corporal Brown, who was acting sergeant and platoon guide.

Pausing to await further orders, we found Gunny Taylor directing other advancing elements and keeping them from bunching up. The Japs had been driven from that area only the day before. A few hundred yards ahead machine gun and rifle fire fights were in progress, and artillery and mortar shells were exploding.

"Keep watching the ridges for snipes or a counter-attack," said Taylor.

Joe Dube introduced me to Corporal Brown and Gunny Taylor. I recognized in them unusual qualities of leadership. Taylor looked at me with quizzical eyes, and pondered before answering my question. His thoughts ran deep, and true.

"Yes. We really took a pounding last night," said the 32-year-old Taylor. "We were shaking in our fox holes all night. When the shells screamed over we'd tighten up. Then they'd land and we'd begin shaking again. We had the shakes all night."

Artillery shells exploded only 15 feet from Taylor's fox holes on both sides, and showered him with dirt and rocks. Eight men of "I" Company were wounded and two killed by the heavy barrage. PFC John W. Moneypenny of Akron, O., and PFC John Zuk Jr., or New Market, N.H., were killed. The wounded were Sergeant Clarence C. Willoughby of Clarence City, N. C., Corporal Carl Cook Jr., of Hurricane, W. Va., Corporal Jesse N. Johnson of Follansbee, W. Va., PFC Francis J. Lally of Philadelphia, Pa., PFC Henry E. La Voie of Salem, Mass., PFC James P. Menefee, PFC Richard C. Woodard of Dundie, N.Y., and Private Hollis R. Nichols of Ashland, Mo.

Word was passed from the front for us to move up. I met First Lieutenant Lawrence P. Sullivan, leader of the third platoon, and Sergeant Robert A. Sioss of Jamaica, N.Y., the acting platoon sergeant. Joe and I went ahead to an observation post, and a few minutes later Lieutenant Sullivan and Sergeant Sioss both were wounded by sniper fire. Private Augustine Perez of New Orleans also was wounded that day.

Captain Walter E. Jorgenson had been advanced from company commander to battalion executive officer. The new commander of "I" Company was tall, wiry Captain Philip J. Mylod of Glen Ridge, N.J., a courageous aggressive leader who exposed himself constantly to enemy fire. His men would follow him anywhere. Captain Mylod called Corporal Brown forward and made him leader of the third platoon in place of Lieutenant Sullivan, who was evacuated.

Brown had been outstanding in combat at Green Hill on the Motobu peninsula. Wounded, he went over the hill from the hospital to rejoin his outfit. He knew combat tactics. He had attended the Marine Corps officer's candidate school—one of the most rigorous military training courses ever devised. Two days before graduation he was "busted." He failed a map reading test by a fraction of a point.

Jim Brown longed for another chance to become an officer. At Camp Le June, N.C., he met charming Kitsy Pepper, daughter of Marine Colonel Claude W. Pepper, who later became Brigadier General.

"I think a lot of Kitsy," Jim told me. "But it was a bit difficult for me as an enlisted man to court her when she lived in officer's country with her father."

Lieutenant Colonel Wright had set up Third Battalion headquarters in front of one of the ever-present tombs. Medical corpsman were busy giving first aid to the wounded, then placing them on ambulances and stretcher-carrying jeeps for movement to field hospitals over roads which were constantly under Jap sniper, mortar and shell fire. Some of the wounded were sheltered inside the big triple-compartment tomb, beside the bones of dead Okinawans.

There was a steady stream of stretcher cases. One was Corporal Robert V. Bastin, A 19-year-old Leatherneck from Reading, O. The day before, his knee was smashed by enemy machine gun fire. Through the long, hot afternoon he played dead, only 100 yards from three Jap machine gun nests.

When darkness came the sandy-haired marine arranged his pack and helmet on the trail, then painfully edged away. About midnight two souvenir-hunting Japs crept up. He killed both with his Browning automatic rifle. An hour later another Jap prowler approached and was shot. Bastin waited, and another Jap emerged from a cave to stalk him. His BAR spoke, and raised his score to four dead Japs.

An advancing patrol found Bastin about noon. He was nonchalantly lying on his stretcher and eating a can of pork and beans when I saw him arrive at the battalion headquarters aid station.

Lieutenant Colonel Wright was marking maps, directing his three companies and coordinating their attack with flanking Units. He ordered Captain Mylod to assault with "I" Company toward a village west of Queen hill. The Third Battalion's "H" Company was advancing toward the village against stiff opposition up the Asa river draw on the left, while "G" Company was battling fiercely at the south end of Queen hill.

In single file we moved out, Captain Mylod and a guide at the head of the column. Then came Corporal Brown, Gunny Taylor and myself. I carried a revolver and a camera. We moved along a protective bank and then across an open field. Captain Mylod sprinted like a deer across the opening, and the rest of us followed suit. After half a dozen had crossed, Nambu machine gun fire began, sweeping the field. Leathernecks would hit the deck for a few seconds; then get up and run rapidly forward. More did the same until all were across. They moved so fast none was hit. We had the same experience crossing two more open fields.

I used my remaining film and started back. I guess I set some new speed records running back across those openings. I wormed along on my belly like a snake to get part of the way across the first opening. The last one was toughest. It was a full 75 yards. I sat at the edge of a tomb with a small cluster of marines and thought things over a bit. A heavy Jap mortar barrage started. At first the shells exploded to the rear, near the command post. But each succeeding blast came closer. Then one landed on the knoll above us. We breathed easier. The barrage had hurdled over us and missed our position.

It was late afternoon. We had been fired on heavily by hidden Japs, but we hadn't seen a live Jap all day.

"How can you fight them when you can't see them?" asked several marines.

Still pinned down by enemy fire, we started to sing "Happy Birthday" to Corporal Philip F. Zito of Newark, N.J., who was 20 years of age that day. But we started on the wrong key, and then were interrupted by a dull explosion which made the ground beneath us quiver.

"What was that?" I asked.

"Oh, just a Jap in a cave below this hill committing hari kari," said Zito. "That went on all last night back on that other ridge."

Time was wasting, and I had a long ways to go to be back at Fighter Command headquarters by 6 o'clock the next morning. I dashed across the last 75-yard field alone, taking cover briefly in a deep ditch at the halfway mark. Next time I visited the "I" Company men, one remarked:

"There's that cameramen who runs so fast."

Ironically, it was a borrowed camera and all the film had been previously fogged. Not a picture was good.

Back on the next slope another marine and I suddenly became the target of Nambu fire. Before I realized what was happening he shouted:

"Hit the deck."

We flattened ourselves on the exposed slope while a dozen machine gun bullets danced within six feet of us.

"Run for the road." he said in a few seconds.

It was a good 50- yard dash, and I relaxed as we reached the road.

"Hit the deck." he ordered.

Down I dived, and not a second too soon. Machine gun bullets whizzed directly over me, cutting blades on grass and kicking dust on me. But I was safely sheltered by a two-foot bank. I took a helmet from a dead Jap for a souvenir and departed.

"I" Company remained that night where I had left them, but after dark Corporal Brown moved the third platoon close to the village and somewhat to the right, where he had the men dig in. Some were a bit reluctant, because marines seldom move at night. No sooner had they moved than a heavy artillery and mortar barrage began falling in the positions they had vacated. There wasn't a casualty in the platoon that night.

Captain Mylod tied in his "I" Company lines in with "H" Company on the left and "G" Company on the right, dashing repeatedly across open fields and drawing heavy fire from machine guns. Then he returned to the command post to confer with Lieutenant Colonel Wright.

Corporal Brown sent his runner, Private John O'Leary, for water and entrenching tools, which he obtained at a supply dump which Gunny Taylor set up just to the rear. When all were dug in, Brown called a meeting of his squad leaders.

"We'll function just as we have been," said Brown, who has assumed the full responsibilities of a commissioned officer in leading the third platoon.

"The better we get along, the more of us will come out. We want to gain ground and keep casualties to a minimum. When daylight comes keep everyone in his fox hole until we get orders to assault."

In the morning PFC John F. Rossi, an Italian boy from Syracuse, N.Y., who had lots of moxy, raised up to look for enemy gun positions and was fatally wounded in the chest.

Captain Mylod joined Brown and led the third platoon in a fast assault against the village. Lieutenant Stone assaulted with his first platoon through the village on the left flank and joined his lines with "H" Company. The marines were under withering machine gun fire as they charged. Ten men of the first platoon were wounded, while in Brown's platoon 10 were wounded and three killed.

Captain Mylod joined Brown and led the third platoon in a fast assault against the village. Lieutenant Stone assaulted with his first platoon through the village on the left flank and joined his lines with "H" Company. The Marines were under withering machinegun fire as they charged.

After advancing 300 yards, the third platoon set up a skirmish line and put up a heavy field of fire while casualties were removed. At the start of the advance Brown killed a Nambu machine gunner with bazooka fire. The big push drove the Japs back from most of the village. The first platoon sealed a number in caves with demolition charges.

Captain Mylod returned to check the position of supporting units, and Brown led the third platoon in a fast charge up the saddle of Queen's ridge. Although under constant fire, his platoon gained the saddle without further casualties.

"G" Company assaulting up the east side of Queen's hill, was under flanking fire from nearby Sugar Loaf hill, and casualties ran high. The third platoon was ordered to advance, and Brown moved his men, two at a time top speed, across the area under fire from Sugar Loaf. Then he led a rifle and BAR squad which charged with fixed bayonets and drove the remaining Nips off the nose of Queen's ridge. Demolition men and a flame thrower followed rapidly, cleaning out and sealing caves. They knocked out two Japs 47 millimeter anti-tank guns. The advance cost two more casualties.

On the face of Queen's hill Corporal Brown set up a firing line with two men in each fox hole. They were exposed to enemy fire from the front and from both flanks.

Brown returned to confer with Captain Mylod and Captain Jorgenson, and found that fire from Sugar Loaf hill had wounded Captain Mylod and Second Lieutenant Thomas J. Melcher of Philadelphia, leader of the second platoon. Even while being evacuated Captain Mylod was waving encouragement to his men and telling his stretcher bearers to take their time and not work too hard.

Placing Lieutenant Brooks in charge of "I" Company, Captain Jorgenson jumped off with "G" Company on an assault against Charley hill to give support to the 22nd Marine Regiment's Second Battalion, which was assaulting Sugar Loaf hill that evening.

Major Courtney, executive officer of the Second Battalion, had only 40 men, the remnants of three rifle companies which had been all but wiped out during several days of constant battling.

Sugar Loaf hill, overlooking Okinawa's capital city of Naha, was honeycombed with caves and pillboxes, and covered by flanking fire from nearby Half-Moon hill. Here the Japs made their most bitter stand. On the crest of Sugar Loaf hill were dozens of heavy batteries of mortars. Several thousand Japs were entrenched in the immediate area.

Major Courtney and Captain Jorgenson coordinated their attack plans. Then the major turned to his troops and said:

"Come on men, let's go."

At top speed they raced across an opening under withering machine gun and rifle fire, and assaulted the forward slope of Sugar Loaf hill, the major in the lead.

"Forward," shouted Captain Jorgenson.

Pistol in hand, he led "G" Company in an assault on Charley hill just to the north of Sugar Loaf. With him went Lieutenant Brooks and two squads from "I" Company's second platoon.

Captain Jorgenson took Charley hill and dug his men in on its southern tip under the guns of Sugar Loaf, while Major Courtney and his men captured the forward slope of Sugar Loaf under terrific machine gun, rifle and mortar fire. Big artillery shells from Shuri exploded in their midst. Japs on top of the ridge hurled hundreds of hand grenades down on Major Courtney and his men, but they held their positions. A constant stream of Jap parachute flares made the battlefield light as day. Casualties ran high.

With this battle raging, Jim Brown returned to his men who were dug in and holding the point of Queen hill.

"We're exposed in front and on both flanks, but we're going to hold this hill," Brown told his men. "Don't fire more than one shot a Jap. We don't want to reveal our position."

By the light of almost constant flares they saw the battle raging on Sugar Loaf and Charley hills. About 10:30 p.m., a Jap patrol moved out from Sugar Loaf hill toward Queen hill. Brown had just returned from making a lone dash more than half a mile back to the command post to report his platoon's position to the incredulous officers in charge. Armed only with a pistol and a knife, he ran swiftly and silently, freezing in his tracks when the Japs fired flares. His men were glad to see him return.

"Hey, men, ain't we having ourselves a time on this hill?" asked Brown, repeating the words Corporal Miller said when he was wounded at Green hill on the Motobu peninsula. That became a by-phrase with the third platoon, and brought much-needed laugher and relaxation in many tight spots.

A single shot rang out. One of Brown's men wounded a Jap approaching up the trail. The Jap wounded soldier lay a few paces away, moaning and squirming. At any instant he might recover and toss a hand grenade into the cave where Brown had set up his machine gunners and aid station.

Knife in hand, Brown crawled stealthily forward. Then he lunged and drove his knife into the Jap's side. Twice more the blade flashed, each time plunging into the Jap's throat. Jim took the Jap's hand to check his pulse. It had almost stopped. Another flare lighted the sky, and Jim darted back into the cave.

Now another shot rang out, and another moaning and wriggling form lay beside the first Jap, who now was motionless. Jim's heart still pounded from his last ordeal. But again there was danger of a hand grenade.

With his bloody bowie knife in hand, he again crept forward. The form raised up and wild eyes glared at Brown from a bushy, hairy head. It looked like a wild man, or an animal. Brown recoiled and scrambled back into the cave. It was the most terrifying moment of his life.

Was it an animal, or a Jap? He pondered. If it was a Jap, they could expect a hand grenade. He took a sip of water; then made up his mind.

Again he crawled forward. Then he lunged and buried his knife to the hilt in the thing's stomach. He held it there an instant, and the body went limp. He started to withdraw the knife, but it was stuck. He returned to the cave without it. His men looked at him with drawn faces and wondering but admiring eyes.

It was raining hard now, and water trickled into their fox holes. Artillery shells were exploding nearby. Japs were on three sides of them, and on the prowl. In three days more than a third of the platoon had been killed or wounded. They could see that the battle was going tough for the marines on Sugar Loaf and Charley hills. The Japs might make a breakthrough at any time. It was a night of horror.

"Now fellows, I want to tell you something," said Brown. "I'm going to sleep. Don't wake me up unless there's something REALLY important."

Again they laughed, and Brown relaxed in his first sleep for two nights. At day breaker O'Leary awakened him.

"Brown! Get up! What is that?"

The second Jap he had stabbed was a beautiful nurse. She had removed the knife from her stomach and bandaged the wound, as well as bandaging another wound where the rifle shot had broken her leg. Jim crept forward with another knife. The Jap woman looked at him with big, blurry eyes. He didn't have the heart to kill her. So decided to hold her for intelligence. She began dragging herself slowly back toward the Jap lines, but didn't go far. She died, with unused hand grenades on her belt.

It was Tuesday, May 15. Gunny Taylor brought up food and water and helped install a telephone line. While he was there the third platoon underwent a thunderous shelling by the Japs' eight-inch naval guns from Naha. Shells fell at the rate of one a minute. Gunny's deep laugh was a reassuring sound. The big guns were registered in on them, and continued firing. Helpless, there was nothing to do but wait... and hope... and pray. Most marines in battle pray.

When the artillery barrage lifted, Lieutenant Stone's first platoon gave supporting fire for an advance by "H" Company on the left, and killed dozens of routed Japs. Then Lieutenant Colonel Wright came up and told Lieutenant Stone:

"Move forward and assault through that draw. Tie in with "G" Company on Charley ridge. "H" Company will advance later and tie in on your left flank. Move up as fast as you can. And by the way, you're commander of "I" Company now. Brooks was wounded last night."

"My God! They got Brooks," said Lieutenant Stone. "Okay, colonel. We'll move out immediately."

Lieutenant Stone advised Corporal Brown by phone of the plan, and asked for supporting fire from the nose of queen hill. Brown's third platoon unleashed a heavy barrage of rifle and machine gun fire, and Lieutenant Stone's men drove the Japs back and advanced to their objective without further casualties.

Meanwhile the battle for Sugar Loaf hill went bad for the marines. Captain Jorgenson and his men held their positions all day Tuesday on the exposed forward nose of Charley hill. They were pinned down by fire from Sugar Loaf hill and were under terrific barrages of mortars and artillery. Strong men were at the point of breaking.

Unleashing a powerful attack, the Japs tossed hand grenades down onto the marines and sprayed them with machine gun and rifle fire. Major Courtney was killed on the bald, forward slope of Sugar Loaf hill Tuesday morning, and every one of his men was killed or wounded. Captain Lee Mable of the 29th Regiment went to the aid of Major Courtney's force and assaulted Sugar Loaf hill with a platoon of men. They were repulsed with heavy casualties. Murderous flanking fire came from nearby Half-Moon hill and other Jap-held ridges.

At dusk Captain Jorgenson put up a smoke screen and moved his men back to more protected positions on top of Charley hill, and evacuated the wounded. Lieutenant Brooks, who had been wounded by shrapnel the night before and was delirious, was struck twice more by small arms fire while being evacuated. On the crest of Charley hill, Captain Jorgenson set up machine gun and rifle positions to sweep the top of Sugar Loaf hill.

That night First Lieutenant Sherman B. Ruth, 23, of Glochester, Mass., the commanding officer of "G" Company, was wounded by exploding artillery fire. Hurt pretty badly, but in good spirits, he came hobbling down a path with the aid of two men and greeted Lieutenant Stone.

"Babe, how about trying to eat something?" asked Lieutenant Stone.

"Thanks. I guess I haven't eaten for 36 hours," replied the wounded officer.

He told Second Lieutenant Owens to take over as "G" Company commander. A bit of fat from Lieutenant Ruth's wounded knee worked into his blood stream, and he died three days later.

Gunny Taylor was there helping evacuate other "G" Company casualties and loading them into Amtracks which had brought up supplies. Lieutenant Stone ordered Corporal Brown to hold his position on Queen hill another night. Then he reformed his "I" Company in preparation for a big push all along the lines on Wednesday.

The 22nd Marines were scheduled to assault Sugar Loaf hill again, and Lieutenant Colonel Wright's Third Battalion was committed to attack heavily-defended Half-Moon hill, from which heavy machine gun and mortar fire had been directed against leathernecks who previously assaulted Sugar Loaf hill.

Lieutenant Stone, First Sergeant Berry and Gunny Taylor sat down and listed the "I" Company casualties for the two days just ended. Killed or fatally wounded were PFC Thomas A. Lenahan of Girardville, Pa., PFC Earl D. Whatley of Alexander, La., Private Harold E. Richardson, Corpsman "Chick" Demuth, Private Robert E. Myers of Mercersburg, Pa., Private James K. Schrock and Private Jean Winchester of Smithville, Ark.

Wounded during those two days were Captain Mylod, Second Lieutenant Melcher, First Lieutenant Brooks, Sergeant William E. Cromling, Corporal Ralph M. Heller of Dewitt, Neb., Corporal Harold L. Nichols of Wayne, Mich., Corporal Samuel D. Shotwell of Ocean View, Va., Corporal Gerald A. Tellinghuisen of Lenox, S. D., Corporal Floyd D. Terry of Charlotte, N C., Corporal Clark A. Thornton, PFC William C. Cherry of Johnsonburg, Pa., PFC Paul R. Miller, PFC Vernon Rogers, PFC Dominick J. Simone of New York City, PFC Lorenzo D. Sparks, PFC Woodrow Steedly of Charleston, S.C., PFC Martin Sucoff of Brooklyn, N.Y., PFC Paul E. Voelker of Monongahela, Pa., Corporal Marcel J. Wicka of Arlington, Va., Corporal Richard O. Stucker of Columbus, O., PFC Harrison F. Hanzlik, Private Charles G. Katavolos, Private Francis J. Kearney, Private Walter G. Nangano, Private James R. Peebles of New Castle, Pa., Private Grover C. Shankle, PFC George M. Breaux of Houma, La., PFC Samuel A. Mullett of Middlefield, O., PFC Donald G. Shakeshaft of New York City, PFC Daniel B. Steedly of Charleston, S.C., Private Paul A. Nelson and Private Vernon W. Mohrman.

Evacuated because of sickness was Private William H. Davidson of Baltimore, Md. Shrapnel struck Corporal Brown on the nose, but he remained with his third platoon.

Since arriving at Okinawa, "I" Company had suffered almost 50 per cent casualties. Replacements filled the ranks after the Motobu peninsula battles, but again big gaps were appearing. Casualties since the start of the Okinawa campaign now ran 76 per cent in Corporal Brown's third platoon.

The Leathernecks were bartering blood for victory... killing Japs rapidly, but gaining ground slowly. And the worst fighting was yet to come!

Chapter 16

The Fall of Sugar Loaf and Half-Moon Hills

The bloody battle for Sugar Loaf hill was renewed on Wednesday, May 16. The Third Battalion, 22nd Marines, assaulted that Jap stronghold, while Lieutenant Colonel Wright's Third Battalion of the 29th Marine Regiment pushed across the narrow gauge railroad running from Kadena to Naha and attacked Half-Moon hill, several hundred yards northeast of Sugar Loaf hill. The First Battalion advanced on the left flank toward Woody hill, north of Half Moon hill.

Lieutenant Colonel Wright was at an advanced command and observation post on top of Charley hill to help direct the coordinated push, which started at 1 p.m.

A few hours earlier a Jap mortar shell exploded at the command post, wounding Captain Jorgensen in the stomach. After hospital treatment, he returned to the Third battalion a week later. Platoon Sergeant John D. Heim, who had been acting leader of the first platoon, was wounded that morning by sniper fire.

"I felt like I had lost my right arm," said Lieutenant Stone. "Heim was so well liked that three men cried when he was hit."

Lieutenant Stone placed Corporal Frenchy Francoeur in charge of the first platoon.

Supported by tanks and heavy artillery and mortar fire, the Third Battalion pushed forward. "G" Company, with only 100 remaining men, crossed the railroad tracks and moved up the southwest side of Half Moon hill. Lieutenant Stone advanced to the base of Half Moon hill with his first and second platoons, and "G" Company pushed upward to the top of Half Moon ridge.

The Japs withheld their fire as the Marines advanced into exposed areas. Then they unleashed a terrific counter-attack. Japs suddenly appeared on the ridges of Sugar Loaf and Half-Moon hills, tossing grenades and firing with rifles and Nambu machine guns. Cross-fire from well-camouflaged machine guns on Woody hill poured into the backs of the marines. From narrow slits in pillboxes boomed anti-tank shells from Jap 47 millimeter guns. And from the reverse slopes of half a dozen hills came Jap mortar fire.

On the left flank of the mile-long assault front the First Battalion was getting cross-fire from the hills surrounding Shuri Castle and from Woody hill. Lieutenant Stone placed his "I" Company men in skirmish positions and built up heavy fire at the flanks and against the top of Half-Moon hill. Then he ran back to the command post.

"Our flanks aren't covered," he told Lieutenant Colonel Wright. "They're shooting into our backs and cutting us to ribbons. I request permission to pull back to last night's position."

Half-Moon hill was 600 yards out ahead of either flank.

"Yes, I can see that your position is untenable," replied Lieutenant Colonel Wright. "Start an orderly withdrawal, but keep up a heavy field of fire and be sure to get all of your casualties out."

In small sections, all units withdrew to their previous positions while others kept up a heavy hail of fire. Those who returned first took new positions on Charley hill and helped cover the withdrawal. The 22nd Marines also had to pull back from Sugar Loaf hill.

After three hours of bloody battling there was a big job evacuating wounded. PFC Vernon N. "Chief" Haynes, an Indian heavy-weight boxer, made three trips, each time carrying a wounded buddy 500 yards back to the aid station under heavy enemy fire. The gallant Indian, from Moshpee, Mass., went back to evacuate another wounded buddy, but was killed by enemy fire.

Half-Moon hill and Sugar Loaf hill overlooking Naha were the gates to that city, as well as the key to Shuri Castle. The Japs continued their battle of attrition there, apparently being more interested in killing marines than in holding defensive positions. Losses were heavy on both sides. Each day the marines were exacting a heavy toll from the Jap garrison, but the Nips kept sending up more reserves.

Gunny Taylor brought supplies to Corporal Brown's men Wednesday afternoon with the aid of Pop Leach and PFC Glen Tincher, whose jeep seemed to go anywhere there was a marine. John O'Leary, runner for the third platoon and Brown's closest buddy, was shot in the head by a sniper and died while Pop Leach was taking him to an aid station.

Others of "I" Company who paid with their lives that day were Corporal George D. Carson of Newton Center, Mass., Corporal Ralph C. Shinn of Elba, Neb., and Chief Haynes.

The wounded were Platoon Sergeant Heim, Sergeant Jack L. Elliott, Sergeant Martin Presser, PFC Hydra S. Best, PFC William R.

Brew of Chepachek, R.I., PFC Arthur D. Brown of Montmorenci, S.C., PFC Julian C. Casey of Spartanburg, S.C., PFC Wade H. Cooper of Beaver Fall, Pa., PFC Malcolm Farrell, PFC Chester Gunn of Atamore, Ala., PFC Leo. E. Hartman of Baltimore, Ma., PFC Joseph Hogan of Audubon, N.J., PFC John A Marz of New Brunswick, N.J., PFC James H. Myers of Silver Springs, Md., Private Dalton F. Phillips of Atalissa, Ia., and Private Oscar F. Schaub.

Three others worn down by the incessant hell around them broke down and were evacuated because of battle fatigue, another name for combat shock.

That night Corporal Brown heard voices of marines far beyond the front lines.

He slipped into the darkness alone and between flares ran toward them. After going more than a quarter of a mile he shouted:

"Hey, marines!"

They recognized his voice.

"Brown, I knew if you were anywhere around you'd get us," said Corporal R.R. Miller, one of Brown's boot camp buddies.

Miller was shot in the stomach, and was returning with PFC Maurcie F. Vail of Little Falls, N.Y., who was wounded in the thigh. With them was PFC William J. Keaney.

No sooner had Brown gone to the aid of the wounded men than Gunny Taylor asked Pauk:

"Where's Brown?"

"Out there after some wounded men," replied Pauk.

Gunny Taylor and another marine plunged into the darkness after them. Pauk followed, although Taylor had repeated Brown's order for the corpsman to remain behind the lines in accordance with combat regulations. Corpsmen are too valuable to take unnecessary risks.

After going 300 yards, Taylor called to Brown:

"J.V., this is Zachariah. I'm coming out."

"Okay, Gunny, come on over," replied Brown.

Armed only with a pistol, two grenades and a knife, he had been trailing the other three marines to protect them from the rear. Brown sent Pauk ahead with the wounded. He and Taylor waited a few minutes, then followed. All returned safely.

There was only one way to victory. That was over the bodies of dead Japs. So back to the bloody slopes of Half Moon hill and Sugar Loaf hill the Leathernecks assaulted the next day—Thursday.

Field artillery units and warships surrounding southern Okinawa shelled the reverse slopes of the Jap-held hills Thursday morning, and our planes bombed, rocketed and strafed the positions heavily. The Japs with their "rat hole" defense holed up in their elaborate caves during the bombardment, then returned to their battle stations.

The reorganized Second Battalion of the 22nd Marine Regiment again assaulted Sugar Loaf hill, and "H" and "I" Companies renewed the attack on Half-Moon hill. The First Battalion moved forward and attacked the left flank of Half-Moon hill.

The third platoon spearheaded the assault up the face of Half-Moon hill, with Corporal Brown as leader. "H" Company assaulted on the right flank.

"I won't be off," Brown told Lieutenant Stone. "I'm going to hold the hill."

"You can do it," said the Lieutenant.

Sergeant Joe Sheer, a broad-shouldered, six-foot-one Leatherneck from Beaver Meadows, Pa., had taken over the machine gunners after the death of Gunnery Sergeant Doerr at Green Hill. Joe's machine gunners sprayed the ridge of Half-Moon hill while the marines charged rapidly to the top. Tanks also were brought up and added their fire.

Brown and his men were under heavy fire going up the barren face of Half-Moon hill. With his sub-machine gun, Sergeant Frank Lilly knocked out a Nambu machine gun nest on the flank.

The machine guns and tanks had to stop firing when the Leathernecks reached the top of the hill. Then the Japs counter-attacked.

A Jap officer charged over the hill, brandishing a Samarian sword. Private Walter J. Avelin brought his flame thrower into action. A stream of fire roasted the Jap officer to a crisp. More Japs followed, throwing grenades. As the Japs showed themselves the marines shot, and meanwhile tossed grenades like mad across the ridge.

Nambu cross-fire raked them from Woody hill and Sugar Loaf hill. Corporal Brown pulled half a dozen men from the adjoining first platoon and placed them in his lines to replace wounded and build up more strength where the Japs were directing their heaviest attack. Then he sent PFC George Gardner of Washington D.C. back to ask Gunny Taylor for more hand grenades, and to ask Lieutenant Stone to direct mortar fire against the reverse slope.

Jim placed two riflemen and a BAR-man at key points on the bald slope to cover the ridges, while the others deployed just below the ridge to pitch hand grenades. While he was busy directing this switch someone shouted:

"Brown! Look behind you."

He wheeled and saw five Nips poking rifles and Nambu machine guns over the ridge. He dropped down and fired rapidly. The Japs were only 10 yards away. He shot three through the face. Other marines picked off the remaining two.

Private Avelin was wounded by Nambu fire. Corpsman John Pauk gave him first aid and told him to stay there and keep the flame thrower going.

PFC Gardner was wounded in his dash back for more grenades, but continued. Soon First Lieutenant William G. Vellman's "I" Company mortar crews were raining shells into the Japs on Half-Moon hill's reverse slope.

Supply men ran the gauntlet of machine gun fire to bring more grenades up to the battling Leathernecks on the ridge. The toll of killed and wounded was mounting. More fire power was needed. Corporal Brown shouted for a machine gun to be sent up. He couldn't make himself heard, but one of the "H" Company men at his right found a caliber .30 machine gun which had been abandoned the day before by the "G" Company when it was repulsed.

The Leatherneck handed the gun across a trench to Brown, and while exposed was struck by three machine gun slugs from Woody hill. He fell back, but Brown held the gun. A machine gunner from "H" Company manned the weapon to sweep the ridges where the Japs kept appearing. Soon he was wounded, and a squad leader form "H" Company took over the gun and kept it firing. A bullet hit his belt buckle.

In the thick of battle he ripped off his shirt and showed everyone that his stomach was not hit.

"Boy, I'm going to keep that buckle for a souvenir," he said, a big grin on his face.

Later PFC Jack Moon of "H" Company dashed over to help Brown who was his cousin. Moon manned the machine gun. Brown placed several wounded marines in a cave and had them load rifle bullets into machine gun belts.

Under this added fire, the Japs drew back from the ridge and began arching mortar shells into the marine lines. Casualties continued. Only one man was left in the center of the line. Corporal Brown pulled four more from his right flank to bolster the line. Then he charged directly over the ridge by himself to check the enemy positions.

In a quick glance he saw the city of Naha a mile and a half to the southwest, and saw a hillside teeming with Japs. Wounded Nips were being evacuated on makeshift stretchers. Only a few yards in front of him were half a dozen Japs around a mortar, firing rapidly. He tossed a grenade into their midst, silencing the weapon and killing four of its crew.

Jim ducked back from the ridge. A Nip followed and hurled a grenade at him. He caught it in both hands and threw it back. It exploded on top of the ridge.

Gunny Taylor was sending all available grenades up to Brown's men, but there weren't enough. He called for more to be sent up from a supply base. Soon an amtrack arrived, but instead of grenades it brought mortar flare shells. Knowing how desperately Brown and his men needed grenades, Gunny was broken hearted. He loaded the amtrack with wounded marines and sent it back.

Now out of grenades and running low on bullets. Brown sent word for Joe Sheer's machine gunners to sweep the ridge while reinforcements could be brought up.

But no reserves came, so Brown left Sergeant Frank Lilly in command and ran back to the command post to ask for more men.

"Give me two platoons and we'll assault over the top of the ridge and save the lives of a lot of marines who are counting on us," he said.

Up the slope he dashed with two platoons following. But now the fire grew heavier from Woody hill at the rear, and also from Sugar Loaf where the marines again had been driven back. Halfway up the hill Brown looked back. Only 12 men were following him. The others had been killed, wounded or pinned down by deadly fire. He continued with the few remaining men, and again bolstered his lines.

Meanwhile Corporal Frenchy Francoeur, leader of the First platoon, kept his men on the ridge line battling the Japs feverishly. Casualties continued to mount. The Marines ran out of hand grenades, but hurled rocks at the enemy.

Brown made another trip back to the command post.

"Don't put any mortar fire on the crest of the hill, because we'll stay there and hold it tonight," he told Lieutenant Stone.

Under increasingly heavy fire, the First Battalion forces soon were compelled to withdraw from the left flank of Half-Moon hill. This left "I" and "H" Companies even more exposed than ever, and with less fire power, so they too were ordered to pull back off Half-Moon hill.

Jim was not advised of this, because he was rerouted back to the crest of the hill on the enemy side. Moving rapidly and picking protective terrain for cover, he wanted to check enemy positions further. Near the top of the ridge he was fired upon by Nambu, which hit another marine who had joined him. Brown placed the wounded marine in a cave on the Jap side and instructed him to crawl down to "H" Company lines when darkness came. It was dusk then.

Then Jim dashed quickly over the ridge to rejoin his outfit. But his men had received their orders and withdrawn. Only the dead remained.

His own machine gunners thought him a Jap, and opened fire from their positions 200 yards down the slope. Jim dived behind a mound of dirt. The machine gun bullets began ripping it away. Each slug came closer.

The big assault had failed. His men were ordered to withdraw. Nips were just over the ridge. And now his own men were firing on him. He was bitterly disappointed... broken hearted... indescribably lonely.

Two more machine gun slugs kicked dust in his face. A bullet crashed through his helmet, but missed his head. Then the firing ceased. Brown raced full-speed through the darkness, identified himself and rejoined his troops.

Although their full objectives were not reached, the marines made substantial gains and again took a big toll of Japs. The Third battalion set up lines representing a 300-yard advance for the day, and the 22nd Marines dug in closer to Sugar Loaf hill.

They had pushed tanks at both flanks of Sugar Loaf while riflemen stormed up the west slope and over the crest. The attack had penetrated farther than any previously, and more Japs had been slaughtered than before. The marines were in better position to launch another assault the next day.

A number of our tanks were knocked out by Jap mortars and antitank guns, and 10 armored amtracks bringing in supplies and evacuating wounded were disabled.

All hands worked until late that night evacuating killed and wounded.

It was the darkest day of the campaign for "I" Company with 33 casualties. Six were killed, 23 wounded and four evacuated with combat fatigue. They just couldn't take it any longer. Casualties also ran high in "H" Company.

"I" Company men killed were Corporal Jackson W. Bennett of Philadelphia, Pa., Corporal Gerald J. Tardiff of Waterville, Maine, PFC Elmer Patterson of Blue Ridge, Ga., PFC James V Aardo of Ansonia, Conn., Private Edwin A. Schumacher and Private Rex. M. Scott.

Wounded were Corporal William M. Rapp of Raymondville, Tex., Corporal Edward J. Sullivan of Youngstown, O., Corporal Edwin C.

Timanus, II, of Washington, D.C., PFC Edward J. Blevins, PFC Clyde W. Keller, PFC James D. Player of Banberg, S.C., PFC John F. Palding of East Newark, N.J., PFC Don A. Schinnerer of Albany, N.Y, PFC Donald Slade of Brooklyn, N.Y., Private Avelin, Private Harold E. Carlson of Newton Center, Mass., Private Edward S. Finkbeiner, Private Ralph L. Nokes, Private Charles E. Northcote of Franklin Park, Ill, Private Michael L. Nappi, Private York Payne of Marchall, N.C., Private Richard W. Ross, Private Medford M. Shorts, Private Randall E. Snyder, PFC Harry E. Stockwell and PFC William O. Vasilion.

"They never would have run us off the hill if we hadn't run out of hand grenades," said Brown.

"I know it, Jim," replied Gunny Taylor. "But we'll have plenty tomorrow. Lieutenant Stone has gone back to order two more loads of grenades sent forward."

Gunny Taylor had taken over as acting company commander for the night and set "I" Company men into their positions. Soon supplies began rolling up in amtracks.

With a few replacements injected into their ranks, the marines charged back into the Jap lines again Friday, May 18, determined to run the Nips clear off Half-Moon and Sugar Loaf hills.

The First Battalion drove the Japs from positions around Woody hill on the left flank and took up stronger supporting positions than they occupied the day before.

The 22nd Regiment's Second Battalion again attacked Sugar Loaf hill, assaulting from the flank and up the reverse slope. They charged so rapidly that the Nips were taken by surprise and found the marines right in their midst. The Leathernecks, tossing hand grenades furiously, and firing savagely and accurately with their rifles and sub-machine guns, blasted the Nips right off Sugar Loaf hill. Many of the Japs were killed in their tracks, or as they fled. Others dived into caves where they were sealed by demolition charges.

It was the eleventh and final assault of Sugar Loaf hill. The marines had gained another major objective in one of their bitterest campaigns.

On one of the many Sugar Loaf hill assaults Lieutenant Bayer picked up a caliber .30 machine gun to hold the counter-attacking Japs at bay while the tiny handful of surviving marines was being evacuated. A bullet hit him in the thigh and knocked him down. Still he fired.

Another bullet hit him in the knee. Mortar shells burst all around him. He continued to fire. A third bullet struck him in the hip. Lying prone, he kept his machine gun chattering until the other wounded were evacuated. It required seven corpsmen to remove his 225-pound hulk.

One company assaulting Sugar Loaf lost all but two men. Another had only eight survivors.

While the 22nd Marine Regiment was capturing Sugar Loaf hill, "H" and "I" Companies attacked Half-Moon hill, which had been nicknamed Hand Grenade hill. Captain William Gamble of New Haven, Conn., led "H" Company on an assault up the reverse slope on the southwest side, and Corporal Brown followed rapidly with the "I" Company riflemen, charging higher on the ridge and across to the reverse side. This time every man carried half a dozen or more hand grenades.

With grenades, rifle fire and demolition charges they blasted the Japs right off the hill, or sealed them in caves. Three-fourths of the hill was secured by dusk. Quickly they set up lines to hold the hill for the night. More men were needed, so Corporal Brown went after them, accompanied by PFC Bill Cunningham, a tall, blonde youth from New Haven, Conn. Nambu fire swept the open field they must cross.

"Come on, Bill," said Brown. "Those Nip sons of bitches can't hit us."

They ran at top speed and eluded the bullets which flew around them. They returned in an amtrack with two more squads which filled the gap just in time to help repulse a Jap counter-attack. A number of infiltrating Nips were killed that night, but there were no more marine casualties.

The next day the Fourth Marine regiment relieved the 29th Marines, and there were a number of casualties during the shift. After going through a week of hell without being injured, PFC Edwin P. Shaughnessy of Philadelphia was hit by a mortar shell and killed as he was returning from the front battle lines. Corporal Cecil R. Utley of Daytona Beach, Fla., and PFC Charles L. Thibeault were wounded, and PFC Joseph J. Anderson of Macomb, Miss., had been wounded the day before. But the new lines held, and the Fourth Marines continued the advance. A number of Jap mortar and artillery positions were sighted farther back and knocked out.

I saw Gunny Taylor, Jim Brown and others of "I" Company the next day at a bivouac area where they were sent for a week of rest and shore defense duty while replacements were poured into their ranks.

A week before there were 51 in the third platoon. Now only six remained. They were Sergeant Frank Lilly, Corporal Frank J. Kakuchka, PFC Bill Cunningham, PFC Ivan G. Zahler, PFC Charles

J. Miller and Corporal Brown. Also with them was Corpsman John Pauk.

Big Joe Sheer brought back only six of his 15 machine gunners. The others were wounded or killed.

I saw drawn, haggard faces. But it was their eyes which were the most pitiful... sad, staring eyes which kept seeing their wounded and killed buddies. The men were dazed, and seemed to be still living in some hellish nightmare. In subdued tones they talked of their week of hell, and praised their fallen comrades.

They were physically and mentally exhausted. They had gotten out of the habit of eating and sleeping. They slept lightly and nervously, if at all. Death had been staring them in the face for days. It now was hard for them to force food down. Appetites had to be re-cultivated. Most of the week they had lived chiefly on tropical chocolate bars, and nerve.

They knew the ghastly price for victory, and were paying it. They wondered why a comparatively few from our nation had to pay with everything they had—their lives. But there wasn't a word of complaint.

Chapter 17

Japan's Empire Crumbles

While capturing Sugar Loaf and Half-Moon hills, the Sixth Marine Division drove simultaneously into the city off Naha and set up strong positions along the Asato river.

At the same time the Gung-Ho Leathernecks of the First Marine Division blasted ahead toward Shuri Castle through the heaviest and most concentrated defenses of the island.

In a four-day assault on "Martha Rae ridge" the First Marine Division battled through the heaviest machine gun and rifle fire encountered in the Division's history. The Devil Dogs had to silence a thousand light and heavy machine guns on the double pronged ridge and overrun scores of anti-tank gun and mortar positions. And the Japs always had an endless supply of hand grenades.

Slashing onward toward Shuri Castle, the marines poured fuel oil over the reverse slopes of Jap-held hills and exploded grenades to ignite it and roast holed-up Japs in their caves. Anti-tank gunners used their big weapons like rifles, firing them point blank at slits in pillboxes.

In Naha the 22nd Marine Regiment, commanded by Colonel Harold C. Roberts of Buffalo, N.Y., set up a regimental command post in a two-story concrete schoolhouse and in a few days secured all the area north of the Ksato river. The 22nd drove eastward two thousand yards and joined forces with the Fourth Marine Regiment which swept southward from Half-Moon and Sugar Loaf hills.

In this school house on May 20 I found PFC W.G. Dawson, a youthful marine from Baltimore, Md., calmly playing "Danny Boy" on a captured piano while Jap bullets and mortar shells were striking the building and two machine guns upstairs were blasting away at Japs trying to make a counter-attack.

"I used to play piano in church," he said.

A half dozen grenade-carrying Japs had attempted to infiltrate into the marine lines in front of the school the night before. PFC Daniel J. Stokes of Mt. Vernon, O., killed two with a machine gun. Another Leatherneck sleeping in a cave killed two who were so close that their bodies fell on his bed of blankets. Riflemen killed the other Japs. I saw the six bodies, none more than 20 yards from the lines.

Upstairs in the school directing the assault were Colonel Roberts and Major General Geiger, commanding General of the Marine Third Amphibious Corps.

The Okinawa campaign was the first for the Sixth Division, although most of its troops had been through other campaigns. After conquering all of northern Okinawa, they were hurling themselves savagely at the Japs in southern Okinawa and had entered the capital city of Naha.

"It's a pretty damned good division," said Major General Geiger proudly. "It has done excellent work. You couldn't possibly ask for any more than the men of the Sixth Division have been doing. The same goes for the First Marine Division."

Major General Geiger was a flier in World War I. I asked if he had any luck in that conflict.

"Yes," he replied with a big smile. "I got back."

His First and sixth Marine divisions were pushing ahead aggressively and killing thousands of Japs. He was in good spirits. Both he and Colonel Roberts who as a youth fought with the First Regiment at Belleau Woods in World War I, were scornful of Jap fire. They stood at the large windows studying the terrain, checking maps and watching the assault.

Japs were running one at a time over the shoulder of a ridge 900 yards east of us and hitting the deck quickly. One of our machine guns was sighted in on them and greeting each with a hail of lead. One of the Leathernecks loaned me his M-1 rifle which was loaded with tracers and sighted in for that distance. I took a lot of satisfaction out of putting a dozen shots into the area where the Japs hit the deck. At that distance we couldn't see the results. Probably the Japs were crawling to cover. But it was great sport for me, just the same, after having been a target for Jap Nambu fire a week previously.

Three days later the Fourth and 22nd Marines forced a bridgehead across the Asato river and began attacking the main part of Naha itself. The Japs continued to make heavy counter-attacks almost daily all along the lengthening Okinawa battle line, and their losses were tremendous.

The Seventh Army Division stormed across the Yonabaru airfield on the east coast and then captured the town of Yonabaru. The 96th Army Division was assaulting on the Seventh's right flank, while the 77th Army Division drove southward in the center of the line toward Shuri Castle. The three Army and two Marine Corps divisions were keeping constant pressure on the Japs, and driving them slowly but steadily backward.

The Sixth Marine Division widened its bridgehead in the devastated city of Naha which was a flattened mass of ruins following constant bombing and shelling since the start of the campaign. Many snipers had to be cleared from the ruins, but the Marines captured most of the city by May 28.

Now the foundations of the Jap defenses were trembling. On May 23 the 77th Division had taken the town of Taira, 500 yards from Shuri. The Japs fought fanatically to keep Shuri.

The First Marine Division, driving southward, pulled one of the biggest surprises of the campaign on May 29. In a pre-dawn attack a company of Leathernecks slashed through the Japs' outer defenses and drove a mile eastward. In driving rain the marines advanced up a slippery draw, killing the few surprised Nips who blocked their path, and captured the crumbling ruins of Shuri Castle, the military capital of the island.

The routed Japs quickly began fleeing southward to build up another defensive line south of Naha on the Oroku peninsula.

After a week of rest the 29th Marines relieved the Fourth Regiment in the southward push in the eastern outskirts of Naha on May 28. Although still below strength, "I" Company had received a number of replacements. Second Lieutenant James McCormick Jr., son of Admiral McCormick, became leader of the third platoon.

Lieutenant Stone sent the first platoon in an assault against a hill and ordered the third platoon to follow and extend the line to the right. The attack moved rapidly, and in a hot fire fight the marines killed a number of Japs and sealed many more in caves, while advancing 400 yards.

Jim was returning to the command post to report his platoon's position when men of the first platoon pointed to a group of soldiers 400 yards away.

"Are those marines, or Nips?" one asked.

"Gimme that BAR and get me all the magazines you've got," said Brown. "Get 'em over quick."

Then he flung himself full length on a knoll and emptied six clips—120 rounds—into the surprised Nips.

"Pour all the fire you can on those bastards," he said.

Nips fell like cordwood. A few escaped and fled southward. Jim returned to his platoon.

Masters at mortar fire, the Japs exploded a phosphorous shell right in front of Brown, burning his hands. All that night Private Robert E. "Devil" Parsons, 33, of Johns, Alabama, poured water on Jim's hands to keep them from burning more deeply.

The next morning a doctor treated them and ordered Brown to remain at the aid station. But his platoon was ready to assault again, so Brown returned to the lines. In two days "I" Company sustained 15 casualties, but killed 35 Japs.

The incessant Jap artillery and mortar fire, hand grenade attacks at night and bonsai charges continued. Six of the casualties were combat fatigue. PFC Maurcie E. Bryson of Sylva, N.C., was killed. The wounded were Private Howard E. Tuma of Chicago, Ill., PFC Carleton K. Smith of Brigton, Maine, PFC Warren T. Hinkley of Dickersfield, Maine, PFC George S. Gardner Jr., of Washington, D.C., Private Roland A. Tremblay, Private Charles L. Sowers of Washington, Pa., Private Major Summerford Jr., and Private Roger R. Vanrycheghem.

Second Lieutenant McCormick led a scouting party forward 500 yards to feel out the Jap defenses. His party got pinned down and Lieutenant McCormick's leg was broken with Nambu fire. He was evacuated under a smoke screen. Once more Corporal Brown became the leader of the third platoon.

The following morning Lieutenant Stone sent Brown's platoon on an assault which gained 600 yards, during which the Leathernecks knocked out a knee mortar and two 20 millimeter guns, and sealed a number of caves. They tossed a grenade into one cave, and for good measure pitched in another. The cave was full of Jap ammunition which exploded, injuring seven.

The marines had the Nips on the run, so Brown asked and received permission to assault to the next ridge. This attack took the third platoon 400 yards farther, to the edge of a village. Again Brown got permission to continue, and his men assaulted through the village to the top of a ridge.

There they encountered heavy rifle and machine gun fire. Quickly they set up a skirmish line and began picking off Japs.

PFC Bill Cunningham dived behind a boulder and was unable to fire without exposing himself. So he became a switch-shooter. Firing left-handed, he killed four Nips. One remained, with only his head visible. Bill raised upright, put the rifle back to his right shoulder and shot the Jap between the eyes. The remaining Japs began to run.

"There go those sons of bitches," shouted Brown. "Let's get 'em."

He charged forward and the entire platoon followed, having a field day mowing down Nips. Brown set up a new skirmish line on the next ridge and had his men dig in there, after an advance of more than a mile that day.

That evening PFC Otto V. Trignano of Nutley, N.J., who had been helping Gunny Taylor move up food and ammunition under fire all week, saw a Jap, dressed only in a kimono, emerge from a cave. "Trig" leaped on the Jap's back and pinned his arms to his side. Then he reached for his knife, the only weapon he had at that time.

But another marine stepped up and covered the Jap with his rifle while Gunny Taylor, who had just arrived, helped frisk the prisoner. Taylor bound the Jap and turned him over to intelligence.

Many-a-marine has sung the old familiar lines:

"Someday, I'm gonna murder the bugler."

But Corporal Joe "Stinky" Stelmach, 25, of Allentown, Pa., probably is one of the few ever to accomplish the feat. He shot a Jap and immediately laid claim to all souvenirs on the body. The haul included a short, stubby Jap bugle.

The First Marine Division, driving southward after capturing Shuri Castle, extended its lines on the left flank of the 29th Marines, and on June 2 relieved them to participate in a surprise flanking attack.

With Naha completely secured and a stiff battle raging on a high escarpment south of the city, the Fourth Marine Regiment made an amphibious crossing of Naha bay in LVT's and assaulted the beaches of the Oroku peninsula. The 29th Marines followed a few hours later and tied in their lines with the Fourth Marines. This bold maneuver took the Nips by surprise, and the marines advanced to strong positions with low casualties.

Within a few days the Sixth Marine Division had taken Naha airfield and driven the Japs remaining on the Oroku peninsula into a small pocket. The First Marine Division boomed rapidly southward, sweeping past the Oroku peninsula and driving down the west side toward the southern tip of the island, while the Army divisions drove southward and eastward over a large area.

The Japs quickly reorganized and continued their fanatical defense in hills and ridges.

On June 7 "I" Company moved against the Japs in the pocket on the Oroku peninsula. Led by two regular tanks and two flame-throwing tanks, they captured a small but high hill and blitzed a small village, killing 50 Japs in the open and sealing 100 more in caves.

Gunny Taylor, who each day grew more contemptuous of Jap sniper fire, was exposed, as usual, watching demolition teams sealing a cave. A sniper put a bullet through Gunny's leg.

"I'm sorry," he said apologetically to Lieutenant Stone. "I guess I should have been behind cover where I belonged."

"Gunny knew he was likely to get it," Brown told me later. "In fact he was surprised he hadn't been wounded previously. But those kids on the line were going through so much hell that Taylor kept exposing himself and laughing at the Japs just to give the kids more courage."

Gunny Taylor was father-confessor to every man in the company. He knew them all, and talked over personal problems with each one. He was a tireless warhorse, and dozens of times dashed forward with hand grenades and bandoliers of ammunition when the troops leading assaults were pinned down. From his hospital bed Gunny wrote encouraging letters to just about every man in the company. I saw several of those letters, and they were wonderful.

Gunny Taylor, with his reassuring laugh and his horse sense advice, pulled many of the men through when they were near the cracking point. During the training days he was a stern, G.I. individual who had to carry out the orders of the company commander and maintain strict military discipline. But in combat the old gunny sergeant proved to have a heart of gold. The men loved him.

Gunny's presence was needed badly a few days later. The company was having a rough time, because the Japs were occupying a dozen tiny hills honeycombed with caves, and rained cross-fire from half a dozen angles at every assaulting unit. Corporal "Stinky" Stelmach, leader of a machine gun squad, was placing PFC Marvin A. Long, a machine gunner from Washington, D.C., into a new machine gun position to give supporting fire for an assault. A sniper pinned them down. A bullet struck Long in the head and killed him.

"He was my closest buddy," Stinky told me the next day. "He's the seventh man killed in my eight-man squad. And we've had three wounded. We keep getting replacements, but they keep getting killed."

Stinky sat dejectedly at the command post 200 yards behind the lines. Battle-weary, he was near the breaking point.

"I just don't have the heart to be up there fighting today," he continued. "Maybe it's my fault those men got killed. Maybe I didn't put them in the right positions. And then... my own life line is getting pretty thin..."

He always had been laughing and joking before when I had seen him.

"Stinky, it's not your fault," I assured him. "You know machine guns; you know the Japs and their tactics, and you know how to pick the best firing points. Why, someone else might have lost three times as many men as you. It's just the hellish price of victory."

Up at the observation post I saw Sergeant Joe Sheer, leader of the machine gun section. A big smile was on his unshaven face.

"Boy, we've really been killing Japs this week," he said.

The next day Joe started to set up a machine gun in the same area where Long was killed. More fire power was needed badly there to protect the flank of Corporal Brown's platoon, which was assaulting Flat Top hill 300 yards ahead of the lines, and was getting fire from all sides. Joe moved up with his machine gun. The same sniper shot him through the head and killed him.

With Sheer gone, Stinky went back to the front lines and fought courageously to the end of the campaign.

Corporal Brown and Corporal Eugene D. Diamond of Jamestown, N.Y., with a squad of 10 men, killed 25 Japs and sealed many more in caves on June 8. They also captured a base from which the Japs had been launching their big spigot mortars, known to the doughboys as G.I. cans, and to the marines as "Screaming Mimis."

That night Jim Brown and Jesse Morley slipped out ahead of the lines to blow more Jap caves. The night was black, and they moved down the reverse side of the hill. Suddenly Morley shouted:

"Jump, Jim!"

Brown jumped to the left and Morley shot and killed a Jap who was in the act of throwing a hand grenade. They tossed a couple of grenades just in case any more Nips were following; then returned to their lines.

On June 10 the Third platoon assaulted Flat Top hill, but pulled back under smoke screen in the evening after battling all day and knocking out several Nambu machine guns. They were pinned down most of the day, and several marines were wounded trying to bring supplies forward. Private Floyd E. Sykes, a runner from Coronado, Calif., was killed while loading a bazooka for Corporal Diamond.

The next day Brown led his platoon back to the previous day's position beside a small hill in front of Flat Top hill. Then at full speed he ran through an opening in the Jap lines. With his platoon following closely in column formation, he charged to the top of Flat Top Hill. Second Lieutenant August L. Camarata led the second platoon through the same gap and set up a skirmish line lower on the forward slope of Flat Top to rain fire at the reverse slope of the previous hill. Several were wounded, including Lieutenant Camarata.

From the crest of Flat Top the third platoon directed rifle, submachine gun and bazooka fire at Japs on other nearby small hills, and Corporal Diamond began lighting demolition bundles and tossing them down the reverse slope of the hill to clear the Japs from that area. Inside the hill the Japs had an elaborate cave system with half a dozen opening on the reverse side.

With the capture of Flat Top hill, the Jap pocket resistance crumbled on the Oroku peninsula. On June 13 "I" and "G" Companies formed a broad skirmish line and swept across an open field toward the seawall east of Naha. Elements of the Fourth Marines joined the drive. Standing straight up, the Leathernecks walked slowly across the field, flushing concealed Japs. Those who offered resistance were killed, while others were taken prisoner.

Some of the Japs tried desperate hand grenade attacks, but were mowed down. Some Japs who tried to surrender were killed by other Japs, who then committed hari kari. "I" Company took 41 prisoners that day, and the Third Battalion killed 225 Japs.

Rifles and machine guns had become scarce among the remaining Japs, but they never did run out of hand grenades. Upon finding a Jap hiding in a cave or in tall grass, the marines would shout "data coy," (come out) and "shimpa shinade," (don't be afraid.)

The Japs who surrendered were ordered to strip off all their clothes. That was the only way to be sure they were not concealing hand grenades. Corporal Brown was leading both the third and second platoons that day. His men captured 25 of the Nips and killed 130.

Jim killed seven. It was ticklish business. Most of the killing was done at 10 yards or less when Japs suddenly rose from the grass and tried to toss grenades. The Leathernecks were quick on the trigger and sure with their aim. Most of the Japs were covered by camouflage nets. They were practically under foot before discovered.

After a few more days of mopping up and sealing Japs in caves in that area, Lieutenant Colonel Wright's 29th Marine Regiment moved southward on June 19 to seek out remnants of enemy forces hiding in the Mozado and Kuwanga ridges and the open fields between the ridges. The Kuwanga ridge was only two miles from the island's southern tip.

With the 29th Marines I had the pleasure of a surprise meeting with my boot camp drill instructor, PFC T.J. Muse of Central Point,

Oreg. He would have been a corporal and possibly a sergeant had he remained at San Diego as a D.I., but he asked for overseas duty. We respected him as a D.I., because he was strict but fair, and led us instead of driving us.

An expert with the M-1 and the Browning Automatic Rifle, he more than kept up with the kids in his outfit despite his 34 years. One night on Okinawa he awakened to see a Jap assaulting him with a bayonet. The Jap stabbed him in the arm and then in the leg. Muse doubled up his legs and kicked the Nip out of the fox hole; then killed him with his rifle. He killed 10 Nips during the campaign.

With doughboys and marines battling fiercely and squeezing the remaining Japs into a small pocket on the high ridges of southern Okinawa, Lieutenant General Buckner went to an advanced marine observation post on June 18 to view the fighting. An artillery shell exploded beside him and killed the general, who had directed one of the biggest and bloodiest battles of the Pacific.

Admiral Nimits, the overall commander of the Okinawa operation, praised Lieutenant General Buckner's generalship in directing the land campaign, saying:

"Officers and men of all armed services in the Pacific ocean areas are greatly shocked at the death by enemy shell fire of Lieutenant General Simon Bolivar Buckner. His loss comes on the eve of the complete capture of Okinawa. That operation which General Buckner conducted with such skill and courage will have a profound influence on the war against Japan.

Major General Geiger immediately was named commanding general of the Tenth Army. It was the first time in history that a Marine Corps officer became general of an Army.

Then Tenth Army included four Army divisions and three Marine Corps divisions. The Second Marine Division was standing by during the campaign, and its Eighth Regiment was used in the final drive to the southern tip of Okinawa. On June 19 Major General Geiger was promoted to Lieutenant General. The only other three-star general in the Marine Corps at that time was Lieutenant General Holland M. Smith.

Even to the end the Japs offered fanatical resistance, although they began surrendering in increasing numbers. A corpsman giving first aid to a captured Japanese naval officer who had been wounded, didn't like the sneer on the Japs' face.

"Where's your navy now, Tojo?" asked the corpsman.

With a sweeping gesture the officer, who had been captured in a cave, pointed to the fleet lying off southern Okinawa.

"Oh yeah?" retorted the Corpsman. "Take a look with those field glasses."

The officer focused the glasses and looked from one ship to another. He recognized the United States Fleet battleships, cruisers, destroyers, landing craft, freighters and tankers. Laying the field glasses down, he shook his head and said sadly:

"Poor Japan. Poor Japan."

Holed up in caves like rats, the Jap troops had been told that those were Japanese ships off shore.

In mid-June Lieutenant General Buckner had called upon the remaining Japanese garrison to surrender. This plea was ignored by the Jap leaders, but increasing numbers of Japs began complying.

During the final days of the campaign the Sixth Marine Division captured 700 prisoners along the steep cliff at the southern tip of the island. Some 40 Nips retreated to a ledge above the water and committed hari-kari.

Doughboys and Leathernecks battled fiercely to scale the high escarpments in the final drive. Tremendous artillery barrages pounded the dwindling Jap forces.

Always hovering over the battle lines throughout the entire campaign were spotter planes to direct artillery fire. Hedge-hoping over the battle lines, the two-seater aircraft were under constant fire by Jap rifles, machine guns and anti-aircraft guns, and always faced the danger of being struck by the very shellfire they were directing against target.

For protection the pilots would dive, bank split-S or climb, or zip down some convenient valley. But always they returned, exposing themselves by the hour to spot the masterfully-concealed Jap gun positions and direct artillery fire against them.

VMO-3, a marine observation squadron, had a rough time during the Okinawa campaign, and did an outstanding job. A small outfit, you couldn't beat it for spirit.

"Say, we've got the hottest pilots in the Pacific," said Corporal Bill Charlton of Philadelphia, Pa., a squadron operations clerk. "We've got the best cook in the Pacific. In fact, we're the hottest outfit in the Pacific."

Circling low over the area where the Japs had their heaviest artillery concentrations, First Lieutenant Herbert Fincel of Frankfort, Ky., and his observer located a battery of eight to 10 Jap cannons. He called for heavy fire, and hovered over the targets to give corrections on the gun range.

The Japs put up a demoralizing barrage of anti-aircraft fire. Flak was bursting behind him, so he gave full throttle. Then a burst exploded in front of him. He did a split-S turn and headed the opposite direction. Ack-ack followed him. He changed altitude, and continued to direct the fire of marine five-inch guns. Then a Jap 40 millimeter shell exploded in the plane's tail, blowing half of the tail away, severing the rudder control and ripping off most of the fabric on the rear part of the plane.

With superb airmanship Lieutenant Fincel kept his plane flying and dodging, and remained over the target an hour. He directed more than 250 rounds of artillery fire onto the Jap gun positions, leaving only when his gas supply was almost gone. Then he returned and landed in the dark on an unlighted field.

One of the hottest spotter pilots who ever mowed the tops of Okinawa trees with propeller was First Lieutenant Robert C. Jackson of Webster Grove, Mo. Ruddy of complexion, he talked and looked like Bob Burns, and had phenomenal success at scrounging equipment for the squadron.

Once he spotted a few Japs in a tiny village, and immediately made a strafing run at them. Of course spotter planes have no weapons, but Lieutenant Jackson blazed away with his .45 pistol, and his observer cut loose with a Tommy gun. But instead of a few Jap soldiers, there were 30. A few went down under the surprise attack. On the second strafing run the Japs riddled the little Stinson's fuselage with rifle fire, but several more Japs were killed or wounded. On the third strafing run the Japs had taken a powder, and a fourth run showed the village deserted.

"I reckon we won that battle," said Lieutenant Jackson.

Once he kept flying back and forth past a sheer cliff to get photos of caves in which Japs kept their suicide crash boats and landing craft for surprise landings behind our troops. Despite heavy fire from the caves, he continued to fly past to study the camouflaged positions, until finally he was wounded in the side by a bullet. Two days later he was back flying again, and with just as much daring. He had been wounded twice before during the Peleliu campaign.

Later, while flying as observer for First Lieutenant William C. Parvis of Wilmington, Del., he killed at least one Jap in a cave on the high cliff rising from the sea on the south tip of Okinawa.

Lieutenant Parvis, the squadron's operation officer, once directed a 72-gun barrage which practically annihilated a village. On another occasion he knocked out a battery of four Jap five-inch guns near the Yonabaru airfield.

A 40-millimeter shell exploded in the tail of First Lieutenant Donald W. Manley's plane, jamming the rudder and trim tab controls and wounding him in the neck. It took full throttle to keep the plane flying. Lieutenant Manley, whose home is St. Joseph, Mich., was the first American pilot to touch wheels on the Naha airfield. Just to tantalize the Japs, who held the field at that time, he swept down, touched his wheels on the runway and then sped away before the Japs could line up his plane with their fire.

Commanding officer of the squadron was Captain Wallace J. Slappey Jr., of Perry, Ga., who also took his turns at spotter flying. Easy going, he had a happy and efficient outfit. The only time he ever got perturbed was when his relief officer joined the squadron. Captain Peter Fritz of Jamaica, Long Island, N.Y., no sooner arrived to snap in as the squadron's new skipper than he began flying. Captain Slappey read him off sternly. Having received his orders to return to the States, Captain Slappey didn't want his relief wounded. It might delay his return by many months.

First Lieutenant Lawrence J. Stien of Minneapolis and Second Lieutenant David M. Bidwell of Batesville, Ar., both helped capture Jap prisoners, directing marine troops by dropping notes. Lieutenant Stien and another pilot were the first American fliers to land on Okinawa, setting their planes down on Yontan airfield on L-plus one-day.

First Lieutenant S. L. Fraser of Pontiac, Mich., the squadron adjutant, and Lieutenant Jackson had landed with the assault troops on L-Day to set up headquarters, get bulldozers to fill bomb craters and prepare a landing strip, and to contact marine artillery units. Lieutenant Fraser's rifle helped kill the Jap fighter pilot who made the mistake of landing at Yontan field the evening of L-day.

"Halt!" someone ordered as the Jap pilot climbed from the Tojo's cockpit.

The Jap's hand started for his pistol, but never got there. A volley of shots riddled his body.

During the campaign every squadron plane was struck by enemy fire, and six of the 12 planes assigned to VMO 3 were lost or had to be junked.

"Everything under nine slugs through the fuselage is a bad day," said Corporal Charlton. "And our pilots fly so low that they start using oxygen at 100 feet. Yep, we've got the hottest outfit in the Pacific."

For a week VMO 3 performed double duty when another squadron was temporarily grounded. Pilots flew as much as nine or ten hours a day, and throughout they had outstanding success in spotting targets and directing fire. The secret of this success was the pilot's determination to stay over enemy territory and do a job despite heavy fire. There's no substitute for guts. The Japs shot everything they had at our grasshopper boys, and one Jap even threw rocks at low-flying Lieutenant Fincel.

One pilot was killed in an operational accident, and First Lieutenant Harold Saastad was missing in action. No trace was found of him, even after the island was secured. Possibly his plane crashed into the sea, or into jungle-thick undergrowth. Or maybe it got in the way of some of the heavy artillery fire which he was directing, and was blown to bits. Flying spotter planes in combat is rough duty.

Lieutenant Bidwell took me on an aerial Cook's Tour of southern Okinawa after the campaign was over, and showed me scores of knocked out gun positions. In the area surrounding Sugar Loaf hill, Half-Moon hill and Shuri Castle we counted the rusting, mangled carcasses of 45 of our tanks which the Japs knocked out during the bitter struggle.

During the final stages of the campaign Lieutenant Fincel flew me over the huge escarpment south of Itoman where bitter fighting was raging. It was spooky sitting up there 200 feet above a raging tank, artillery and mortar duel. Ships' guns and field pieces were pounding the Jap positions, and the Japs were arching mortars back at doughboys and marines. One of our tanks had been knocked out, but three remained, firing at point-blank range. Marines assaulting the west end of the ridge along the coast highway had just been driven back.

A few days later I climbed the ridge and talked to the marines who held it.

"We were run off twice," said Second Lieutenant W. G. Loftis of Durham, N.C., commanding officer of "C" Company, First Battalion, 22nd Marine Regiment. "After battling all day we finally captured the crest of the ridge at 7 p.m. The Japs counter-attacked at 8 p.m., and we had another red hot hand grenade fight.

"We held the top of the ridge all night, and the next day won the reverse slope. Six of our men were killed, and 29 wounded. We killed 150 Nips."

Battles like this raged to the last. Corporal Brown and his platoon were in the thick of fighting to the last, killing and capturing numerous Japs near the island's southern tip. Fortunately there were no further casualties in "I" Company.

On June 21 the Sixth Marine Division concluded its first campaign by hoisting the Stars and Stripes on the southern tip of Okinawa. Army Divisions had cleared the heavily-defended areas to the east.

Shortly after noon on June 21 Lieutenant General Geiger announced:

"Organized resistance has ceased on Okinawa. Two small pockets on the southern portion of the island are being mopped up."

Victory had come on Okinawa.

Prime Minister Winston Churchill sent to President Truman a "salute" to the land, sea and air forces which fought at Okinawa, saying the campaign was "among the most intense and famous in military history. It is in profound admiration of American valor and resolve to conquer at whatever cost might be necessary, that I send you this tribute."

Okinawa was part of the Japanese empire, and was considered almost as part of the homeland. Japan's empire was crumbling... the homeland was shaking.

Chapter 18

The Atomic Bomb and Victory

Okinawa was one of the greatest prizes of the Pacific war. It became the mightiest air base in the Pacific. The Seabees, who began pouring ashore on L-day shortly after the first assault troops landed, soon were at work widening and lengthening airfields and air strips, and building new ones. By July thousands of planes were at Okinawa, smashing Japan's resources and military installations.

So close to Japan is Okinawa that even medium-range fighter planes carried big "pay loads" of bombs and rockets to rain on the enemy homeland, and medium and heavy bombers carried ponderous loads.

Okinawa became the battle parade grounds for the newest and best United States aircraft with the arrival of Boeing B-29 Superforts, Consolidated B-32 Dominators, Douglas A-26 Invaders, Northrop P-61 Black Widow night fighters, Chance Vought's new and more powerful F4U-4 Corsairs, Grumman F7F twin-engine Tigercat night fighters, numerous other combat planes and all manner of transport planes.

The price of victory at Okinawa was high. There were 7,316 marines and soldiers of the Tenth Army who paid with their lives, and total casualties were 70,971. This included the Tactical Air Force, comprised chiefly of Marine Aviation units but also including Army Air Corps units.

But the Leathernecks and Doughboys were rough on the Japs. They killed 107,760 Japs and took 7,492 prisoners plus 3,393 labor troops, accounting for a total of 116,345 Jap troops. That was more prisoners than had been taken previously during the entire Pacific war.

The Jap soldiers, who once believed propaganda that Japan had conquered California, now began to see the light. Increasingly large numbers realized their cause was hopeless. Their visions of domination faded and their instincts of self-preservation began to predominate. Life began to look good to them. Surrender followed.

The U.S. Pacific Fleet also paid a high price while turning in a magnificent performance during the operation. Naval casualties in the Okinawa theater of action during the first three weeks of the campaign exceeded the combined Army and Marine Corps casualties, although in the end the ground troops, as usual, paid heaviest.

Twenty-four of our destroyers and smaller ships were sunk during the first seven weeks of the campaign. During that time 1,131 naval personnel were killed, 2,816 wounded and 1604 were missing in action—a total of 5,551 casualties.

Jap Kamikaze planes made ours ships their number one targets, with airfields a close second. Ships anchored off Okinawa shelling Jap land positions or discharging cargo, and ships on picket patrol were subjected to repeated suicide plane attacks. Jap planes scored two direct hits on Vice-Admiral Mitscher's flagship, the carrier Bunker Hill, causing 656 casualties. The attack occurred near Okinawa on May 18. Determined fire fighters put out the blaze, and the flattop reached Puget Sound under her own power.

Another Kamikaze plane—a vulture of hate—hit one of our hospital ships, the U. S. S. Comfort, while it was traveling at night, fully lighted, 50 miles southwest of Okinawa. The crash and explosion killed 29 and wounded 33 more.

First Lieutenant Stone's "I" Company landed on Okinawa with 242 officers and men. Forty-four were killed and 197 wounded, a total of 241 casualties—virtually 100 per cent. In Corporal Brown's third platoon the casualties totaled 114 per cent.

During the campaign Jim Brown led his men with outstanding courage and skill, and with deadly effect on the enemy. He was a master of close combat tactics. He knew the Japs and their every trick. Frequently he used improvisations of his own, and with great success. He took much greater risks himself than he asked his men to take, and his utter disregard of danger was a constant inspiration to them.

Time and again he exposed himself to enemy fire to evacuate wounded buddies. As platoon leader he never left a wounded man from his platoon in the battlefield, and frequently risked his own life to evacuate men from other outfits.

Yet he knew fear, but always overcame it. He loved life, and had a dread of being wounded and disfigured. A week after his outfit returned from capturing Half-Moon hill he told me:

"We're going back into the line in Naha tomorrow, and I've got butterflies in my stomach tonight. I'm not afraid of any Jap. We like to meet them face to face. We'll beat him to the draw. But it's tough when you can't see them. I'd rather be dead than disfigured."

Once back in action he dismissed all thoughts of self and returned to his task of killing Japs...gaining ground with as few casualties as possible...always killing Japs. Corporal Jim Brown, descendant of the feudin' McCoy's, killed 43 Japs on Okinawa—43 for sure—and probably many more.

"Why Brown killed at least 60 or 70 Japs," one of his platoon members told me. "When in command he led every charge, and always was the first man to assault. We'd follow him anywhere."

After the island was secured, Corporal Jim Brown was nominated for officer's candidate school. Lieutenant Stone was intensely proud of all his men.

"They had a great esprit de corps and a feeling of comradeship," he said. "When one got hit, the others determined to fight that much harder. Words can't seem to express it... the unity...the way they disregarded personal safety to help a wounded buddy.

"While under fire and fighting back, your own personal safety doesn't seem to enter into it much. But sitting, thinking, waiting and wondering when under shell fire—that tears a man's heart and soul out and rips his nerves and fibers apart.

"My men had intense pride in the Marine Corps and "I" Company. And I have intense pride in them."

After the island was secured, Brown told me:

"During all the fighting I prayed for the Japs to see the light—but when they got in my way I had to kill them. I prayed that if I was right to let me go, and if not the let me stop. The Lord must have been on my side."

The day before the Sixth Division left Okinawa for a rear area, he said:

"I'm leaving some wonderful buddies here... in the Sixth Division cemetery. Jim, there must be some way to prevent wars, and if there is we must find it."

In MAG 43 headquarters squadron we lost another buddy. One night a string of Jap bombs hit our area. We heard the missiles swooshing downward. One landed in a tree, spraying shrapnel over a wide area. Corporal Harold C. "Red" Burgess was wounded in the leg; PFC John Donavan dived for shelter and broke his collar bone, and Corporal William C. Garrity, who was on night duty, was struck in the stomach as he dived into his fox hole. A few days later he died.

On April 29 The Sergeant Don Houseman, who with Bill Carver was wounded during our beach landing operation, returned and moved into the tent with Dick Koch-Church, Bill Gibson and myself. At first Houseman was high strung and nervous. Even the test firing of our anti-aircraft guns caused him to jump at every blast. But in a few days he completely overcame his nervousness, and became one of the calmest during air raids.

One of the most appalling mishaps of the campaign befell big staff Sergeant John Thomaselli of MAG 43. An ordinance expert, he was disarming captured Jap anti-personnel bombs when one exploded and blew off one of his hands and three fingers from the other. We felt very badly about it, and I know it was a cruel blow to Tommy. But I know that Tommy, with his keen intellect and fighting spirit, won't be stopped by that handicap.

Our squadron's duties kept us away from most of the ground action against the Japs. However, Shamrock Coyne and several others from the communications section captured two prisoners in a cave near our area, and PFC John F. Lenz of Seattle helped kill four Japs at our new camp area during the mop up period after the island was secured. The Japs had hidden in caves and were attempting to reach the wilds of the northern Okinawa.

A weird, fantastic episode occurred during the mop up period. First Lieutenant George Thompson of Dorchester, Mass., and four other marines of the 29th Regiment were chasing 16 Japs along a trail overlooking a sheer bluff. Abruptly they found themselves in a clearing filled with 350 enemy troops.

Their plight appeared hopeless. To give battle would be suicide.

"Tobakko!" shouted Lieutenant Thompson, grinning, bowing and waving.

Several Japs held out their hands and the marines quickly handed out cigarettes. Meanwhile Lieutenant Thompson kept chattering over his walkie-talkie radio to his battalion headquarters.

"Don't interrupt," he said. "If I stop talking the Japs may kills us."

Then a mass suicide orgy began. A Jap officer killed the women with him, then stepped up to the PFC Rufus E. Randall of Augusta, Ga., and saluted. He handed the Leatherneck two sabers and a wrist watch, then backed off 10 yards and blew off his head with a grenade.

Other officers did the same, killing their women and then blowing their own heads off after presenting sabers, watches and flags to the amazed marines. Suicides continued at the rate of one per minute.

The cigarettes soon were gone, and four Japs carrying grenades approached the marines and insolently demanded:

"Tobakko!"

Thompson grinned widely, pointed up the cliff toward the American lines and shouted:

"Lots of Tobakko there!"

He advised the approaching marine patrols to hide their weapons. When the patrols arrived, 150 Japs surrendered without resistance. The others were dead.

The commander of all Jap troops on Okinawa was dejected and broodish after his defense broke down on June 21. The commander, Lieutenant General Ushijima and his chief of staff, Lieutenant General Cho, indulged in a night of revelry with liquor and geisha girls in their command headquarters—a cave at the southern tip of the island.

At 3:40 in the morning their aides spread blankets in front of the cave. Dressed in full field uniforms, replete with medals and insignia, the two officers knelt to commit hari-kari. Both took daggers and made arch-like slashes across their stomach, in keeping with the best hari-kari traditions. And, true to the traditions which demand that the best friend assist in case the subject lacks the strength or courage to complete the deed, the adjutant swung a heavy saber twice and severed the heads from the bodies of the two generals.

Three orderlies then carried the bodies to shallow graves, which was only 100 yards from the fox holes in which Yanks were crouching. A few days later the graves were discovered by a patrol from the 32nd Regiment. A captured Jap officer who had witnessed the scene identified the officers, and broke into uncontrollable sobs as the Doughboys moved the bodies for positive identification.

With General Cho's remains was buried his white silk mattress cover upon which he wrote the following epitaph:

"22nd Day, 6th Month, 20th Year of the Showah Era: I depart without regret, fear, shame or obligation. Army Chief of Staff, Lt. General Cho Isamu. Age of departure, 51 years. At this time and place I hereby certify the foregoing."

By mid-July Japan was rocking under the thunderous bombardment of Army, Navy and Marine planes. By the first of August, with thousands of combat planes now based on Okinawa, as many as 1500 planes in one day were smashing Japan's industry, airfields and cities.

Now we were calling our shots. Superforts dropped leaflets warning that 11 Japanese cities faced total destruction in future incendiary strikes. It was explained that American policy was to give warning and permit evacuation of civilians before the cities were obliterated. The raids went off on schedule.

Japan was reeling and cringing from the weight of the most concentrated bombings in history. Transportation was virtually at a standstill in much of Japan. Our planes bombed and strafed trains, trucks and shipping. A mounting wave of hunger, sickness and despair was sweeping Japan. Military leaders knew the hopelessness of the situation, but doggedly prepared to defend their shores against the inevitable invasion.

Then came the atomic bomb. One bomb, equal in destructive power to the combined bomb loads of 200 Boeing Superforts, swished from a B-29 and devastated wide areas in Hiroshima, a city of 343,968 persons in 1940. This one missile spread a mysterious, terrifying malady which killed 90,000 persons and injured thousands of others. Ultra violet rays burned persons within a two-mile radius of the explosion, and others almost twice as far away broke out with painful skin blisters about two hours later.

Japan refused to surrender, so another atomic bomb fell two days later on Nagasaki, a city of 252,000 persons. The atomic bomb burned so instantaneously that it produced a strange pulverizing effect which reduced buildings to neat rows of ashes. There were 120,000 casualties in Nagasaki. The B-29's which dropped the atomic bombs flew from Saipan, and the second one landed at Okinawa on its return flight.

Man now had a ghastly, monstrous weapon which could annihilate civilization, and the weapon was a closely guarded secret of the United States government.

At chow time the atomic bomb always was the topic of conversation for days.

"The United States has the atomic bomb now, but other nations probably will discover it," said Tech Sergeant Herman Markowitz of Philadelphia. "Within the next quarter of a century we'll have new weapons which will make present weapons largely obsolete. We've got to discover defenses against the atomic bombs and other new weapons."

"There's only one defense against it," said Shamrock Coyne. "That's common sense. The United Nations charter can be the answer if we give it full support and make it work.

"We're perfecting the science of death. Now we must perfect the art of life. Instead of learning better methods to kill each other, nations must learn how to live with each other."

"You're absolutely right," said PFC McLeod. "We'll have a lot of problems, but I believe we can solve them and have peace for a long time."

On the heels of the two atomic bombings, Russia declared war against Japan on August 9, and unleashed a mighty land offensive against Manchuria and Korea.

On August 10 at 9:13 p.m., we received a radio broadcast at Okinawa saying:

"Tokyo expresses the desire to surrender according to the Potsdam ultimatum."

The announcement broke up a movie showing in our area. A roar of exultation resounded over Okinawa. Soon the sky was full of signal flares and tracers.

To us the war was over. We knew a haggling period was in store, but the war was over. And we also knew we were stuck in the Pacific for months to come. During the next few days we still had nightly air raids.

At 8 a.m., August 15 (August 14 in the United States) we received President Truman's announcement that Japan had surrendered unconditionally.

"I wish I was back in the States to celebrate," said Tech Sergeant Shamrock Coyne.

"Texas, here I come, just as fast as I can," said First Lieutenant John Farmer.

"The war's over, but the Seabees keep on building airfields," said Dick Koch-Church. "Nobody told them to stop. Give me a sport jacket, slacks and the Stork Club in good old New York."

"I came into the Marine Corps right out of high school," said PFC Gilbert E. Pennington of Martinsville, Ind. "I wonder how it feels to be a civilian?"

"They'll need men in the service for a long time, but they should get us out as fast as possible," said Coyne. "They shouldn't keep anyone in just because there happens to be an unemployment problem. If jobs are scarce, we should be permitted to get out and have an equal chance scrambling for them."

Waiting is the thing we do most in the service, and we knew we were in for more of it before getting discharged. Instead of years, it had become a matter of months, but impatient months.

Then we would be home, and with a much better appreciation of the liberties and privileges which formerly we took for granted. And we would know the price they cost...

We knew that some must die to assure freedom and happiness for many.

We saw our buddies pay the price.

Addendum

At the end of the 82 day battle, the longest of the Pacific war, more than 100,00 Japanese soldiers and their Okinawan conscripts had been killed. U.S. casualties of all kinds numbered 65,000, with 12,500 dead.

In this lengthy battle, U.S. forces suffered their highest-ever casualty rate, 48%, for combat stress reaction, formerly shell shock, known today as PTSD, post traumatic stress disorder. Some 14,000 soldiers were retired due to "nervous breakdown."

Jim Nutter, my father, entered Agnew State Hospital, California, in 1949 with a "nervous breakdown." He died there a year later, just forty years old.

www.ingramcontent.com/pod-product-compliance
Lightning Source LLC
Chambersburg PA
CBHW061638040426
42446CB00010B/1472